Modern Language Association of America

Approaches to Teaching
World Literature

Joseph Gibaldi, Series Editor

1. Joseph Gibaldi, ed. *Approaches to Teaching Chaucer's* Canterbury Tales. 1980.
2. Carole Slade, ed. *Approaches to Teaching Dante's* Divine Comedy. 1982.
3. Richard Bjornson, ed. *Approaches to Teaching Cervantes'* Don Quixote. 1984.
4. Jess B. Bessinger, Jr., and Robert F. Yeager, eds. *Approaches to Teaching* Beowulf. 1984.
5. Richard J. Dunn, ed. *Approaches to Teaching Dickens'* David Copperfield. 1984.
6. Steven G. Kellman, ed. *Approaches to Teaching Camus's* The Plague. 1985.
7. Yvonne Shafer, ed. *Approaches to Teaching Ibsen's* A Doll House. 1985.
8. Martin Bickman, ed. *Approaches to Teaching Melville's* Moby-Dick. 1985.
9. Miriam Youngerman Miller and Jane Chance, eds. *Approaches to Teaching* Sir Gawain and the Green Knight. 1986.
10. Galbraith M. Crump, ed. *Approaches to Teaching Milton's* Paradise Lost. 1986.
11. Spencer Hall, with Jonathan Ramsey, eds. *Approaches to Teaching Wordsworth's Poetry.* 1986.
12. Robert H. Ray, ed. *Approaches to Teaching Shakespeare's* King Lear. 1986.
13. Kostas Myrsiades, ed. *Approaches to Teaching Homer's* Iliad *and* Odyssey. 1987.
14. Douglas J. McMillan, ed. *Approaches to Teaching Goethe's* Faust. 1987.
15. Renée Waldinger, ed. *Approaches to Teaching Voltaire's* Candide. 1987.
16. Bernard Koloski, ed. *Approaches to Teaching Chopin's* The Awakening. 1988.
17. Kenneth M. Roemer, ed. *Approaches to Teaching Momaday's* The Way to Rainy Mountain. 1988.
18. Edward J. Rielly, ed. *Approaches to Teaching Swift's* Gulliver's Travels. 1988.
19. Jewel Spears Brooker, ed. *Approaches to Teaching Eliot's Poetry and Plays.* 1988.
20. Melvyn New, ed. *Approaches to Teaching Sterne's* Tristram Shandy. 1989.
21. Robert F. Gleckner and Mark L. Greenberg, eds. *Approaches to Teaching Blake's* Songs of Innocence and of Experience. 1989.
22. Susan J. Rosowski, ed. *Approaches to Teaching Cather's* My Ántonia. 1989.
23. Carey Kaplan and Ellen Cronan Rose, eds. *Approaches to Teaching Lessing's* The Golden Notebook. 1989.
24. Susan Resneck Parr and Pancho Savery, eds. *Approaches to Teaching Ellison's* Invisible Man. 1989.
25. Barry N. Olshen and Yael S. Feldman, eds. *Approaches to Teaching the Hebrew Bible as Literature in Translation.* 1989.
26. Robin Riley Fast and Christine Mack Gordon, eds. *Approaches to Teaching Dickinson's Poetry.* 1989.

27. Spencer Hall, ed. *Approaches to Teaching Shelley's Poetry*. 1990.
28. Sidney Gottlieb, ed. *Approaches to Teaching the Metaphysical Poets*. 1990.
29. Richard K. Emmerson, ed. *Approaches to Teaching Medieval English Drama*. 1990.
30. Kathleen Blake, ed. *Approaches to Teaching Eliot's* Middlemarch. 1990.
31. María Elena de Valdés and Mario J. Valdés, eds. *Approaches to Teaching García Márquez's* One Hundred Years of Solitude. 1990.
32. Donald D. Kummings, ed. *Approaches to Teaching Whitman's* Leaves of Grass. 1990.
33. Stephen C. Behrendt, ed. *Approaches to Teaching Shelley's* Frankenstein. 1990.
34. June Schlueter and Enoch Brater, eds. *Approaches to Teaching Beckett's* Waiting for Godot. 1991.
35. Walter H. Evert and Jack W. Rhodes, eds. *Approaches to Teaching Keats's Poetry*. 1991.
36. Frederick W. Shilstone, ed. *Approaches to Teaching Byron's Poetry*. 1991.
37. Bernth Lindfors, ed. *Approaches to Teaching Achebe's* Things Fall Apart. 1991.
38. Richard E. Matlak, ed. *Approaches to Teaching Coleridge's Poetry and Prose*. 1991.
39. Shirley Geok-lin Lim, ed. *Approaches to Teaching Kingston's* The Woman Warrior. 1991.
40. Maureen Fries and Jeanie Watson, eds. *Approaches to Teaching the Arthurian Tradition*. 1992.

Approaches to Teaching the Hebrew Bible as Literature in Translation

Edited by

Barry N. Olshen

and

Yael S. Feldman

The Modern Language Association of America
New York   1989

© 1989 by The Modern Language Association of America

Library of Congress Cataloging-in-Publication Data

Approaches to teaching the Hebrew Bible as literature in translation /
    edited by Barry N. Olshen and Yael S. Feldman.
      p. cm. — (Approaches to teaching world literature ; 25)
    Bibliography: p.
    Includes index.
    ISBN 0-87352-523-X   ISBN 0-87352-524-8 (pbk.)
    1. Bible as literature. 2. Bible. O.T.—Study. I. Olshen, Barry N. II. Feldman,
Yael S., 1941– . III. Series.
BS535.A6 1989
809′.935221—dc20   89-32332

BS
535
.A6
1989

Cover illustration of the paperback edition: Initial word panel, Jonah, *Xanten
Bible*, Germany, 1294, Spencer Hebrew ms. 1. Spencer Collection, New York
Public Library, Astor, Lenox, and Tilden Foundations. Used with permission.

Second printing 1992   **APR 1 9 1994**

Published by The Modern Language Association of America
10 Astor Place, New York, NY 10003-6981

CONTENTS

PREFACE TO THE SERIES

In *The Art of Teaching* Gilbert Highet wrote, "Bad teaching wastes a great deal of effort, and spoils many lives which might have been full of energy and happiness." All too many teachers have failed in their work, Highet argued, simply "because they have not thought about it." We hope that the Approaches to Teaching World Literature series, sponsored by the Modern Language Association's Committee on Teaching and Related Professional Activities, will not only improve the craft—as well as the art—of teaching but also encourage serious and continuing discussion of the aims and methods of teaching literature.

The principal objective of the series is to collect within each volume different points of view on teaching a specific literary work, a literary tradition, or a writer widely taught at the undergraduate level. The preparation of each volume begins with a wide-ranging survey of instructors, thus enabling us to include in the volume the philosophies and approaches, thoughts and methods of scores of experienced teachers. The result is a sourcebook of material, information, and ideas on teaching the subject of the volume to undergraduates.

The series is intended to serve nonspecialists as well as specialists, inexperienced as well as experienced teachers, graduate students who wish to learn effective ways of teaching as well as senior professors who wish to compare their own approaches with the approaches of colleagues in other schools. Of course, no volume in the series can ever substitute for erudition, intelligence, creativity, and sensitivity in teaching. We hope merely that each book will point readers in useful directions; at most each will offer only a first step in the long journey to successful teaching.

Joseph Gibaldi
Series Editor

PREFACE TO THE VOLUME

Contemporary literary-critical study of the Bible is arguably the most exciting recent development in Bible scholarship. This, of course, is very different from what used to be known as "literary criticism" of the Bible, that is, the source-critical and form-critical studies of the previous century. The new literary approaches to the Bible have found their way into courses in secondary schools, colleges, and universities throughout North America, under the auspices of departments of English, comparative literature, humanities, and religious studies. Parts of the Bible are also taught in numerous other courses in a wide variety of academic fields and disciplines. Yet many of us who have been using a literary-critical approach to teach the Bible have been doing so in virtual isolation, benefiting little or not at all from the experience of others. While the Bible has stimulated more scholarship and commentary than any of us can or cares to read, few sources guide us in applying this learning in the classroom. *Approaches to Teaching the Hebrew Bible as Literature in Translation* has been compiled to help redress this pedagogical deficiency.

The volume is addressed principally to beginning instructors and non-specialists in the field, but it is anticipated that seasoned scholars and senior professors will also find much of interest. This Approaches book will guide instructors who incorporate parts of the Bible into other literature courses and clerics, theologians, historians, and others who teach the Bible in one way but wish to know and teach it in another. It should also be of value to teachers of the New Testament, as they share many concerns and interests with those who teach the Hebrew Bible.

A few words on the title may be appropriate at this point. The term "Hebrew Bible" combines the most accurate denotation with the most neutral connotations for the corpus of texts covered in this book. "Old Testament" is a Christian designation carrying a traditional set of assumptions concerning the relation of Judaism to Christianity. Its use begs questions central to the teaching of the Bible, questions of approach and context discussed throughout. The phrase "as literature" need not bother those who consider the Bible to be literature or those who believe it is not literature. By now a conventional designation, the term simply suggests the volume's general orientation. I hasten to add, however, that the study or teaching of literature need not be separated from the study of history, theology, anthropology, and the many other related areas of interest to biblicists, and this approach is consistently maintained in the volume. (For more on this matter, see the introductory paragraphs of the section "Recent Literary Criticism.") Finally, the phrase "in translation" is not intended to exclude readers who teach the texts in the original Hebrew. It is there only to indicate our chief teaching context. While "translation" refers specifically to English translation and while the bibliographical information is designed mainly for readers of English, the theoretical and pedagogical considerations should be of interest to teachers of the Bible in any language.

In certain important ways this volume is an anomaly in the Approaches series. For one thing, the Hebrew Bible is not a single literary work but an anthology. Nearly any one of its "books" might on its own provide the subject for a volume. For series volumes like that on *The Canterbury Tales* or Wordsworth's poetry, where more than one literary work may be said to be included, the facts of single authorship, similar period and provenance, and so on provide ready-made categories of unity, coherence, and cohesion less easy to impose on the Hebrew Bible. Like *Beowulf* or *The Prelude*, each of the scriptural books assumes a rich and complex place in our literary and cultural heritage, but the books play such a role in our scriptural religious heritage as well.

This fact leads to the next point, which is that, in Bible study, we must always, in some way, contend with the added dimension of faith—regardless of whether or not one is a believer or what sort of a believer one is. The more usual study of imaginative literature, even of so-called religious literature like *The Divine Comedy* or *Paradise Lost*, does not involve us so centrally and so crucially in questions concerning the relation of faith and fact. To classify the creation stories as "myths" or Jonah as "fiction" or to state that Exodus is not "history" has an impact far more profound and disturbing than do the classifications of the Mesopotamian creation stories or *David Copperfield* or Gibbon's *History of the Decline and Fall of the Roman Empire*. The entire matter of classification and analysis, whether of the canon, a book, or a part of a book, is in Scripture an issue quite different from what it is in other written works. In what sense, in fact, can we regard the Bible as imaginative literature at all? And, if it is not literature (or history, or biography, and so on), then what is it? To what extent is the treatment of the Bible "as literature" different from its treatment as history, theology, or "divine revelation"? These are the largest and most difficult questions. They are questions provoked by this project, discussed in this volume, but, I must confess, hardly answered or resolved.

The variety of biblical texts is nearly matched by the variety of training, backgrounds, and fields of interest represented by the participants in this project. Whereas most of the volumes in the series could count on a certain degree of homogeneity within the ranks of their participants, this volume draws from the full range of humanistic and social scientific fields within academe and from the full range of North American religious and cultural experience. Nonetheless, our essay contributors, the many other participants in the project, and our readers are brought together by common problems and concerns; by shared, often passionate interests; and by abiding commitments to teaching the Hebrew Bible and matters related to it. In this way, of course, *Approaches to Teaching the Hebrew Bible* is not at all anomalous within the series.

As with previous volumes, the preparation of this one began with a questionnaire distributed by the Modern Language Association in 1984 to a broad sampling of Bible instructors, representing the full spectrum of American and Canadian academic institutions. Respondents provided information on preferred translations and editions of the Bible, reference and critical works regularly assigned or recommended to students and those recommended to beginning teachers, audiovisual aids used with success, helpful approaches to the Bible and its parts, syllabi and apportionment of class time, and other relevant pedagogical details. The gracious support and encouragement of so many colleagues across the continent offered ample evidence of the value of the work and the need for the volume.

Also like the other volumes, this one is divided into two main parts. The first, "Materials," contains five bibliographic essays covering important teaching and reference material available in English. Some of the information and issues in part 1 was culled from the responses to our survey. Part 2, "Approaches," consists of nineteen essays written by respondents to the questionnaire. They deal with general considerations in Bible instruction, discuss pedagogical and theoretical orientations to the Hebrew Bible, and present many pedagogical approaches to the scriptural books and passages that instructors would be most likely to teach. The essayists are broadly representative in geographical distribution, academic and religious affiliation, and critical or pedagogical approach, and they offer insights and practical suggestions for teachers at all levels within the educational system.

In addition to the survey respondents and essay contributors, many others have assisted with this project, and it is with pleasure and appreciation that I now acknowledge that assistance. Joseph Gibaldi, general editor of the series, contributed valuable suggestions at every stage of the project. My colleague Baruch Halpern read and commented wisely and copiously on the first part of the manuscript. The librarians of York University provided invaluable assistance with the research. I am grateful to York University's Research Grants Committee and its Graduate Program in English for their generous support of the project. The bibliographic research and editing were greatly facilitated by the diligence and intelligence of my graduate research assistants, especially Rod Lohin, Jamie Dopp, Cheryl Manny, and Angela Gawel. Special thanks are also offered to Paule Cotter and the members of her research office, who worked so hard to prepare the typescript for part 1 and the list of works cited.

This work is dedicated to the beloved memory of my parents, Henry B. and Ethel H. Olshen.

BNO

I dedicate this book, with love and thanks, to my husband, Peter, for his help and unfailing support, and to my students in the Bible as Literature courses at Columbia University (1982–89), for their enthusiasm and interest in this project.

YSF

Part One

MATERIALS

Barry N. Olshen

English Translations, Versions, and Special Editions

The choice of translation and edition is the principal decision in planning a course on the Bible. The text that is used influences every aspect of study and affects every concern of teacher and student. The professional Bible scholar may be quite aware of these influences and effects; the student only rarely. The choice of scriptural version may be influenced by a variety of factors, such as the place or function of a course in the curriculum; the theological and philosophical biases of the institution or instructor; the values, needs, and intellectual resources of the students; and so on. No translation is free from theological bias and special ideological or stylistic orientation. Each edition has its own format, catering to a particular readership, with unique advantages and disadvantages only sometimes apparent. No version or edition, therefore, can be equally appropriate to all pedagogical contexts, or to all matters and concerns within the context for which it is chosen.

Fortunately for those instructors without sufficient philological preparation, there are at least two sound and readable guides to the many versions and editions available today. *The Word of God: A Guide to English Versions of the Bible*, edited by Lloyd R. Bailey, is an anthology of essays by scholars in the field. It includes an introductory piece on Bible translation, a chapter on so-called study Bibles, an appendix comparing various translations, an annotated bibliography, and essays on the following versions: the Revised Standard Version, the New English Bible, the New Jewish Version, the New American Standard Bible, the Jerusalem Bible, Today's English Version or "the Good News Bible," the Living Bible, the New American Bible, the New International Version, and (in an appendix) the King James or "Authorized" Version. Jack P. Lewis's *English Bible from KJV to NIV: A History and Evaluation* devotes chapters to most of the above, with the omission of the New Jewish Version and the addition of the New Testament in the New King James Version. An extensive bibliography of English Bible translation follows these chapters. The "evaluation" of the subtitle is partly from an evangelical point of view.

An earlier, annotated bibliography of scriptural translation and style is provided by Samuel Hornsby, "Style in the Bible: A Bibliography." Always useful is the standard *Cambridge History of the Bible*, discussed in the section on reference works. Also interesting in this regard are Edward Greenstein's "Theories of Modern Bible Translation" and Barry Hoberman's popular article "Translating the Bible." What follows here is a short discussion of the key pedagogical issues to be confronted in selecting a Bible, including a brief guide to some of the English versions and editions and a summary of the responses of participants in the MLA survey of Bible instructors.

Despite the obvious logistical problems for classroom discussion and exegesis, a surprisingly large number of respondents (about 15%) state a preference for using a variety of translations in the classroom rather than a single prescribed version. This approach allows the instructor more occasion to emphasize the original Hebrew and to illustrate the nature and importance of translating and editing. The virtues of this approach are seen especially in the students' enlightened views on the interrelationship of translation, commentary, and interpretation; in their perceived need for at least some knowledge of Hebrew; and in their increasing ability to make both stylistic and substantive discriminations among different versions of the same passage, episode, or book. To "undercut the authority of the translations" is a stated desideratum on more than one questionnaire. A similar goal may be achieved, from time to time, by distributing copies of different versions of the same passage for comparison in class or at home. Exercises like this are recommended by many of our respondents and exemplified in Raymond-Jean Frontain's "Teaching Psalm 23" in part 2 of this volume.

The most frequently cited English translation of the Bible in modern scholarship, the Revised Standard Version, is also the one most often used in academic courses. Over one-third of our respondents require or strongly recommend it. Like the King James Version that it was designed to update, it attempts a "formal correspondence" translation. It tries to preserve the tone of the earlier version, while silently correcting errors of translation and seeking a more modern idiom than that of 1611. The language of the RSV is modern but, its detractors say, far from contemporary, and this is a major disadvantage from the point of view of many academics today. Its committee of translators, however, are engaged in an ongoing process of revision, and they seem to be aiming for a more contemporary style, one that eliminates obvious archaisms and gratuitous male-oriented language. It might just be noted here in passing that the very important and topical feminist issue of inclusive language remains almost entirely unreflected in Bible translation to date, partly because all the recent projects, even the New International Version published in 1978, were begun before the male-oriented language of the Bible became so prominent a social issue.

Teachers and scholars depend on the RSV for two principal features: its reliable English lexical equivalence and sentence structure that usually follows the original Hebrew. It is among the least expensive clothbound editions of the Bible and, like most of these versions, is also published in paperback.

A large number of respondents—just a few less than those favoring the RSV—still prefer the King James Version, often admittedly in spite of its typographical format, its many philological errors, and the difficulty (even unintelligibility for some students) of its archaisms. The KJV is almost always preferred for its so-called literalism ("they were trying to translate, not interpret") and the undeniable beauty and familiarity of its style, especially its cadences. English literature and other humanities courses, but hardly ever courses in religious studies or theology, use the KJV. The same reasons are reiterated: for "its integral relation to our literature and cultural tradition"; "because it is one of the greatest books in English and . . . the source for biblical allusion in English"; "because it influenced most writers in English until 1945."

This is the version that teachers of English know best and the one most often and most amply represented in anthologies of English prose and poetry. Volume 1 of *The Norton Anthology of World Masterpieces*, for example, includes parts of Genesis, Job, Psalms, and Isaiah from the KJV.

Some of its obvious drawbacks for classroom use may have been overcome by the New KJV, both testaments of which are now available in one volume. Its new format—including frequent subject headings, conventional typographical layout for passages identified as verse, and short, clear footnotes—makes for much easier reading. Its many modernizations are most obvious in the replacement of the pronouns *thee, thou,* and *ye* by *you,* and *thy* and *thine* by *you* and *yours,* and in the substitution of contemporary usage for the obsolete verb suffixes *eth* and *est*. The many other modernizations of lexis, grammar, and punctuation make the NKJV something different from the KJV, but still nothing like a contemporary English rendering. The effort to replace archaic words and inaccurate translations with more accurate twentieth-century equivalents is manifest everywhere in the text. The result, however, is an often infelicitous mix of Jacobean style and modern lexical usage, which has led one reviewer to call its New Testament "the hand of Esau but the voice of Jacob" (Lewis 350). It is difficult, therefore, to imagine an academic audience for the NKJV, which leads me to speculate on a most uncertain academic destiny.

The New Jewish Version (issued by the Jewish Publication Society of America, hence often called the New JPS Version), since the publication of its third and final volume in 1982, has begun to rival the popularity of the RSV Old Testament, especially among Jewish scholars and students in search of a reliable, but still flexible, formal-correspondence translation. Being the only recent translation of the "Hebrew Bible" as distinct from the "Old Testament," it is especially attractive to those who consider this distinction personally or pedagogically important. (More on this distinction may be found in the essays by Thompson and Olshen in part 2.) This principal advantage for some, however, is also a disadvantage for others: lacking a New Testament, the NJV has limited use in courses that cover both testaments.

The NJV represents the joint effort of the three main branches of modern Judaism (Orthodox, Conservative, Reform) and so enjoys consensus within the English-speaking Jewish community. Christian scholars also seem to admire it as a faithful yet creative rendering of the Hebrew, with a readable format and a readily accessible style. Compared to the RSV, the NJV makes much greater use of contemporary English idiom and flexible lexical equivalence, while still attempting as literal a translation as contemporary English can bear. The recent appearance (1985) of an edition of the three volumes in one will certainly increase its use in the classroom. A number of respondents to our survey remark that, if less expensive and more readily available, the NJV would be the preferred text for their courses. "I have always used the RSV; now, if the JPS version becomes available in a less expensive form," promises one respondent, "I will use it. The RSV is dull but generally accurate. The JPS is generally accurate and not so dull." Another says, "The

RSV is the best of the worst, generally reliable if unexciting. . . . I'd use the new JPS if available in one volume, despite its uneven character." The three separate volumes of the Hebrew Bible (Torah, Prophets, Writings) remain in print for more advanced courses.

The unabashedly idiomatic English of the latest work of British Protestant scholarship, the New English Bible, is the choice of about ten percent of our respondents. It is used, however, only by those who favor a very contemporary English equivalence of the ancient Hebrew, what is now called a "dynamic equivalence." Those who value formal correspondence in their translations regard the departure from literalness in the NEB as a major fault. Often in the translations of the Old Testament, the panel members of the NEB have been too quick to emend the Hebrew and too reliant on the use of comparative philology for new-found meanings in the text. Of special concern to scholars is the tendency in the NEB to transpose material from its generally accepted "canonical" place in the text. In a chapter on the NEB in Bailey's *Word of God*, for example, Roger A. Bullard has counted some twenty-three transpositions in the book of Job alone (60).

Among Catholics, the Jerusalem Bible (1966) is the most popular modern English version. It is the preferred or recommended text of about ten percent of survey participants. This Old Testament, of course, includes those books that are part of the traditional Catholic canon, the deuterocanonical books, excluded from the Jewish canon and set apart as the Apocrypha in many Protestant versions. The JB translation is widely praised as felicitous and dignified; the format, with its headings, subheadings, and paragraphing, and its excellent cross-referencing system in the margins, is universally applauded as readable and useful. Both format and translation are greatly dependent on the earlier French version, *La Bible de Jérusalem*. More than one respondent comments on its introductions and annotations, usually modest yet scholarly and only rarely apologetic. The JB is available in paperback from Oxford University Press; in 1968 a Reader's Edition first appeared in which the notes and introductions are minimized to facilitate the reading of the narrative and poetic sections by the so-called ordinary reader.

Mention of essays and annotations, standard features of the JB, introduces the contentious issue of the value and purpose in using the various "study helps" (footnotes, endnotes, headnotes, marginalia, introductions, essays, appendixes, maps, illustrations, etc.) that are appearing in more and more contemporary editions of the Bible. While textual variants, alternative renderings, and cross-referencing are now standard features of most Bibles, many instructors prefer editions with fewer notations, thus introducing less cultural and theological bias into the classroom and perhaps requiring greater interpretive effort because of the relatively unmediated quality of the text. Some, however, make good use of the "study" or "annotated" Bibles, especially by saving precious class time otherwise devoted to introductory lectures and by substituting the study aids for other kinds of background reading. Teachers find the rather limited introductions and annotations of these texts most useful for the beginning student in the introductory survey course.

There are three such study Bibles popular in colleges and universities today: the JB, *The New Oxford Annotated Bible with the Apocrypha: RSV,* and *The NEB with the Apocrypha: Oxford Study Edition.* Although the theological biases of these books are apparent to the scholar, they are rarely if ever offensive, and so the scholarship contained in them is generally of sound value to the student. If not always of the highest distinction, the introductions and notes provide at least "modest orientation and exegetical clarification," as one of our respondents puts it. The following are also study Bibles, but they are only rarely recommended within the academic environment: *The New Chain-Reference Bible, The New Scofield Reference Bible: KJV Text,* and *The Ryrie Study Bible: New American Standard Translation.*

Lacking space to review each of these, I quote the concluding summary in Robert G. Bratcher's chapter on study Bibles:

> Of the Study Bibles examined in this survey [the six titles above], the JB provides more valuable helps for the readers than any of the others. The study editions of the RSV and the NEB are extremely useful; no person should read the Bible without the minimum helps provided by these two editions. As for the other Bibles, it is clear that each one has certain features which are useful and helpful, particularly for preachers. But the overall attitude toward the biblical literature is so dominated by theological and philosophical biases as to nullify much of the good qualities that these editions possess. In this reviewer's opinion they certainly do not provide an adequate guide for a person who wants to learn what the Bible really means.   (Bailey 182)

One participant in the survey recommends Today's English Version (more commonly called "The Good News Bible") for its "simple syntax and diction." While this version may come closer than others to a colloquial American idiom, I think it is fair to say that nearly all academics avoid it as a principal class text. Also, a brief caveat concerning the Living Bible may well be appropriate here, although no one has suggested its use in the classroom. Repudiated by responsible scholars of every religious persuasion, the LB represents no more than an inaccurate paraphrase of that Bible most of us know and love. To add a personal note, I myself have made good use of both these versions — as components of comparative translation exercises, not as principal classroom texts.

Especially valuable for readers with little or even no understanding of ancient Hebrew is the three-volume *Interlinear Bible,* edited and translated by Jay P. Green, Sr. The Masoretic Hebrew text is here printed (wherever possible) with an interlinear, word-for-word English equivalence, placed beneath the Hebrew and read, as is the Hebrew, from right to left. Another formal-correspondence translation is placed in a column on the left side of each page. This second translation allows for easy access to the English text, while the literal translation enables the reader to find, at a glance, both lexical equivalence and grammatical sequence. Scholars of Hebrew will know the theoretical and practical difficulties of such a work. Nonetheless, it seems to me that *The Interlinear Bible* can be of invaluable assistance to teachers, clerics, students, and ordinary readers lacking the linguistic skills to analyze the original Hebrew text. Those who work from the Hebrew will undoubtedly be familiar with the text and critical apparatus of *Biblia Hebraica Stuttgartensia*, edited by Elliger and Rudolph and based on the famous *Biblia Hebraica* of Rudolf Kittel.

There are, finally, two new and remarkable Torah translations that must be mentioned. *The Living Torah*, translated with extensive notes and other explanatory material by Aryeh Kaplan, attempts to produce a translation that is "accurate, clear, modern, readable, and above all, in consonance with the living tradition of Judaism" (vii). In addition to clear notation of chapter and verse, this edition divides the Five Books of Moses into the traditional Jewish *sedarot* (singular *sidrah*), the weekly portions read in the synagogue, and *parashiot* (singular *parashah*), the smaller divisions of text. The comprehensive and exceptionally clear footnotes include scores of illustrations as part of the exegetical and explanatory material. Interspersed throughout the pages of the text are maps, diagrams, charts, and illustrations of value for all levels of study and scholarship. An extensive, annotated bibliography mainly of traditional Jewish sources and a comprehensive index of every name, place, law, and concept appearing in either the text or the notes conclude this praiseworthy addition to contemporary Torah translation and scholarship. Only one of our respondents requires it in his classes, but, as it becomes better known, it is certain to be more widely recommended.

The other rendition is by Everett Fox, who has so far completed but two of the Five Books of Moses. Although *In the Beginning* was published as a book in 1983, Fox's initial translation of Genesis appeared years ago as an entire issue of the journal *Response* (Summer 1972), and so his approach has already exerted considerable influence on contemporary translation practice and scriptural criticism. It is based on the translation principles enunciated by Martin Buber and Franz Rosenzweig in their celebrated German rendition, and is coupled with an extensive commentary. Colleagues everywhere are familiar with *In the Beginning,* and at least four of our respondents require or strongly recommend it for their courses. Fox faithfully translates into English the major linguistic features of Genesis, most notably what he calls its oral qualities, its unique structure of echo and allusion (based on the recurrence of "leading-words" and word stems), and the symbolism of its names (conveyed by transliteration and explanation). His recent rendering of Exodus, *Now These Are the Names,* follows similar format and principles. Fox's translations best complement contemporary literary and stylistic criticism of the Bible. They come closest to providing, and show the clearest understanding of, the commonplace as well as the unique stylistic elements of the Hebrew Torah. As such they offer an otherwise unobtainable resource for students with little or no sense of the Hebrew language or style.

Required and Recommended
Reading for Students

The assignment of secondary reading varies greatly from instructor to instructor, depending on particular course goals and approaches. Courses that contextualize the Bible within the literature of the ancient Near East or that focus on the relation of the Bible to later literature and culture usually include much additional reading and treat such material as primary. Instructors with a literary-critical approach to Bible study tend to assign fewer secondary texts. Nearly a fifth of the respondents to our questionnaire who teach a survey or introductory course on the Bible require no additional readings. These instructors profess the regular use of a close-reading approach to the Bible, and some declare that their objective is to minimize mediation between student and text. New Critical and reader-response approaches represent the predominant theoretical positions in their pedagogy. Courses with greater emphasis on theology, history, and historical methodology understandably contain more secondary reading for political, cultural, geographical, and methodological background.

Of the single-volume introductory textbooks required or strongly recommended, Bernhard W. Anderson's *Understanding the Old Testament* continues to be the most popular work of its kind for undergraduate and nonspecialist use. It offers a far-ranging cultural introduction to ancient Israel and the Old Testament, making use of the latest findings in archeological research and blending historical, theological, and literary approaches to the Bible. It is well illustrated with maps, charts, and photographs and contains a clear and helpful annotated bibliography of sources in English for students and teachers. The suggested scriptural readings that accompany each of its chapters make it easier for the first-time teacher using the book to construct a detailed syllabus. A number of nonspecialists teaching surveys or parts of the Hebrew Bible have declared Anderson's text to be essential reading.

Somewhat less popular than Anderson's text for undergraduate and seminary use are the following: John H. Hayes, *An Introduction to Old Testament Study*, actually more of an introduction to "issues and approaches involved in contemporary Old Testament study" (13); J. A. Soggin, *Introduction to the Old Testament . . .*; Brevard S. Childs, *Introduction to the Old Testament as Scripture*, especially helpful for redaction and canonical criticisms; J. Kenneth Kuntz, *The People of Ancient Israel*; Samuel Sandmel, *The Hebrew Scriptures*, slightly older but still rewarding. Surprisingly, Isaac Asimov's informal and uneven *Old Testament* appears as recommended reading on more than one syllabus for introductory courses. However engaging the style and story, more reliable and scholary sources of information should be used for college and university students. Finally, too recent to appear on responses to our survey, but very promising for use as an introductory textbook, is Norman K. Gottwald's *Hebrew Bible: A Socio-Literary Introduction*, which, as the subtitle suggests, employs an interdisciplinary approach bridging the social-scientific and literary fields. Gottwald explains this approach to teaching the Bible in part 2 of the present volume.

Regarding one-volume history books, John Bright's *History of Israel* continues to be more generally recommended for undergraduates than any other single volume. It is clear, however, that some instructors now prefer—for themselves as well as their students—the essays contained in John H. Hayes and J. Maxwell Miller's *Israelite and Judaean History*. This large and impressive volume counts a number of eminent scholars among its more than a dozen contributors. Not "simply another proposed reconstruction of Israelite and Judaean history," it is, as the editors note in their preface, "a handbook for the study of that history and one in which the reader can see different leading historians at work" (xv–xvi). Scholarly bibliographies accompany each section of the volume. Some instructors still assign parts or all of Martin Noth's classic *History of Israel*, undoubtedly a major work in the field, but more difficult to follow than Bright's very readable *History*. An excellent short history is Siegfried Herrmann's *History of Israel in Old Testament Times*. Even more concise, but still perceptive and useful, especially for undergraduates, are William F. Albright's *Biblical Period from Abraham to Ezra* and Harry M. Orlinsky's *Ancient Israel*. The most promising recent text seems to be *A History of Ancient Israel and Judah*, coauthored by Miller and Hayes.

For introductory readings concerning the methods of biblical study, many colleagues require or recommend Fortress Press Guides to Biblical Scholarship, Old Testament Series (ed. Gene M. Tucker). Each volume contains a short introduction to a basic approach to Scripture with exemplary analyses especially suited for undergraduate reading. Colleagues comment that one or another of these monographs succeeds where alternative texts prove too difficult for their students. Most often recommended are the first two pioneer volumes of the following list: Norman C. Habel, *Literary Criticism of the Old Testament*; Gene M. Tucker, *Form Criticism of the Old Testament*; Walter E. Rast, *Tradition History and the Old Testament*; Ralph W. Klein, *Textual Criticism of the Old Testament*; Edgar Krentz, *The Historical-Critical Method*; J. Maxwell Miller, *The Old Testament and the Historian*; David Robertson, *The Old Testament and the Literary Critic*; H. Darrell Lance, *The Old Testament and the Archaeologist*; James A. Sanders, *Canon and Community: A Guide to Canonical Criticism*; Robert R. Wilson, *Sociological Approaches to the Old Testament*. From the New Testament Series (ed. Dan O. Via, Jr.) are three monographs also helpful for Old Testament study: Norman Perrin, *What Is Redaction Criticism?*; Edgar V. McKnight, *What Is Form Criticism?*; Daniel Patte, *What Is Structural Exegesis?*

There are single-volume works that attempt to cover the same methodology. The first two hundred pages of Hayes's *Introduction to Old Testament Study* focus on the history and methods of scriptural interpretation. Daniel J. Harrington's *Interpreting the Old Testament* is an introduction to exegesis, in which each chapter explains a method, illustrates it, and makes suggestions for further reading. Harrington considers the major critical approaches of our century. John Hayes and Carl R. Holladay's *Biblical Exegesis: A Beginner's Handbook* is similar but shorter and in paperback. Its ten brief chapters cover textual, historical, grammatical, literary, form, tradition, and redaction criticism; they also discuss integrating exegetical procedures and using biblical exegesis. Bibliographies valuable for both teachers and students appear at the end of each chapter.

A basic book on form criticism—for scholars and students alike—is still Klaus Koch's *Growth of the Biblical Tradition*; see also *Old Testament Form Criticism*, edited by John Hayes. For a comprehensive collection of essays using social science approaches, see Norman Gottwald, *The Bible and Liberation*. Finally, Richard N. Soulen's recently revised paperback, *Handbook of Biblical Criticism*, contains brief entries about all the above areas and much more. Concentrating on fields of study, the handbook offers students abbreviated introductions to the critical methodologies and established tools of scholarly research for both testaments and related literature. In addition, it defines and explains other technical terms; provides bibliography; identifies scholars, their works, schools, movements, and so on; explains abbreviations; and clarifies (when possible) the complexities of biblical criticism in general. As the field gets more and more complicated and the terminology more and more perplexing, the novice—and, alas, the expert—will be more and more dependent on works such as Soulen's.

For documentary background to the Bible that is specially suited for student use, the fullest and the favored text is James B. Pritchard's *Ancient Near East: An Anthology of Texts and Pictures*. This is a one-volume paperback abridgment of his *Ancient Near Eastern Texts Relating to the Old Testament* and *The Ancient Near East in Pictures*. A paperback abridgment of the supplementary materials in the latest, revised edition of these two volumes may be found in Pritchard's *Ancient Near East: A New Anthology of Texts and Pictures*, but this second collection is much less frequently used in courses. For many years Pritchard's only rival in the field was D. Winton Thomas's briefer *Documents from Old Testament Times*. Another text has more recently appeared: *Near Eastern Religious Texts Relating to the Old Testament*, edited by Walter Beyerlin et al., but it too is more limited in scope than Pritchard's. The documents found in all three volumes are usually read for comparison with Scripture, especially with the early chapters of Genesis and the law codes of the Torah. The splendid illustrations in Pritchard's volumes are often selected for presentation in slide shows or employed for other illustrative purposes. For an account of two specific examples of comparative literary study of the Bible and other Near Eastern texts, see Stephen A. Geller's essay in part 2 of this volume.

Among the many literary-critical studies of the Bible, there are a few especially noteworthy for their usefulness to students and their adaptability to the classroom and course syllabus. For a much fuller discussion of literary-critical approaches, see the section entitled "Recent Literary Criticism." The literary essay cited most often by survey respondents is Erich Auerbach's celebrated "Odysseus' Scar," the first chapter of his classic collection *Mimesis*. This essay analyzes the Homeric and biblical styles by comparing an episode in book 19 of *The Odyssey* with chapter 22 of Genesis (the binding of Isaac). Having already had an important influence on two generations of scholars, Auerbach's piece is now frequently required reading for undergraduate students. Three other pioneering essays have proved especially valuable for instructors and still regularly appear as recommendations for student reading. Two are by James Muilenburg: "A Study in Hebrew Rhetoric: Repetition and Style" and "Form Criticism and Beyond," a defense of the exploration of structural patterning and unifying devices characteristic of "rhetorical criticism." The other is by Kenneth Burke: "The First Three Chapters of Genesis."

There are three more recent essays I have found particularly useful in establishing essential categories and very helpful for students as well as instructors. The oldest of these, "The Law, the Prophets, and Wisdom" by John E. Becker, should be better known than it is. It provides an introduction to the literature of the Hebrew Bible, particularly in relation to American literature, and discusses the purposes of literature more generally. Concise and lucid, loaded with insights, this essay comes highly recommended by one of our respondents as "a splendid meditation on the purpose of the Bible." The next, Matitiahu Tsevat's "Israelite History and the Historical Books of the Old Testament," argues for the clear differentiation between historical and literary approaches. It distinguishes between "biblical history," which is the literature of the Bible, and "Israelite history," which is the history of Israel. Tsevat favors analyzing the Bible as the tradition of Israel and referring to history in order to elucidate that tradition. The most recent of the essays, P. Joseph Cahill's "Literary Criticism, Religious Literature, and Theology," argues for the primacy of literary criticism in the study of religious traditions. Both literary criticism and theological discourse, says Cahill, "emerge" from the religious literature that is at the "center of religion." The goal of literary criticism is "participation in [that] literature" (54–55).

Among the synchronic and generic introductions to the literature of the Bible of which I am aware, Leonard L. Thompson's *Introducing Biblical Literature* is by far the most competent and interesting. Thompson's book deals with the Christian Bible, treating both testaments as a unity and focusing especially on its linguistic and symbolic structure. The first three of its five parts are devoted to the Old Testament: part 1 covers introductory material and the "syntax" of "song," "story," and "saying"; part 2 deals with the Psalms and the narrative books; part 3 with "sayings"—legal, proverbial, prophetic, apocalyptic. Thompson's book is especially good for instructors who need an overview of the literature and structural patterns of the Bible and for students at undergraduate and seminary levels. His essay in part 2 of this volume clearly summarizes his basic typological framework. More specifically directed toward the general reader and undergraduate student are Leland Ryken's *Literature of the Bible* and *How to Read the Bible as Literature*, as well as Woodrow Ohlsen's *Perspectives on Old Testament Literature*. Ryken's books contain simple literary theory, a framework of literary types, and discussion of the activities that different literary forms require of the reader. Ohlsen's *Perspectives* is conceived as a supplementary text for Hebrew Bible courses. Each chapter on one of nineteen Hebrew books provides a summary of contents, a selection of essays and commentaries, and a brief list of readings and questions for further discussion and writing (both uninspired).

There are at least three excellent paperback anthologies of essays and other pieces devoted to the literature and literary study of the Bible. These may be used as textbooks for undergraduate and graduate courses or as handy references for one essay or another. *The Bible in Its Literary Milieu*, edited by John R. Maier and Vincent L. Tollers, provides a wide variety of synchronic and diachronic approaches. Compiled and edited with great care, the anthology includes tables, maps, a general introduction, and shorter orientational introductions to each of its five sections. The scholarship of the twenty-five pieces is uniformly excellent. The standard critical anthology for narrative is the two-volume *Literary Interpretations of Biblical Narratives*, edited by Kenneth R. R. Gros Louis et al. The first volume was a ground-breaking collection, with most of its seventeen pieces written by the editors themselves. The second volume, still dominated by its editors, adds a number of other impressive scholar-critics to its list of contributors.

The most notable advances in recent years have been in the area of biblical narrative, and the book most widely read and recommended to students is Robert Alter's *Art of Biblical Narrative*. For a discussion of this and other valuable studies of narrative and narratology, see the opening pages of "Recent Literary Criticism."

Very few instructors make special pedagogical use of the vast periodical literature about which so many of us feel obliged to remain informed, except insofar as they assign an occasional article for reading or require students to do a periodical search for a paper. Only one of our respondents regularly includes assignments from scholarly journals, these being mainly précis and evaluations of journal articles. Interesting, nontechnical journals for beginning students and generalists would surely include *Interpretation*, the monthly *Expository Times*, *Biblical Archaeologist*, and *Biblical Archaeology Review*. The *Journal of Biblical Literature*, devoted largely to diachronic studies, is the most important technical journal in North America; it is at least matched in quality by *Vetus Testamentum*. *Semeia* and *Journal for the Study of the Old Testament* are best for advanced synchronic and structuralist literary studies. The more recent *Prooftexts* frequently publishes nontechnical articles on the Bible.

Reference, Commentary, Background, and Critical Works

Despite serious professional disagreement concerning the background reading and research considered desirable for students, there is consensus where the teacher is concerned. No one disagrees that instructors must know more than the scriptural text and that the richer their backgrounds, the richer their courses are likely to be. Without the background knowledge and proper reference tools, the task can hardly be done; some would say the text cannot properly be read.

A full survey of reference material on the Hebrew Bible would extend considerably beyond the limits of this volume. Exigencies of space require that most of the entries here be restricted to publications in book form with broad scope or general subject matter. Very few studies of individual biblical books or passages can be listed. With only a few exceptions, the works here are written in, or translated into, English. They represent essential, highly regarded, frequently cited, or especially useful scholarly, critical, or pedagogical works. For the basic foreign language research tools, especially in Hebrew and German, see Stanley B. Marrow's *Basic Tools of Biblical Exegesis*.

The new or future instructor, or the nonspecialist teaching parts of the Hebrew Bible in one course or more, is urged to read the previous section. Many titles there contain the best of recent scholarship in readable format and style—exactly what all of us need at least some of the time. Indeed, in a field like the Hebrew Bible, with a tradition that goes back three millennia and that produces the most copious forms of scholarship and theory today, we must all be generalists in the true sense of the word much of the time. The days of the specialist in "the Bible" have long since passed. Everyone working and teaching in the area requires sound, general, and easily assimilated material on many aspects of Scripture. The Fortress Guides to Biblical Scholarship, listed in the previous section, for example, have been equally recommended by teachers for other teachers. The needs of instructors and students are often much closer than some of us care to admit, and this fact is reflected in the interrelation of these two sections.

I proceed here from general to specific, beginning with the major books on books. Considering the enormous range of biblical scholarship, it is surprising that more bibliographic resources are not available and that many instructors have not made their way through the essential bibliographic and research tools that are. *Elenchus Bibliographicus Biblicus*, published by Rome's Pontifical Biblical Institute, is the most comprehensive annual bibliography, listing published material (books, articles, and reviews) on both testaments as well as intertestamental and patristic literatures. Titles and information about entries are given in the languages of the entries; editorial matter is in Latin. The "Book List" found in each quarterly issue of *Vetus Testamentum* provides a well annotated, often critical bibliography of recent books of interest to Hebrew Bible scholars. *Old Testament Abstracts*, a thrice-yearly annotated bibliography published by the Catholic Biblical Association, is more valuable for articles than for books. The Society for Old Testament Study publishes an annotated review of books each year, called *Book List*. The following are composites made from previous *Book Lists: Eleven Years of Bible Bibliography* (1946–56), edited by H. H. Rowley; *A Decade of Bible Bibliography* (1957–66), edited by G. W. Anderson; *Bible Bibliography 1967–73, Old Testament*, edited by Peter R. Ackroyd. Relatively easy access to a vast field of biblical literature has recently been created by Paul-Emile Langevin, in his prodigious three-volume *Biblical Bibliography 1930–1983*. This work of thousands of pages systematically analyzes 163 journals in five modern languages and over 1,500 collective works and recent books with special, though by no means exclusive, concern for exegesis and biblical theology. The journal languages are French, English, German, Italian, and Spanish, the same languages in which all its thousands of headings are written.

Two useful, though selective, bibliographies are Brevard S. Childs's *Old Testament Books for Pastor and Teacher* and John H. Gottcent's *Bible as Literature*. The latter is well annotated and especially pertinent for the literary study of both testaments. It was published just before much of the most exciting and important of contemporary studies appeared, and so is unfortunately limited. Also of value specifically for literary study is *Bible-Related Curriculum Materials*, edited by Thayer S. Warshaw, Betty Lou Miller, and James S. Ackerman. Part of the series The Bible in Literature Courses, this bibliography is designed mainly for, and compiled mainly by, schoolteachers, but it holds something of value for college, university, and seminary teachers as well. Its listings come under the following categories: the Bible in literature, the Bible as literature, the Bible and literature, and the Bible in/and other media. Samuel Hornsby's "Style in the Bible" is an extensive, annotated bibliography of material on the style of English Bible translation.

English language concordances for the major Bible translations can be located in good reference libraries everywhere, but four in particular are favored by scholars because of their special or exhaustive coverage. *Cruden's Complete Concordance*, originally published in 1737, revised many times, and now available in a number of editions including paperback, is the classic concordance to the KJV. John W. Ellison's *Nelson's Complete Concordance*, compiled by computer, is the standard concordance to the RSV. James Strong's *Exhaustive Concordance* offers, among other things, a "comparative concordance of the Authorized [KJV] and Revised Versions, including the American variations." Robert Young's *Analytical Concordance* (originally published in 1879 and frequently revised since then), based on the KJV, claims to list the original Hebrew or Greek for every English word, the literal meaning of every original word, and the "thoroughly true and reliable parallel passages." A multivolume series of concordances for individual books of the Bible, called *The Computer Bible* (Baird and Freedman), has been under way since 1970. The indispensable concordance to the Hebrew text is Salomon Mandelkern's *Kon-dordantsyah la-Tanakh* (*Veteris Testamenti Concordantiae Hebraicae atque Chal-daicae*). The lexicon to use is *A Hebrew and English Lexicon of the Old Testament* by Francis Brown, S. R. Driver, and Charles Briggs.

Of the older one-volume commentaries available to the scholar and student, the Catholic *Jerome Biblical Commentary* (Brown, Fitzmyer, and Murphy) is the best, in both its general essays and commentaries. In the Protestant tradition, there is *Peake's Commentary*, revised by Matthew Black and H. H. Rowley, and *The Interpreter's One-Volume Commentary* (Layman). Nothing comparable to these exists in the Jewish tradition. Some instructors, however, achieve similar ends using books like Walter Harrelson's *Interpreting the Old Testament* and Samuel Sandmel's *Hebrew Scriptures*, one-volume commentaries based on the structure of the Hebrew Bible. The twelve-volume *Interpreter's Bible* (Buttrick), printing both KJV and RSV, still has much merit and still is widely used among academics and Protestant clergy. The novice using these and other commentaries would be well advised to develop a sensitivity to their theological biases, for no matter how reliable and supposedly "objective" the research may be, each exhibits at least some subjectivity in approach and interpretation.

Special note should be made of the recently published *Harper's Bible Commentary*. Under the general editorship of James L. Mays and in association with the Society of Biblical Literature, this single-volume commentary contains the best scholarship currently available and the best coverage of its kind in the social science and literary fields.

Space does not permit a comprehensive description of the standard English commentaries on the Bible or detailed reference to commentaries on specific scriptural books. The best way for beginning instructors to familiarize themselves with these series is by browsing through a collection of them and by comparing a few of their translations, introductions, and commentaries on specific books and pericopes. The most often used and highly recommended within academic circles, although uneven in quality from volume to volume, is the Anchor Bible (1964–   ). Each volume of this series in progress consists of a new English translation of a scriptural book with an extensive introduction and critical notes. The series Hermeneia: A Critical and Historical Commentary (1971–   ), based on Hebrew texts, too often translates older material and is for more technical study, as is the now somewhat outdated International Critical Commentary (1896–1937). The Old Testament Library (1961–   ), another series of commentaries and monographs, is scholarly without being so technical, but it also translates older studies. More popular, but of limited academic use, is the Cambridge Bible Commentary (1963–   ) based on the NEB.

Among the many Bible dictionaries available today, all agree that *The Interpreter's Dictionary of the Bible* (Buttrick), with the supplementary volume, is still the finest for scholarly use — the most balanced, reliable, and objective tool of its kind. Some instructors prefer, especially for their students, the handier, one-volume *Dictionary of the Bible*, compiled entirely by John L. McKenzie. *The Theological Dictionary of the Old Testament*, edited by G. J. Botterweck and Helmer Ringgren (5 vols.), should become the standard reference of its kind. For encyclopedias, *The Encyclopaedia Judaica* is superior to its rivals for reliable information, sound coverage, and Jewish interpretation of the Hebrew Bible and related areas. *The International Standard Bible Encyclopedia* has again been thoroughly revised and reset by a team of evangelical scholars headed by Geoffrey W. Bromiley. Finally, of special interest to teachers of English literature will be the projected work entitled *A Dictionary of the Bible and Biblical Tradition in English Literature*, under the general editorship of David L. Jeffrey. The cooperative effort of some three hundred scholars of the Bible, English literature, and related areas will be required to bring to fruition this compendium of the traditioning of biblical motifs, concepts, names, quotations, and themes in English literature from the Middle Ages to the present.

Much of traditional Jewish scholarship is unavailable to those without linguistic skills and at least some traditional training. While many of the great midrashic works, the famous medieval commentaries, and the classic mystical and legal texts have now been translated into English in complete or abridged editions, their meaning is still not fully accessible to the untutored reader. For standard Bible commentary, the fourteen-volume, bilingual *Soncino Books of the Bible* (Cohen) has some utility. Each page contains the Hebrew text, a modern (but not the latest) English translation, and brief textual and critical notes incorporating some Talmudic, medieval, and modern interpretation. Two contemporary one-volume Torah commentaries with bilingual texts should also be noted: Joseph Hertz's *Pentateuch and Haftorahs* in the Orthodox tradition and W. Gunther Plaut's *Torah* in the Reform tradition. Hertz's volume prints an older English translation with commentary in English. The text itself is divided into the weekly Torah portion (*sidrah*) accompanied by the portion from the Former or Latter Prophets recited in the synagogue service directly after the Torah reading (*haftarah*). The format of Plaut's work includes introductory essays, the Hebrew text with NJV translation, textual notes, commentary, and "gleanings." This last feature, appended to each small section of the commentary, offers "gleanings from world literature" (xxvii) that include selections from Midrash as well as other Jewish, Christian, Moslem, and secular sources that cast light on the Torah text. It is an altogether refreshing format, very useful for pedagogy and enlightening for the scholar and general reader alike.

The *Midrash Rabbah* (that is, the "large" or "great" Midrash) has for half a century been available in English, in a ten-volume edition, edited by H. Freedman and Maurice Simon. This vast compendium can often be entirely perplexing to the uninitiated, but the translation nonetheless offers those without linguistic skill an otherwise unavailable opportunity for study. An even more impressive collection of midrashic texts in English translation is the work of Louis Ginzberg, *Legends of the Jews.* This massive and erudite seven-volume anthology of aggadic sources on scriptural themes includes voluminous and invaluable notes, plus an index to the whole. It is easier to work with than other collections and provides the clearest survey of the aggadic tradition available in English today. For a modern application of the midrashic interpretation of a biblical text (Gen. 22), the reader is also referred to Shalom Spiegel's *Last Trial.*

The whole Babylonian Talmud has long been translated (Epstein) and is now being published by Soncino in a bilingual edition. Also under way, with the University of Chicago Press, is the multivolume *Talmud of the Land of Israel* under the general editorship of Jacob Neusner. There are two other translations of the Mishnah alone, one by Herbert Danby and the other, in seven volumes with much more commentary, by Philip Blackman. For the novice, Neusner has written the clear but sophisticated *Invitation to the Talmud*, which leads the reader through a detailed study of *Berakhot* 8 (a chapter of Mishnah) and the two chapters of Talmud that are based on it. For a translation of *The Zohar*, the greatest of Jewish mystical works, see Maurice Simon and Harry Sperling's five-volume edition. Rashi's, the most famous of medieval Jewish Torah commentaries, is available in two translations, the fuller edition entitled *Pentateuch with Targum Onkelos, Haphtaroth and Rashi's Commentary*, translated and edited in five volumes by M. Rosenbaum and A. M. Silbermann.

The last of the Jewish sources that must be mentioned is an incomplete, but nevertheless remarkable, compendium, not often enough referred to in the literature. The English version is called *Encyclopedia of Biblical Interpretation*, a translation and abridgment of Menachem M. Kasher's monumental Hebrew compendium *Torah Shelemah* ("Complete" Torah, that is, the combination of the so-called Written Torah and Oral Torah). Planned for thirty-five volumes, with at least twenty-nine published to date, *Torah Shelemah* attempts to assemble and collate, for every scriptural verse, "every known commentary, homily, parable, and exegetical interpretation . . . from the very earliest" to about 1500, "gathered from every printed source extant" and scores of unpublished manuscripts, and, in addition, commentary from the scholarship of the last four centuries (*Encyclopedia* xiv). English volumes 1 through 9 cover commentary only on Genesis through Exodus 20. This wonderful treasure trove, the novice will be pleased to learn, is generally clear and easy to use.

Since the above discussion only highlights a few works from the tradition, a recent survey of the field of Jewish literature may well be in order as a closing recommendation. *Back to the Sources*, edited by Barry W. Holtz, contains up-to-date introductory essays followed by short bibliographic discussions. The volume contains three essays on the Bible and one on each of the following: Talmud, Midrash, medieval Bible commentaries, medieval Jewish philosophy, Kabbala, Hasidism, and prayer.

Because the geography of the ancient Near East and modern Middle East can be troublesome for the seasoned scholar and is always so for the student, ready access to a reliable atlas is essential for almost everyone studying the Bible. The following are the atlases generally used by instructors and recommended or required for students: *The Westminster Historical Atlas to the Bible*, edited by G. Ernest Wright and Floyd V. Filson; *The Macmillan Bible Atlas*, edited by Yohanan Aharoni and Michael Avi-Yonah; Herbert G. May's *Oxford Bible Atlas*, revised by John Day. The *Macmillan* best illustrates events; the *Oxford* is perhaps best for the climate and physical features of biblical lands. See also Robert L. Cohn's *Shape of Sacred Space*, a study of the religious or symbolic meaning of biblical geography, and Othmar Keel's *Symbolism of the Biblical World*.

Even more important than the geography of the ancient Near East, for many teachers, is the context of its comparative history, religion, and literature. The standard collections of primary extrabiblical texts in English are James B. Pritchard's companion volumes, *Ancient Near Eastern Texts* and *The Ancient Near East in Pictures*. See also the more recent *Near Eastern Religious Texts Relating to the Old Testament*, edited by Walter Beyerlin et al.

Pritchard's *Ancient Near Eastern Texts* prints E. A. Speiser's translation of the *Gilgamesh* epic. The recent translation by John Gardner and John Maier is already recognized as the leading one. A looser verse rendition of *Gilgamesh* has been done by Herbert Mason and a prose rendition by N. K. Sandars, both of which have been popular in Bible and literature courses during the past two decades. Older but still useful is Alexander Heidel's Gilgamesh Epic *and Old Testament Parallels*. See also his *Babylonian Genesis*, which includes the *Enuma Elish*, other Babylonian creation stories, and scriptural parallels.

The standard collection for comparative study of wisdom texts is Wilfred G. Lambert's *Babylonian Wisdom Literature*, and, for a general orientation to the genres and traditions, there is Gerhard von Rad's *Wisdom in Israel*. For comparative material on ancient law, the reader is directed to *The Assyrian Laws* and *The Babylonian Laws*, both edited by G. R. Driver and John C. Miles. Moshe Greenberg's well-known essay entitled "Some Postulates of Biblical Criminal Law" provides easy access to the comparative field, as well as a useful pedagogical aid to the thorny issue of capital punishment for murder and adultery in ancient Israel. Robert C. Denton's *Idea of History in the Ancient Near East* is perhaps the best place to embark on a study of comparative historiography, and Robert R. Wilson's *Genealogy and History in the Biblical World* is best for genealogy.

A first-rate general orientation to the ancient Near East can be found in William F. Albright's classic work of enduring value, *From the Stone Age to Christianity*. Ancient Near Eastern religious and mythical context is succinctly and brilliantly provided by the universally admired, often reprinted *Before Philosophy* (originally *The Intellectual Adventure of Ancient Man*), by Henri Frankfort et al. Theodor H. Gaster's two-volume *Myth, Legend, and Custom in the Old Testament*, a compendium incorporating much of James Frazer's earlier *Folklore in the Old Testament*, gathers the material that bears on the interpretation of the Hebrew Bible. Sidney H. Hooke's earlier works are still of special interest: his two collections of essays by various scholars entitled *Myth and Ritual* and *Myth, Ritual, and Kingship*, and his *Middle Eastern Mythology*, describing the mythologies of Mesopotamian, Egyptian, Canaanite, Hittite, Hebrew, and Christian cultures. Consult also Driver's *Canaanite Myths and Legends* and the works of Samuel Noah Kramer: *Mythologies of the Ancient World*, *The Sumerians*, and the popular *History Begins at Sumer*.

This Near Eastern framework finds an even larger context in comparative religion and mythology more generally. Works of this still broader scope usually have only limited practical application to the Bible itself. They are, however, among the most stimulating for teachers and students, encouraging us, as they do, to view the Bible from a perspective wider than our traditions will normally allow, and so a few of the most highly regarded of these works are mentioned below. The books of the very prolific Mircea Eliade should perhaps head the list, especially *Cosmos and History: The Myth of the Eternal Return*, *Patterns in Comparative Religion*, and—his best-known work in English—*The Sacred and the Profane*. Joseph Campbell, equally prolific author of the four-volume *Masks of God*, is probably best known among Bible teachers for *The Hero with a Thousand Faces*, which traces the standard path of the adventures of the "mythical hero." See also Rudolph Otto's *Idea of the Holy* and the Victorian classic of comparative anthropology, James G. Frazer's *Golden Bough*, now available and nearly always read in a one-volume, paperback abridgment by Gaster. Finally, an unusual book, harder to categorize, Herbert N. Schneidau's *Sacred Discontent* locates the ancient Israelites within their geographical and cultural milieu but concerns itself more with their influence on later civilization. The fundamental and ubiquitous message of the Hebrew Bible, according to Schneidau, is the need for change that derives from the ancient Israelite ambivalence toward culture of any kind. Ancient Israel "desacralized" culture as well as nature, and, by doing so, the tradition of the Bible paved the way for the scientific view of nature and the historic view of culture.

Usually only courses specifically concerned with theology require the reading of scholarly theological studies. Many instructors, however, encourage the reading of books covering the religion of Israel more generally, its history and its development. Among the most impressive and most often recommended of these are the following: Albright's classic, *Archaeology and the Religion of Israel*; Greenberg's abridged translation of Yehezkel Kaufmann's provocative, multivolume *Religion of Israel*; Helmer Ringgren's *Israelite Religion*; Frank Moore Cross's sober and convincing assessment of the connections between Canaanite myth and biblical literature, *Canaanite Myth and Hebrew Epic*.

Of even more general application are the two well-known, massive scholarly undertakings by Johannes Pedersen and Roland de Vaux. Pedersen's *Israel: Its Life and Culture* is a thorough exposition of the sociopsychological characteristics of ancient Israel. De Vaux's *Ancient Israel* devotes one volume to social institutions and another to religious institutions. Both texts provide valuable introductory sources of information, though Pedersen's is now somewhat dated.

There is, of course, an enormous body of theological writing, but the two most impressive works of Old Testament theology in our time and the most useful as reference for our courses are Walther Eichrodt's two-volume *Theology of the Old Testament* and Gerhard von Rad's two-volume *Old Testament Theology*. A simpler book, sometimes recommended for students though instructive to all, is Walther Zimmerli's *Old Testament Theology in Outline*.

Feminist scholarship of the seventies and eighties is likely to be introduced into numerous Bible courses, and so a few of the best works in this field that attend particularly to the Hebrew Bible should also be mentioned. Because of their dynamic quality and widespread influence, Phyllis Trible's companion books will head the list: *God and the Rhetoric of Sexuality* and *Texts of Terror*. See also Mary Daly's relatively early study, *Beyond God the Father*, Sallie McFague's *Metaphorical Theology*, and Mieke Bal's recent *Lethal Love* and *Death and Dissymmetry*. (See her essay in part 2 of this book.) Rosemary Radford Ruether's influential anthology entitled *Religion and Sexism* contains essays applicable to a wide range of academic study. Other, more recent collections of essays are *The Bible and Feminist Hermeneutics*, edited by Mary Ann Tolbert; *The Liberating Word* and *Feminist Interpretation of the Bible*, both edited by Letty M. Russell.

History books have been discussed in greater detail in "Recommended and Required Reading for Students." Among one-volume histories, Bright's *History of Israel* continues to be the most thoroughly read and frequently recommended and referred to within the academic community. Noth's *History of Israel* and Herrmann's briefer *History of Israel in Old Testament Times* are the other titles most often appearing on our questionnaires.

One-volume introductions to the Bible, especially Anderson's *Understanding the Old Testament*, have also been discussed among the books specifically for students. These can provide easily absorbed overviews of the entire field for beginning instructors and nonspecialists. They offer interesting pedagogical approaches to the text and to many areas and disciplines related to the text. Here I need comment only on the one not normally recommended for undergraduate student use, Otto Eissfeldt's *Old Testament: An Introduction*. This renowned, detailed, and compendious form-critical study covers the Apocrypha, pseudepigrapha, and works from Qumran as well as the Hebrew Bible. "The grand-daddy of critical introductions" is the way one respondent describes it; "the basic book one can always reach for in times of panic" writes another. This daunting and massive work is structured in five parts, which in turn have many subdivisions: part 1 deals with the "preliterary stage" and the "smallest units" of the Bible; part 2 deals with the "literary prehistory" of the books; part 3 analyzes each of the books, basically in the Hebrew Bible order; part 4 discusses the formation of the canon, the deuterocanonical books, and other noncanonical books; part 5 is devoted to the "text" from its "prehistory" through the Vulgate translation.

For the history of biblical interpretation and translation, the primary reference work is *The Cambridge History of the Bible*, which contains, within its three volumes, articles by different scholars on Bible texts and versions in the West, the circulation of the Bible, attitudes toward its authority and interpretation, and its place in the life of the Western Church. An updated, brief history of interpretation may be found in Robert M. Grant and David Tracy, *A Short History of the Interpretation of the Bible*. The one nineteenth-century critical text still recurring on syllabi and still widely read for its (in)famous "Documentary Hypothesis" is Julius Wellhausen's *Prolegomena to the History of Israel*. See also Ronald E. Clements's survey, *A Century of Old Testament Study*, a point of departure and major focus of which is the work and influence of Wellhausen, and John Rogerson's *Old Testament Criticism in the Nineteenth Century*, a study of the previous century concluding with "the triumph of Wellhausen."

A number of our respondents suggested *The Old Testament in Modern Research*, by Herbert F. Hahn and Horace D. Hummel, for a survey of modern approaches to scriptural interpretation. The survey, however, does not include the literary study of the Bible and is, by now, somewhat out-of-date. Better to consult *Tradition and Interpretation*, edited by G. W. Anderson, which contains thirteen essays with bibliographies and an introduction by different members of the Society for Old Testament Study. It tries to provide a general account of the position of scholarship in various branches of Old Testament study, but it too fails to include the field of literary criticism. Lastly, a more recent volume, edited by Douglas A. Knight and Gene M. Tucker, *The Hebrew Bible and Its Modern Interpreters*, deals with the history of biblical interpretation since 1945.

Recent Literary Criticism

I anticipate that readers of this volume will consist primarily of literature teachers with courses, or parts of courses, devoted to the Bible and of biblicists teaching, or wishing to teach, within a literary-critical framework. Given this readership and the fact that synchronic literary-critical study represents one of the most important developments in recent Bible scholarship, I devote an entire section to the field. Entries are limited mainly to studies in English of the past few decades. Listings of the many earlier surveys and other older books and articles may be found annotated throughout the pages of John Gottcent, *The Bible as Literature*. Consult especially the sections entitled "The Bible as Literature: History of" (40–44), "The Bible as Literature: General Studies" (44–52), and "The Old Testament as Literature: General Studies" (76–81). Gottcent also includes bibliographies on individual books of the Hebrew Bible and has quite useful listings for Genesis and Job, books that everyone seems to teach. See also *Bible-Related Curriculum Materials*, edited by Thayer S. Warshaw et al.

Entries in this section, with but few exceptions, are restricted specifically to the literary-critical treatment of the Hebrew Bible, and so the reader will only rarely find reference to works on the Bible *and* literature or the Bible *in* literature. Excluded also are the many apologia for the study of the Bible "as literature." This designation, for some critics and theorists today, is a misnomer, no more appropriate to the study of the Bible than to the study of *The Aeneid* or *The Divine Comedy*. This very point, in fact, is given prominence in the most thorough and one of the best of recent studies, Meir Sternberg's *Poetics of Biblical Narrative*. Sternberg says:

> To offer a poetics of biblical narrative is to claim that biblical narrative is a work of literature. Not just an artful work; . . . not a work resorting to so-called literary devices; not a work that the interpreter may choose (or refuse) to consider from a literary viewpoint or, in that unlovely piece of jargon, as literature; but a literary work. The difference is radical. (2)

A full treatment of this issue is unfortunately beyond the scope and purpose of my essay. To do justice to its complexity, however, I cite one alternative opinion of at least equal authority:

> In dealing with literature we frequently speak of its self-contained unity as "imaginative," and distinguish as "imaginary" its relation to actual events. The Bible, however, . . . evades this antithesis: it is neither literary nor non-literary, or, more positively, it is as literary as it can well be without actually being literature. (Frye, *Great Code* 62)

The Literary Guide to the Bible, edited by Robert Alter and Frank Kermode, with contributions by twenty-four other international scholar-critics, promises to become a standard reference work in the field. It consists of Alter's introduction to the Old Testament followed by twenty-two essays on individual books or groups of books, Kermode's introduction to the New Testament followed by eight such essays, and another group of essays on more general topics. The problem with *The Literary Guide*, a problem common to many essay collections, is that its contributions are of widely disparate quality.

The greatest strides in recent years have been made in the areas of narrative and narratology. The most frequently read and most highly praised of the many works in these areas is surely Alter's *Art of Biblical Narrative*. "The one indispensable book" for students and scholars alike—as one respondent puts it—Alter's study has attracted a wide, enthusiastic readership. Almost fifty percent of our respondents recommend it to their students or use it to prepare their courses. Perceptive, lucid, and relatively jargon-free, Alter's book describes and analyzes the literary conventions of biblical narrative, the emergence of character, the crucial importance of point of view, and much more—all in a way that is credible to nearly everyone who reads it. His most impressive contributions lie in explicating and illustrating the biblical "type-scene" and the various techniques of repetition characteristic of biblical styles.

Sternberg's *Poetics*, referred to above, published after our survey was conducted, also promises to be especially influential, though it is more difficult to read than Alter's book. It covers the full range of a "poetics" of narrative, including a good deal of current literary theory and literary analysis of narrative passages of the Hebrew Bible. Another, more modest "poetics," but easier to read and more adaptable to the classroom, is Adele Berlin's *Poetics and Interpretation of Biblical Narrative*. A useful combination of theory and the close reading of texts, Berlin's book concentrates on character and point of view.

Because Alter's *Art of Biblical Narrative* just preceded the publication of Northrop Frye's long-awaited *Great Code*, the two books were often discussed and even reviewed together. While Alter's is about the Hebrew Bible and very much in the forefront of the new literary-critical approach, Frye's is about the Christian Old and New Testaments and is to be identified with a more traditional typological approach. Despite some disappointment with *The Great Code*, it certainly represents a major achievement of its kind and has been widely read within academic circles. It presents great difficulty for undergraduates and nonspecialists, however, and only a few teachers have used it in or for their courses. Also recurring on our questionnaires are recommendations for parts of Frye's *Anatomy of Criticism*, especially "Theory of Archetypal Meaning (1): Apocalyptic Imagery" (141–46) and "Specific Encyclopaedic Forms" (315–26), and for his essay "History and Myth in the Bible." These are concerned with the operation of myth and archetype as the organizing form of narrative, what Frye calls *mythos*.

Michael A. Fishbane's little-known essay "The Sacred Center: The Symbolic Structure of the Bible," does for Hebrew Scripture what Frye's methodology does for Christian ("a sustained religious imagination has filtered historical facticity through archetypal structures" [7]). Fishbane's clear, perceptive, and ground-breaking collection of pieces entitled *Text and Texture* is especially adaptable to pedagogical purposes but is not as widely used as it ought to be. Of special interest are the first four essays, which are on the early narratives of Genesis, the Jacob cycle, and the early chapters of Exodus, and the last two essays, which are on the Eden and Exodus motifs.

As noted in the section entitled "Required and Recommended Reading for Students," the most often cited literary essay in response to our questionnaire is Erich Auerbach's celebrated "Odysseus' Scar" (*Mimesis* 3–23). For the scholar interested in a lesser-known critique of part of Auerbach's method, see William Whallon's article "Old Testament Poetry and Homeric Epic" and the last two chapters of his book *Formula, Character, and Context*, in which Whallon argues, among many other things, that Auerbach's comparison of Homeric poetry with Hebrew prose is not entirely justified on generic terms. See also Auerbach's equally influential essay, but one much less suited for the classroom, "Figura," a long, erudite piece on classical and Christian figural interpretation.

A very interesting and probing "deconstructive" study (of sorts) is Peter D. Miscall's *Workings of Old Testament Narrative*, the second part of which is expanded in his *1 Samuel: A Literary Reading* (published too recently for anything but a notice here). Miscall works in microcosm, so to speak, devoting 143 pages to the analysis of Genesis 12 and 1 Samuel 16–22, trying to demonstrate "how the biblical text undermines itself, puts its own status and authority into question" (142). Although Miscall never refers to Schneidau's *Sacred Discontent* (described in the preceding section), the two works are allied ideologically, Miscall's analyses silently affirming Schneidau's ideas about the Israelites' devaluation of cultural attainments and their tendency to undercut or interpret their own myths. The fifth and final chapter of *Sacred Discontent*, "The Bible and Literature: Against Positivism," is a literary study in which Schneidau asserts that the West has inherited from Israel its tendency to probe and criticize language, the verbal forms that shape our acts. In ancient times, the prophets and Jesus did this, while today it is the function of our imaginative writers. It is also in this final chapter that Schneidau distinguishes between metaphor and metonymy ("where myth is hypotactic metaphors, the Bible is paratactic metonymies" [292]), a distinction further developed in chapter 1 of Frye's *Great Code* and chapter 2 of Alter's *Art of Biblical Narrative*.

Brief reference to other recent, miscellaneous approaches to biblical literature may be made here. Ulrich Simon's *Story and Faith in the Biblical Narrative* finds relations between "forms of narrative" and "areas of faith." Jacob Licht's *Storytelling in the Bible* distinguishes between historical and storytelling aspects of narrative in the first chapter and goes on to deal briefly with "scenes and basic structures," repetition, point of view, time, and "complex structures." Steven J. Brams's *Biblical Games* analyzes biblical narrative from the standpoint of modern game theory. Yehoshua Gitay's *Prophecy and Persuasion: A Study of Isaiah 40–48* is the study of prophecy most sensitive to contemporary literary concerns.

A few books from the 1960s and early 1970s deserve mention, chief among them being Luis Alonso Schökel's *Inspired Word*. This contains a valiant attempt to synthesize traditional ideas of inspiration with modern ones on the nature of language, literature, and the creative process. Edwin M. Good's *Irony in the Old Testament* was among the first books to apply contemporary methods of literary criticism to the Hebrew Bible. The book contains an introduction on irony and studies of Jonah, Saul, Isaiah, Ecclesiastes, Job, and a number of figures and episodes from Genesis. *Teaching the Old Testament in English Classes*, by James S. Ackerman et al., is very basic but reportedly still useful even at the university level. Consult also Thayer Warshaw's *Handbook for Teaching the Bible in Literature Classes*.

There are two little-known books by Zvi Adar, a genuine pioneer in the field deserving more recognition than he got: *The Biblical Narrative* discusses five "stages of narrative" (short tale, cycle of stories, long story, book, the biblical narrative as a whole); *Humanistic Values in the Bible* is particularly concerned with pedagogy and with the "educational value" of the literature. Mary Ellen Chase's older, popular studies are still to be found on professors' shelves and in their course syllabi: *The Bible and the Common Reader* and thè sequel, *Life and Language in the Old Testament*. See also Elias J. Bickerman, *Four Strange Books of the Bible: Jonah, Daniel, Koheleth, Esther,* and T. R. Henn, *The Bible as Literature*, both of which are still used in academe.

Because of their perceived application to pedagogy, essays containing important literary approaches by James Muilenburg, Kenneth Burke, John Becker, Matitiahu Tsevat, and P. Joseph Cahill have already been discussed in the section devoted to student reading. A few other early essays on biblical imagery are deserving of mention here: H. Fisch, "The Analogy of Nature: A Note on the Structure of Old Testament Imagery"; Dom Aelred Baker, "Visual Imagination and the Bible"; D. F. Payne, "A Perspective on the Use of Simile in the Old Testament"; Dov Rosner, "The Simile and Its Use in the Old Testament." With the exception of Baker's fascinating piece, the titles of these essays are self-explanatory. Baker discusses the paucity of visual details in biblical description and the absence of "portraits" in anything like the modern sense of the term. He then relates these stylistic characteristics to later scriptural interpretation.

Also discussed under student reading are the two best current essay anthologies, edited by Maier and Tollers and by Gros Louis. Robert C. Culley has edited two special issues of *Semeia: Classical Hebrew Narrative* and *Oral Tradition and Old Testament Studies*. Readers unfamiliar with *Semeia* should consult this experimental journal, its special issues, and the monographs published under its auspices for the latest in theoretical and critical approaches to the Bible. See also Semeia Supplements 8, *Encounter with the Text*, edited by Martin J. Buss, and *The Biblical Mosaic*, edited by Robert M. Polzin and

Eugene Rothman. The British *Journal for the Study of the Old Testament* (*JSOT*) and its Supplement Series are equally valuable. See especially *Images of Man and God: Old Testament Short Stories in Literary Focus*, edited by Burke O. Long, and *Art and Meaning: Rhetoric in Biblical Literature*, edited by David J. A. Clines et al.

The omnipresence of "structuralism" in the literary criticism and social sciences of the past decades is clearly reflected in biblical studies. The approach is so important and the studies so numerous as to encourage this subsection devoted exclusively to structuralist approaches and other studies generally concerned with structure. I begin with brief mention of a few works from other fields that have exerted special influence on Bible scholarship. The oldest of these is Vladimir Propp's *Morphology of the Folktale*. Propp isolated thirty-one "functions," or constant features of plot structure, of Russian heroic fairy tales and studied their sequencing and interrelationships. That these fairy tales will, in the end, be of much use for biblical studies is still in doubt, but attempts have already been made to superimpose or adapt Propp's model to biblical literature. Perhaps the best known of these is Jack M. Sasson's use of it to analyze the literary type of the story of Ruth. See Alexander Globe's essay on "Folktale Form" in part 2 of this volume.

The most influential anthropological studies are those by Claude Lévi-Strauss, especially *Structural Anthropology*, *The Elementary Structures of Kinship*, and *The Raw and the Cooked*. The novice may find that Lévi-Strauss's seminal essay "The Structural Study of Myth" provides a more focused and accessible introduction to the process and to some of the main principles of structural mythology.

Many structural anthropological studies are devoted specifically or principally to the Hebrew Bible, the most famous of these being *Genesis as Myth and Other Essays*, written by the doyen of British anthropology, Edmund Leach. His much more recent *Structuralist Interpretations of Biblical Myth*, coauthored with D. Alan Aycock, contains a reprint of a lecture called "Anthropological Approaches to the Study of the Bible during the Twentieth Century," as well as five more specific, not always convincing, pieces, two of which are by Aycock. The basic argument of Leach's work, and indeed of structuralist studies in general, is that the true meaning of these sacred texts is deeply "encoded" in their structures and not easily inferred from the "manifest sense" of the narrative. In this regard, the structuralist approach is somewhat akin to the psychoanalytic, but structuralists focus more on totalities than component parts, more on patterns than particulars.

Three other anthropological essays should at least be mentioned. Their titles describe their contents: Michael P. Carroll's "Leach, Genesis, and Structural Analysis"; Karin R. Andriolo's "Structural Analysis of Genealogy and Worldview in the Old Testament"; and Robert C. Marshall's "Heroes and Hebrews: The Priest in the Promised Land."

For an elementary introduction to literary structuralism, see Robert

Scholes's *Structuralism in Literature*, and, for a general study of its application to the Bible, Daniel Patte's *What Is Structural Exegesis?* and Daniel Patte and Aline Patte's *Structural Exegesis*. For a conceptual and historical overview of the major trends and figures shaping twentieth-century literary criticism and theory, and for suggestions concerning the convergence of criticism and theory with biblical study, consult Edgar V. McKnight, *The Bible and the Reader*. This little book surveys everyone from Barthes and Culler to Sklovskij and Todorov, providing brief remarks on a host of fields and figures for specialist and nonspecialist alike.

There is a plethora of literary structuralist studies of the Hebrew Bible and related areas, but space allows only for a representative sampling of the best. Convenient essay collections are *Structuralism and Biblical Hermeneutics*, edited by Alfred M. Johnson; and Roland Barthes et al., *Structural Analysis and Biblical Exegesis*, which contains Barthes's celebrated and often reprinted "The Struggle with the Angel: Textual Analysis of Genesis 32: 22–32." *Interpretation* 28 published five useful articles on the subject: Robert A. Spivey, "Structuralism and Biblical Studies: *The Uninvited Guest*"; Richard Jacobson, "The Structuralists and the Bible"; Robert Culley, "Structural Analysis: Is It Done with Mirrors?"; Robert M. Polzin, "The Framework of the Book of Job"; Dan O. Via, Jr., "A Structuralist Approach to Paul's Old Testament Hermeneutic."

The study of chiasmus has become an important part of structural approaches, and many analyses of biblical episodes focus on supposed chiastic patterns. Michael Fishbane's studies of "symmetry" in his *Text and Texture* represent some of the earliest and most influential of these. Perhaps the most complex (though not necessarily the most credible) is *Chiasmus in Antiquity*, edited by John W. Welch. The Hebrew Bible is represented in this collection by Yehuda T. Radday's elaborate "Chiasmus in Hebrew Biblical Narrative," which claims to prove that very complicated forms of structuralism have been employed as deliberately in ancient Hebrew narrative as in modern fiction; and by Wilfred G. Watson's "Chiastic Patterns in Biblical Hebrew Poetry." See also Radday's "Chiasm in Kings." A short, provocative book, Isaac M. Kikawada and Arthur Quinn's *Before Abraham Was*, makes credible use of chiastic analysis. The authors construct a stylistic and structuralist argument for the unity of the first eleven chapters of Genesis, and thus an argument against the Documentary Hypothesis. For an older argument, similar but more traditional, consult the following works of the great scholar Umberto Cassuto: *A Commentary on the Book of Genesis* and *The Documentary Hypothesis and the Composition of the Pentateuch*.

Other recent structural studies of the Hebrew Bible are the following: J. P. Fokkelman's *Narrative Art in Genesis* and *Narrative Art and Poetry in the Books of Samuel* (Vol. 1: *King David*); Culley's *Studies in the Structure of Hebrew Narrative*; Charles Conroy's *Absalom Absalom! Narrative and Language in 2 Sam. 13–20*; Polzin's *Biblical Structuralism* and *Moses and the Deuteronomist*; D. M. Gunn's *Story of King David* and *Fate of King Saul*; David Jobling's *Sense of Biblical Narrative*.

Many colleagues have been especially influenced by the hermeneutics of
Paul Ricoeur. His collected essays can be found in *The Conflict of Interpretations* and *Essays on Biblical Interpretation*. A collection of pieces about him
has been edited by John Dominic Crossan for *Semeia, Paul Ricoeur on Biblical Hermeneutics*. See also Ricoeur's *Symbolism of Evil* and *Rule of Metaphor*.

In comparison with the recent literary studies of biblical narrative, those
for poetry or verse are disappointingly few. The theoretical studies are inadequate to varying degrees, and the critical language for discussing the poems
is only beginning to be refined and sophisticated. The best place I know to
begin one's study of biblical poetry is the *Encyclopaedia Judaica*, volume 13.
This contains a brief but insightful section, "Some Principles of Biblical Verse,"
part of the much longer entry by Benjamin Hrushovski entitled "Prosody, Hebrew." Also in this volume, under the general heading "Poetry," is a more sub-
stantial essay, "Biblical Poetry," by James Muilenburg. These relatively painless
pieces offer the rudiments of a state-of-the-art understanding of the subject.
An alternative or supplementary introduction may be found in the *Interpreter's
Dictionary of the Bible*, volume 3, under "Poetry, Hebrew," by Norman Gottwald. This should be read along with the article in the supplementary volume by Mitchell Dahood.

A number of important studies, requiring of the reader little or no Hebrew
knowledge, have recently been published on the subject. James L. Kugel's
major scholarly contribution, *The Idea of Biblical Poetry: Parallelism and Its
History*, is well described by its subtitle. The opening chapters contain a radical reformulation of the description and significance of Hebrew parallelism,
while most of the rest of his book discusses "its history" from midrashic exegesis to Robert Lowth's "discovery" of it. Robert Alter's *Art of Biblical Poetry*,
as the title suggests, is conceived as a companion volume to his earlier book
on narrative. The first three chapters establish the "formal system of biblical
poetry . . . moving from the nature of the poetic line to larger structures"
(ix). The remainder of the book seeks to apply the general conceptions to
the major poetic texts. The main genres are covered: psalms, prophecy, wisdom poetry, proverbs, and love poetry. The close readings of the texts are
illuminating and should prove valuable for pedagogy. Adele Berlin's *Dynamics
of Biblical Parallelism* uses a variety of readily accessible linguistic approaches
to describe what biblical parallelism is and how it operates. Grammatical,
lexical, and phonological language levels are covered concisely yet thoroughly;
citations are mainly of verse but include a good number of prose passages
as well. Her book includes an extensive and helpful bibliography. Other useful studies of parallelism, especially of the grammatical type, are Stephen
Geller's *Parallelism in Early Biblical Poetry* and Edward Greenstein's "How
Does Parallelism Mean?"

The standard texts in English before the above were published will already
be familiar to the experienced teacher, especially George B. Gray's *Forms of
Hebrew Poetry*, reissued with a prolegomenon by David Noel Freedman, and

Theodore H. Robinson's *Poetry of the Old Testament*. A structuralist approach is represented by Ruth apRoberts, "Old Testament Poetry: The Translatable Structure." Hebrew poetry, she argues, is translatable because "the sense unit is the form unit. The units are not phonemic but semantic" (1001). David Noel Freedman's *Pottery, Poetry, and Prophecy* makes available in one volume more than fifteen of his scholarly essays on Hebrew poetry. Very useful, but written principally for readers with knowledge of Hebrew, is Wilfred Watson's *Classical Hebrew Poetry*. This text may serve as a reference guide to such subjects as oral poetry, metrics, parallelism, stanza and strophe, verse patterns, phonology, imagery, and numerous poetic devices. Extensive bibliographies for each topic and helpful indexes are its other important features.

Finally, Edward Greenstein and Alex Preminger's anthology *The Hebrew Bible in Literary Criticism* provides an overview of critical appreciation of the Bible as literature through the ages.

Aids to Teaching

Many college and university teachers of the Bible believe that the "written word" needs no further aural or visual mediation, that there is little time for audiovisual aids in the classroom, and that struggling with the text alone will ultimately produce the results desired. In the end, however, it is the uses to which the Bible is being put, the goals and focuses of one's course, that will determine the need for, or desirability of, aids to teaching. Because the uses to which the Bible is put are so diverse and because so many fields of study can be fruitfully pursued in conjunction with it, the possibilities for employing aids to teaching seem nearly infinite. In what follows a few of the possibilities are suggested and reference sources provided for the instructor interested in pursuing the subject further.

Recommended is the previously referred to *Bible-Related Curriculum Materials*, edited by Warshaw et al., even though the volume was compiled principally for schools. For each scriptural topic covered (such as "Creation," "Noah," "Samson," "Wisdom," "Aprocrypha"), the volume provides listings under the heading "The Bible in/and Other Media—for Pupils." These other media (recordings, sheet music, videocassettes, films, etc.)—as the editors of the bibliography point out—tend to be ephemeral and more difficult to locate than books and articles. The listings, however, do provide a good idea of the biblical books, figures, and episodes on which audiovisual material is available. They also suggest the enormous range of possibilities for enlarging the Bible curriculum with materials from print and nonprint sources.

Among the general media indexes, the best is the National Information Center for Educational Media (NICEM). The indexes most relevant to the Bible cover videotapes, 16mm films, filmstrips, audiotapes, and slides, but all of them locate only materials that are educational, informational, or documentary. The most comprehensive index for reviews of nonbook and nontheatrical material is the annual publication *Media Review Digest*, with sections on film and video, filmstrip, audio media, and "miscellaneous."

Audio media are especially difficult to track down; the *Media Review Digest*, with its alphabetical subject index, should help—but only on an annual basis. There are perhaps a thousand musical settings for biblical texts, and there is no discography dealing with the Bible and music, or even the Bible and the spoken word. *The Gramophone Spoken Word and Miscellaneous Catalogue*, an annual publication, with author and artist indexes (and the Bible under author) is one likely place to start a search. Check also *Schwann*, the monthly periodical of records and tapes, with subject index.

There are two recent filmographies directly relevant to the Bible. *The Bible on Film: A Checklist, 1897–1980*, by Richard H. Campbell and Michael R. Pitts, attempts to list all films largely based on the Bible or containing biblical characters, with "selected" television programs (those that are on film). The arrangement of the checklist is by the year of issue, but a title index may aid a subject search. The compilers offer brief but helpful synopses of each film. *The Middle East and North Africa on Film*, by Marsha Hamilton McClintock, provides a comprehensive listing of films and videotapes produced between 1903 and January 1980. Contents are arranged by general subject and country categories; indexes are by title and series and by producer and distributor. Two other books on film may also be of interest: Jon Solomon's *Ancient World in the Cinema* has long chapters on both testaments; Derek Elley's *Epic Film* is a heavily illustrated survey, with chapters on both testaments and a comprehensive filmography.

Of special note and general interest are at least the following two video series: Northrop Frye, *The Bible and Literature*, a thirty-part video series (each a half-hour long) representing an abridgment of his famous lectures at the University of Toronto; Abba Eban, *Heritage: Civilization and the Jews*, a nine-part documentary for television, the first two episodes of which are most relevant to the Bible: "A People Is Born" (13th–6th centuries BCE) and "The Power of the Word" (6th century BCE–2nd century CE).

The single indispensable resource guide for the use of computers in Bible study (in English, Hebrew, Greek, and Latin) promises to be John J. Hughes's *Bits, Bytes, and Biblical Studies*. Prepublication readers' comments and my own review of parts of the manuscript indicate authoritative description and evaluation of numerous language-learning programs, machine-readable versions of Scripture, word-processing programs, text-retrieval and concording programs, archives and data banks, major online services, and a great deal more practical and helpful material. (Information on the explosion of textual data and computer software is also readily available from the Center for Computer Analysis of Texts [CCAT], University of Pennsylvania. Contact Dr. John Abercrombie [Bitnet address JACKA @ PENNDRLS] or Robert Kraft [KRAFT @ PENNDRLN].)

Among the most helpful aids in traditional Bible courses are maps and charts of the ancient Near East and the contemporary Middle East. These are often adequately represented in the Bibles, atlases, and textbooks that are assigned to students and that are discussed elsewhere in this volume. About one-third of our respondents employ film strips and slide shows on such diverse topics as archeology, ancient art and architecture, Western art influenced by the Bible, flora and fauna, and topography and geography of Israel and its neighbors. The components of these shows are either borrowed from libraries, museums and galleries, and other institutions, or they are gathered by individuals from private photograph collections, book and magazine illustrations, and the like. For those instructors especially wishing to encourage their students to visualize and situate the world in which the scriptural works were composed and collected, slide presentations are often considered essential parts of the course.

The other principal way in which academics use audiovisual material is to help in the explication of the meaning of particular books or episodes or styles of the Bible. This kind of use may range from the unique or occasional aid to the regular employment of the full range of materials, usually associated with courses on the Bible and Western culture. In these courses, audiovisual materials may be used not simply to illustrate or explicate a text but to indicate the vast impact of Scripture on the social life and artistic production of the Western world.

The study of the Bible and visual arts is a vast, fascinating field, for which no one general guide exists. The number of specific reference sources and scholarly studies, however, is legion. For a preliminary search in this area, the most fertile of the Library of Congress subject headings are "Bible-Illustrations" and "Bible-Pictures." Especially helpful for locating reproductions of paintings in books and catalogs are the following reference tools: *World Painting Index* and its first supplement, by Patricia Pate Havlice; *Index to Reproductions of European Paintings*, by Isabel Stevenson Monro and Kate M. Monro; *Index to Reproductions of American Paintings* and its first supplement, also by Monro and Monro; *Index to Reproductions of American Paintings Appearing in More Than Four Hundred Books, Mostly Published since 1960*, by Lyn Wall Smith and Nancy Dustin Wall Moure. A more specific source providing access to a rich collection of slides and photographs of paintings is *Iconographic Index to Old Testament Paintings, . . . Fine Arts Library, Harvard University*, compiled by the curator Helene E. Roberts.

Visual images of Eden, or paradise, or Adam and Eve through the ages may be especially enlightening to students of Genesis interested in the history and variety of scriptural interpretation, and also to those studying comparative culture, art, or other literary works like *Paradise Lost, The Faerie Queen*, and many others. Illustrative images for such a presentation are readily available to all. William Blake's drawings, watercolors, and engravings provide a common adjunct to the study of the book of Job (as does Job to Blake's poetry and pictures); for a teaching approach along these lines see Robert E. Simmons's essay in part 2 of this volume. One of our respondents suggests that a model for a visual commentary on biblical texts is provided by Robert Short's *A Time to Be Born—a Time to Die*, which offers contemporary photographs by way of commenting on the verses of Ecclesiastes. Audio suggestions range from Martin Luther King's speech "I Have a Dream" in connection with an introduction to Israelite prophecy, to Handel's *Messiah* as adjunct to the study of Isaiah (and, indeed, other oratorios for other texts), even to Bill Cosby's "Noah" skit in connection with the Genesis story. As I have said, the possibilities seem almost infinite, depending on time, knowledge, purpose, and inclination.

Part Two

APPROACHES

INTRODUCTION

The essayists presented in the following pages were chosen from among the respondents to our questionnaire and invited to write about some aspect of their Bible teaching that falls broadly within a literary or literary-critical framework. Their essays describe both representative and innovative approaches. Some reflect what scholar-teachers have been and currently are doing in their university, college, and seminary classrooms, while others attempt to guide readers through new pedagogical approaches and perspectives. Theory and criticism enter these pages mainly as they are applied to pedagogy.

In North America and especially the United States, the vast majority of undergraduate and seminary courses on the Hebrew Bible or the Old Testament are taught in a single semester or the first half of a full year course (which frequently includes the New Testament and the Apocrypha). There is, therefore, a generally experienced tension between surveying the full range of material and covering some of it in greater depth. The number of texts to assign, the number of topics to discuss, and the number of approaches and methodologies to introduce are the three fundamental issues in constructing the syllabus of the survey course. Between maximalist and minimalist approaches there remains a gradation of great variety. Questions of breadth versus depth, variety versus intensity, and the like feature in the essays of the first two sections.

The Bible is studied in conjunction with, or used for the study of, Hebrew language, ancient and modern law and ethics, archeology, theology, religious studies, mythology, women's and feminist studies, and social, political, and intellectual history (within which the comparison of ancient Greece and Israel seems a favorite topic). The books most frequently taught seem to be Genesis and Job. The most common focuses for upper-level, specialist courses are the Torah, especially Genesis and Exodus; the prophetic books, including the especially popular Jonah; and poetry and wisdom. The biblical figures most often selected for special attention seem to be one or more of the

Prophets, Saul and David (frequently coupled), and the variety of female figures of both testaments and the Apocrypha.

There exists a huge diversity of content and perspective among approaches that respondents identify as "literary" or "literary-critical," the largest divisions of which are the Bible as literature, the Bible and literature, and the Bible in literature, including comparative literature and even the "biblical tradition in Western culture" more generally. The most frequent request for information among our respondents pertains to biblical genres and styles, reflecting, I think, the confusion that still exists within the minds of many instructors and the vagueness of description and categorization still found in so many books on these subjects. A literary-critical approach is preferred by many instructors as the most efficient way of studying the "coherence" and "integrity" of the texts or of allowing their students to "question the text" without feeling that faith or person is being "threatened."

The responses to our questionnaire suggest, not surprisingly, that North American biblicists are most comfortable using the older historical-critical approaches and literature teachers the older rhetorical or New Critical approaches. A main reason for this, of course, is that these approaches are most familiar to instructors who themselves were students a generation or more ago. Also, in defense of two of these approaches, New Criticism and rhetorical criticism do not require prior knowledge or theory on the students' part, and so, unlike many other approaches, can yield immediate results.

Recent theories of narrative and narratology are also clearly reflected in current pedagogy. Close analysis of narrative strategies and structures, especially that using structuralist methodology, characterizes a very broad spectrum of Bible courses. Today one need not be a literary specialist to deal successfully with scriptural narrative in terms of point of view, genre, archetype, motif, characterization, key-word, and type-scene. Poststructuralist approaches to the text are used much less regularly, mainly by specialists, and all too often with only "limited success" (as more than one instructor has noted).

Bible pedagogy is in the same period of flux as are its theoretical cousins, scriptural hermeneutics and literary theory. Many instructors—including sophisticated scholars and theorists—frankly admit that they are refining their perspectives and techniques and that this process, though challenging and unsettling, is also stimulating and illuminating. Flexibility, variety, and eclecticism seem to be the norm within the literary-critical framework. Unfortunately, however, only a few instructors are sufficiently concerned to inquire into the underpinnings of their basic theoretical approaches or into the exegetical integrity of their generally eclectic positions.

The essays collected here represent approaches and perspectives that respondents suggested. They are grouped in three broad sections. The first, outlining the field of study, contains essays on teaching Scripture in translation, on teaching the Old Testament within the Christian cultural tradition, and on teaching the Hebrew Bible as distinct from the Old Testament. The second section presents a variety of focuses, including the socioliterary, metaphorical, comparative, psychoanalytic, and feminist, as well as two shorter, less easily characterized pieces (by Francis Landy and Herbert Schneidau). The final section contains essays dealing with the teaching of specific genres, books, or chapters of books. Uniting them all are their authors' devotion to the subject and zeal for teaching and learning.

BNO

DEFINING THE FIELD OF STUDY

It Gains a Lot in Translation

Stanley N. Rosenbaum

For my mother, z"l

In the best of all possible worlds, we would be able to recall not only the Greek that Plato implies we all once knew but also our Hebrew. In the second best, we would require students of the Hebrew Bible to take two semesters of the language before turning to serious study of the text. The modern academic world, however, has almost as little room for the second notion as for the first. We are therefore constrained to teach the Bible in translation to students who may be totally lacking in classical languages. But the limits this situation imposes on our teaching can, if properly understood, lead to an appreciation of the Hebrew Bible that is appropriate for most students. What we need to keep uppermost in our minds is that the Bible "gains" a lot in translation.

The first question to be addressed by those who teach the Bible in translation is Whose translation? Students initially do not recognize that all translations contain theological biases imposed by the worldviews of their sponsors. This problem may be dealt with by using three translations at once — say, one Catholic, one Protestant, and one Jewish — and seeing where they differ. For example, in identifying who it is that will crush the head of the serpent (Gen. 3.15), Protestants usually translate "he," prefiguring Jesus, Catholics prefer "she" (Mary, following the Vulgate's *ipsa*), and Jews use "they" meaning "humanity," all of us. Until recently all Protestant and Catholic translations had "a virgin" in Isaiah 7.14; the New International Version still has it. Jewish versions have always had "the young woman."

The New Jewish Publication Society's Torah even upsets that well-loved applecart "In the beginning . . . ," translating instead "When God began to create . . . ." This refinement points up the syntactical anomaly with which Scripture begins. The use of a prepositional phrase to modify a finite verb is rare enough that medieval commentators suggested changing the vocalization of the first word (see Rashi). Moderns such as Ephraim A. Speiser offer a cautious defense of the text but note that it implies serious cosmological problems (12–13). The issue here is nothing less than our time-honored doctrine of *creatio ex nihilo.*

Translating a text may be compared to furnishing a house. In both cases certain dimensions are given. It probably would not do to furnish a Georgian mansion in Danish Modern, or vice versa. The self-styled *Living Bible* or other paraphrastic translations are therefore quite unsuitable, given their authors' penchant for making unauthorized additions to the text. Even Luther's addition of the word *alone* to the statement in Habakkuk 2.4 "The righteous shall live by faith" bends the verse in a direction that might not have been intended.

Just as history needs constantly to be rewritten, so too translations need constantly to be refurbished. German and English are living languages in which individual words may shift in meaning over time. The AV's "voice of the turtle" (Song of Sol. 2.12) conjures up an almost mystical image. Did biblical turtles have the power of speech or was Solomon simply smart enough to "listen"? One may imagine the surprise that such speculations would engender among King James's contemporaries, to whom the word *turtle* merely meant "turtledove."

Another problem for translators, and one not nearly so easy to solve, is that posed by the question of synonyms. As far back as the twelfth century David Kimchi pointed to "a reduplication of the meaning by means of synonymous terms" in Hebrew poetry (Gray *Poetry,* 17). This recognition was also the guiding insight of Robert Lowth's 1754 study of Hebrew poetry, and the term he coined to describe this practice, *parallelism,* continues to hold a prominent place in literary criticism.

In "Parallelomania," a 1962 presidential address to the Society for Biblical Literature, Samuel Sandmel warned biblicists against overdependence on parallelism. James Kugel repeats, emphatically, the caution against looking for complete correspondence between two lines of Hebrew poetry, and Robert Alter takes a middle-of-the-road position (*Art of Biblical Poetry*). It is clear that even Hebrew scholars cannot agree on the extent of synonymity between various pairs of Hebrew words.

Moreover, many linguists are now inclined to believe that in a natural language there are no synonyms, a conclusion increasingly reinforced by semantic field studies. No matter how close in meaning two words may be, they are not synonyms unless either can be used in any text in which the other is found with no change of meaning. Even if we accept the existence of synonyms within a given biblical book, the same words may have different meanings in different texts. After all, the material of our Bible was written over a period of several hundred years, during which time individual words might well have undergone shifts in meaning.

The literary qualities of the various translations merit our closest attention. The AV's rendition of Psalm 23 not only captures the cadences of the original but perhaps "improves" it. "Valley of the shadow of death" is an inspired guess at the meaning of the Hebrew word *ṣalmavet*. The translators thought they saw a conflation of the words for "shadow" (*ṣelem*) and "death" (*mavet*). We now have evidence from cognate literature that *ṣalmavet* is a word that means "valley of deep shadow." The two ideas may be sufficiently close that we are justified in retaining the familiar phrase. In any case, readers will be reluctant to accept changes in translations that, after generations of use, have taken on a life of their own. We should be careful, however, not to cut the chain that anchors us to the originals.

In the opening sentence of *The Great Code*, Northrop Frye notes that "a sacred book is . . . closely involved with the conditions of its language." Since Hebrew is a Semitic language, its universe of discourse differs from that of Indo-European languages. This can be demonstrated by the following examples. In Hebrew the words for "man," "Adam," "ground," "Edom," "red," and perhaps "blood" come from the same root. A reader of Hebrew will hear overtones of all in each, while a reader of English translations will not. Again, English *boy* and *girl* have no etymological relation while the Hebrew *yeled* and *yaldah* are from a single root that means "to give birth." An enormous number of Hebrew nouns signify gender by the presence or absence of the *-ah* ending. The English pair *man* and *wo-man* is a rare parallel example.

The reason for this disparity is that Hebrew is, as it were, a "vertical" language while English is "horizontal." Hebrew derives many meanings from few roots; English carpets creation with wall-to-wall vocabulary. A Hebrew word may have half a dozen English "equivalents." If one therefore changes the English translation according to each context, the reader will not know what Hebrew word stands behind the translation and what associations the Hebrew reader may have at these points. If, however, one uses a straight one-for-one correspondence, the result may be just as unfortunate. For example, one might always translate the Hebrew *nephesh* as "soul." But it is likely that until the Greek period, Hebrew had no word for "soul," in the sense of something in but not of the body. The word *soul* implies a dualism that, at best, was only latent in Hebrew thought. In Deuteronomy 12.23, the RSV (Protestant), the New JPS (Jewish), and the Jerusalem (Catholic) all translate *nephesh* as "life," but there are many verses, such as Psalms 17.9, where a different English word ("desire" or "appetite") is clearly required. Second, no matter which translation scheme one adopts, that part of the Bible's message that is carried by allusion, assonance, and deliberate ambiguity—its "music," if you will—will be lost.

Even without knowing Hebrew, however, one may begin to explore the more salient differences between the Hebrew and English languages, especially differences in the verbal and pronominal systems. Students who have grown up in the three-dimensional (and subtly Christian) time system of past, present, and future and of ancient, medieval, and modern will have delightful difficulties grasping the two-dimensional Hebrew verb system of "complete" and "incomplete" action. The so-called Now Generation may be surprised to find Hebrew lacks a present tense. A similar downshifting may be necessary in confronting the conspicuous absence of the word *it* in the Hebrew pronominal system. It would be fanciful to insist that, if God, in his/her/its infinite wisdom, had seen fit to give us the Bible first in English or German, we would not now have to deal with the matter of inclusive language, but Hebrew cannot refer to God by a genderless pronoun. Hebrew's two-gender discourse, like that of all Semitic languages, has profound sociological ramifications.

Although Hebrew society was generally patriarchal, the Bible's appreciation of "female" qualities is greater than its critics sometimes acknowledge. The Hebrew word for "compassion" is *raḥamim,* from the root /r-ḥ-m, "womb." The Psalmist, in asking for compassion (25.6, 79.8), is asking that God respond as a mother. As Phyllis Trible puts it, "Thus, the female organ becomes a moral and theological event" (*God* 36). In contrast, the much-admired wisdom of the Greeks takes *hyster* "womb," and gives us "hysteria." As another example regarding this point, translations of Genesis 3.16 seem almost to compete with one another in their attempts to banish women to "*Küche, Kirche, Kinder.*" The AV has "he [your husband] will rule over thee"; the Modern Language Bible says, "he will dominate you"; and the 1966 Jerusalem Bible has "he will lord it over you." Inner biblical exegesis strongly suggests that the verse actually deals with the differing regenerative cycles of men and women (cf. Song of Songs 7.11, RSV 7.10). Women's sexual desires will be regulated by the capacity of their menfolk; the curse cuts both ways.

A syllabus that made room for occasional excursuses into key points of Hebrew semantics and the history of translation would provide a good balance to the subjects our courses usually cover. I favor an approach that stresses quality over quantity. A good one-semester introductory course might concentrate on a small number of selected biblical texts, each of which illustrated a particular style of writing, a problem in translation, or a biblical self-contradiction. A very short list might include the following: Genesis 1.1–2.3 (Hebrew ideas of cosmology); Genesis 2.4–3.24 (Eden); the "Ten Commandments" in Exodus *and* Deuteronomy (without an explanation of differences); Judges 13–16 (the apparent historicization of myth in the Samson story); Jeremiah 1 (the prophetic call); the balanced treatment of Solomon in 1 Kings 3–11 compared to the more fulsome account in 2 Chronicles 1–9; Psalms such as 1, 5, 8, 19, and 92 (Hebrew "poetry"); and 2 Chronicles 36, the last chapter in the Bible according to the Jewish ordering of the books.

This approach has certain advantages over the traditional survey found in most religion departments. Doing the entire Hebrew Bible in one semester is a bit like the travel agent's offer of seventeen countries in thirteen days. Greater selectivity allows teachers to concentrate on areas of particular interest to them so that they, and their students, can achieve greater understanding of complex issues. It also prevents students from concluding that their own study of the material has been exhaustive.

An alternative to this approach, or, even better, a complement to it, would be a second-semester course that concentrates on a single text. The prophet Amos helps students understand the sociological, historical, and religious background of eighth-century BCE Israel from which his little book comes. If the Hebrew Bible (and the New Testament, too, for that matter) were taught in a two-semester sequence, a significant language component could be built into both. Students would not become proficient in Hebrew or Greek, but they could become sensitized to problems that are basic to any understanding of biblical texts.

It should be enough to mention the importance of biblical names and their meanings. Genesis 35 implies that Jacob's naming of his son Benjamin is a clumsy attempt to avoid saddling the child with the name Benoni (son of my pain) given him by his dying mother. In fact, the name points to the possibility that the tribe of Benjamin consisted originally of Mesopotamian nomads who allied themselves with Israel just before the conquest of Canaan (Kupper). Similarly, the names of Saul's sons — Jonathan, Ishbaal, and Meribaal — suggest that Israel's first king had two wives, one Israelite and the other Canaanite. "Samson," from the root /š-m-š (sun), has been the object of speculation for nearly a century. The most exciting treatment of this name is in Giorgio de Santillana and Hertha von Dechend's *Hamlet's Mill* (ch. 11), in which the authors argue for an identification of the biblical hero-judge-berserker with the constellation Orion. In the Bible, as in other literature, *nomen est omen.* So it is necessary to unpack the information hiding behind most biblical names.

Every age and condition of Western civilization seems to produce new meanings for the Bible. However valuable these may be to their adherents, the task of teaching is to determine the extent to which the new meanings are inherent in the text. Failure to pay attention to the text at its basic textual level is to invite dilettantes, of which there are no lack, to use the Bible as a Ouija board and so to contact whatever demons lurk in the void where real knowledge fails.

From *Tanakh* to Old Testament

Leonard L. Thompson

In Jorge Luis Borges's "Pierre Menard, Author of *Don Quixote*," Pierre Menard does not want to copy or produce a mechanical transcription of the original *Don Quixote*, nor does he want to compose another *Don Quixote*. Rather, he wants "to produce pages which would coincide—word for word and line for line—with those of Miguel de Cervantes (49). After that arduous and difficult task of coincidence is completed, a passage from Pierre Menard is quoted alongside the "same" passage from Cervantes. Then the critical comment is made that though the two passages are verbally identical, "the second is almost infinitely richer" (52). What in Cervantes is "mere rhetorical eulogy" is in Menard "astounding" (53). In this story Borges displays something more than playful cleverness. He points to the cunning of language as it is used and reused in different verbal contexts. The exact same words take on different meanings as they collude with their new and different friends and neighbors.

Context and Motive for Transforming Tanakh

So, also, when *Tanakh* (Jewish Scriptures) is reproduced as Old Testament (Christian Scriptures), the text remains exactly the same, but the meaning is dramatically changed. *Tanakh* loses its autonomy and becomes subordinated as Old to New. Without the text's changing, *Tanakh* is transformed into a book of promises and scenes of expectation that are fulfilled in the Christian community and the life of the Christian Savior.

For example, the following words appear in Isaiah: "Behold, a young woman shall conceive and bear a son, and you shall call his name Immanuel" (7.14). In Matthew, the same words, translated with minor textual variations, appear in connection with a dream of Joseph, who is puzzled over the pregnancy of his betrothed. He is told that she conceived by the Holy Spirit and that she will bear a son named Jesus: "Behold, a young woman shall conceive and bear a son, and you shall call his name Immanuel" (1.23). The passage in Isaiah reiterated in Matthew thus becomes subordinated to the event of Jesus as promise in relation to fulfillment. No student of the Christian Bible can read the passage in Isaiah without making the association with Jesus, and, more important, the link with Jesus is often unreflectively assumed as essential in the interpretation of Isaiah 7.14.

When Isaiah is read in the context of *Tanakh*, however, the connection with Jesus is inconceivable. Within the immediate context, the message in Isaiah 7.14 is given as a sign to Ahaz, the reigning king of Judah, that he should not be afraid of a military coalition between Syria and northern Israel that threatens him. The king is told that before this child "knows how to refuse the evil and choose the good, the land before whose two kings you are in dread will be deserted" (7.16). In other words, the young woman and the son are characters tied closely to the situation of Ahaz and his political difficulties. The Christian association with Jesus makes no sense at all. In fact, from a historical perspective the Christian reading becomes impossible, for Jesus was born several centuries after Ahaz was king, whereas this sign is directed at a particular situation in his reign.

As this examination of Isaiah 7.14 makes clear, *Tanakh* does not need the New Testament to be understood. Jewish Scriptures require no addition, no supplement for understanding. If one stops reading at the end of the Hebrew Bible, there is no sense of incompleteness. It does not end on a note of expectation or waiting: in 2 Chronicles, the final book, spatial imagery of God's people gathered at rest around the temple dominates over temporal images (see L. L. Thompson 137–41). *Tanakh* ends with the assurance that God will be with his people as they build his house. Jews have for centuries found that ending to be complete and satisfying. Nothing intrinsic to Hebrew Scriptures requires that they be placed in relation to the Christian New Testament. There are, however, good extrinsic reasons for doing so—at least in certain contexts.

Christian theology is one such context. Within the Christian community the church continues the line of the covenantal people chosen to bear witness to God's presence in the world. However sensitive Christian theologians are to the ongoing presence of Judaism and to the special family relationships between Judaism and Christianity, they must claim that the revelation in Jesus Christ supersedes all previous revelation. Terms such as "Judeo-Christian tradition" and "Old Testament" presuppose the finality of Christianity over Judaism. Within the further history of religious movements, that process of scriptural usurpation continues. Islam supersedes Christianity, and the Quran claims a final revelation that subordinates both Old and New Testaments. But for Christian theology the claims for final revelation rest within the New Testament and its witness. All previous revelation of God's activity in Jewish life points to the supreme revelation in Jesus Christ.

That theological position becomes significant for those who study the Hebrew Bible in the context of the humanities, because—put simply—our culture is Christian. Most biblical images in art, literature, drama, music, and even philosophy have been forged from a reading of the Old Testament in relation to the New. For example, the story of Adam and Eve's being driven from the garden is heard or read through the Christian Paul or the church father Augustine, so that the exile from the garden of God is seen as a "fall," resulting in total depravity and original sin. Handel incorporated the phrase from Isaiah "How beautiful upon the mountains are the feet of him who brings good tidings, who publishes peace . . . " because he saw it alluding to the proclamation of the Christian gospel, not because of the Jewish expectation that the exile would soon be over. So, also, in the history of art, the gourd and the large fish (often a dolphin) refer less to Jonah's response to the Ninevites than to the Resurrection of Jesus. One can find many more examples of how images and symbols from the Hebrew Scriptures have entered into our cultural artifacts through the New Testament and Christian theology (see, e.g., Auerbach, "Figura" 60–76). It may be lamented, it may be defied, but an appreciation of Hebrew Scriptures in the context of the humanities and the liberal arts requires that readers wear a Christian lens and read *Tanakh* as Old Testament.

Narrative Structure in Jewish and Christian Scriptures

The narrative sequence of the Hebrew Bible is straightforward as the plot moves from the creation of the world to the rebuilding of the Temple. At Genesis 12, directions are reversed as stories of expulsion (Gen. 1–11) are followed by Abraham's God-given vocation to go "to the land that I will show you." In the sequence of the generations, the chosen are destined to go down to Egypt, where they are eventually oppressed into slavery.

The most fundamental narrative pattern of the Hebrew Scriptures follows: God's merciful deliverance of the people from Egypt, the covenant and law giving at Sinai, and the conquest of the Promised Land. The narrative sequence from life in Egypt to life in the Promised Land is structured temporally as a ritual movement from Passover night in Egypt, through the crossing of water (Red Sea/Jordan River), to the morning after Passover in the Promised Land of Canaan (Josh. 5.10–12). Having wandered through the labyrinthine wilderness path and passed through the larval waters of chaos, the Israelites in Canaan return to the ritual moment that they left off in Egypt. Viewed from the ritual time of Passover, the whole wilderness trek is a time of testing, a wandering maze of conflicts between the wilderness powers and the Lord, a rite of passage from irresponsibility and servitude to maturation and freedom (see L. L. Thompson 101–03).

After a period when judges ruled, kingship is introduced with its zenith in David and Solomon. Jerusalem is established as the capital city, the Temple is built, the empire is extended, and Israel celebrates the high point of life in the Promised Land. Kingship is also a climactic turning point in Hebrew Scriptures, for it brings *galuth* 'exile.' After the dark night of exile in Babylon, where many Jews found it difficult to sing the Lord's song, they return under Ezra and Nehemiah and come to rest around the temple of God.

Christian Scripture assimilates and restructures that narrative line of *Tanakh*. First of all, the narrative extends into the life of Jesus and the early church (see Acts 7). For that reason, the restoration after exile cannot be the final "rest." From a Christian viewpoint, Israel remains in exile, even as it celebrates life around the Temple, for Israel must wait for the once and future king to reign again (Mal. 3–4). That period of exile and waiting then sets the stage for the coming of the Messiah, underlined in the Christian Bible through a fourfold rendition of his life. The four Gospels present the fundamental narrative in Christian Scriptures as they tell the birth, the teaching, the mighty deeds, the death, and the Resurrection of Jesus as understood in the Christian community. Then follow stories about early Christians such as Peter, Paul, and the growth of the Christian Church. Paul and others write letters to various churches in order to guide, teach, and admonish them in the Christian way. The finale to the Christian Bible comes when the seer on Patmos envisions the re-creation of heaven and earth and the manifest rule of God and his Christ.

The Christian addition of new stories into Scripture not only extends the narrative line but also reshapes it. Now the constitutive narrative and climax comes in that extension—with the story of Jesus. Thus, in *Tanakh*, the central narrative moment of Exodus and covenant occurs early on and is looked back to at points throughout Scripture in order to reconstitute that which has gone before. In contrast, the crucial moment of the Christ event occurs late in the narrative of Christian Scriptures. The whole of the Old Testament must be read before coming to the climax of the narrative. As a result, foreshadowing dominates Christian Scriptures, just as reconstituting dominates *Tanakh*. Moreover, that foreshadowing is correlated to the crucial Christ event as promise to fulfillment. So Matthew observes about the passage from Isaiah discussed above: "All this took place to fulfil what the Lord had spoken by the prophet" (1.22). Virtually every character, object, and narrative event in the Old Testament has the potential to be correlated with the Christ event. Jesus is thus a fulfillment of the Exodus (Luke 9.31), the paschal lamb (1 Cor. 5.7), the deliverance in the wilderness (John 3.14), and the Temple and its sacrifices (Heb.). The writer of the Revelation of John recapitulates almost all situations and all symbols of power and deliverance in the Old Testament: garden, Sinai, Jerusalem, royal son, and restoration are fused with Crucifixion into one grand finale (see L. L. Thompson 303–04).

Transformations in the move from Jewish to Christian Scriptures restructure synchronic as well as diachronic or sequential aspects of the narrative. The fundamental narrative sequence in each Scripture patterns other sequences. In Hebrew Scriptures language describing conquest of the Promised Land is similar to that used in God's directions to human beings at the creation: the land is a gift, a blessing from God, to be taken by Israel; human beings (Israelites) are to be fruitful and multiply, and fill the earth (Promised Land) and subdue it (see L. L. Thompson 158). The wilderness sojourn (pre-land) is, by contrast, comparable to primal chaos. Wilderness is there where God has removed his ordering presence; it is curse not blessing, barren not fertile, an evil, threatening place (see Mauser). It thus forms a relation to life in the Promised Land analogous to the relation between primal chaos and the created order, and the movement from wilderness to the Promised Land reiterates a narrative pattern found also in the movement from chaos to creation. The exile (post-land) is described in language similar to both wilderness and chaos, and the restoration from exile to the Promised Land reiterates the same narrative pattern of the Exodus-conquest and chaos-creation (Isa. 51.9–11). In *Tanakh* nothing supersedes Torah and the covenant given at Sinai in connection with Torah, and so both covenant renewal and Torah obedience offer their disclosive power to many other moments in the Hebrew Scriptures (see Fishbane, *Text* 121–40). Celebration of life around the Temple at Jerusalem under a king of the lineage of David structures another significant narrative pattern in the Hebrew Scriptures (see Levenson). Ezekiel, a prophet speaking from exile, envisions the return in terms of the reconstructed Temple established once again on the "high" mountain of Zion (40–48). Haggai and Zechariah link and reiterate the establishment of Davidic kingship and the reconstitution of the Temple.

Christian Scripture traces out a different narrative pattern based on the story of Christ. A key element in that pattern is the combination of glory and humiliation derived from the narration of the crucified Messiah/king. That pattern becomes visible in the way that the heavenly voice conflates Old Testament passages at the baptism of Jesus. Various aspects of the baptism reiterate Old Testament situations. The baptismal waters, especially in connection with the descending Spirit "like a dove," link the baptism of Jesus with cosmogonies in Genesis—both the "brooding spirit" in Genesis 1 and the dissolving and re-creating waters in the time of Noah and the flood. That aquatic symbolism is also connected to the victory of God at the Red Sea/Jordan River in the narrative of the Exodus and conquest. In that baptismal context, the heavenly voice declares, "Thou art my beloved Son; with thee I am well pleased" (Mark 1.11). The baptism of Jesus, as "Son," reiterates the installation of the Israelite king, at which time God declares, "Thou art my Son, today I have begotten you" (Ps. 2.7). The king is thereby granted power and victory over his enemies: "You shall break them with a rod of iron, / And dash them in pieces like a potter's vessel" (Ps. 2.9). The baptismal voice, however, links that image of power and victory to Isaac, Abraham's "beloved son," who is sacrificial victim (Gen. 22.2). Furthermore, the second half of the heavenly saying at the baptism reiterates Isaiah 42.1, a so-called servant song, which describes God's servant as a "bruised reed" and "a dimly burning wick" who will establish justice through nonviolent submission. When the passages about Abraham and Isaac or the suffering servant of Isaiah are read in the Old Testament, they are seen as passages foreshadowing Jesus. Moreover, through that Christian narrative pattern, royalty in Psalm 2 is naturally associated with defeat and crucifixion, just as the "bruised reed" of Isaiah is seen as a royal, messianic designation of glory and power; for both passages foreshadow the messianic activity of Jesus, who dies on the cross. Through such novel combinations, the centrality of the "crucified king" transforms passages of straightforward despair or glory into ironic statements (see L. L. Thompson 224–26), and simple images are taken up recursively into more complex linguistic structures (see Abrams 343).

Sometimes, narrative patterns in *Tanakh* are reiterated in the New Testament. The narrative sequence of the exodus from Egypt to the conquest of the Promised Land, for example, patterns Matthew's portrayal of Jesus's birth and early years (Matt. 1–4). Jesus, son of Abraham, is born in the land of promise and goes to Egypt by means of Joseph. Jesus then retreads the path on which Moses led the children of Israel out of Egypt (Matt. 2.15 = Hos. 11.1), through the waters of the Jordan/Red Sea (Matt. 3.13), into the temptations of the wilderness for forty days, and finally into the Promised Land where Jesus proclaims the message of the kingdom.

Typology

Often the relation between the Old Testament and the New is said to be typological or figural (see Auerbach, "Figura" 14; Frye, *Great Code* 78–101). Broadly conceived, a figure emerges as a common element in passages from the Old and New Testaments: commonality, for example, between narrative events, character traits, ritual acts, or legal-ethical situations. Those common elements draw Old and New Testaments together. In 1 Corinthians 10 Paul makes a typological connection between Israel's sojourn through the wilderness and Christian existence. The common element of passing through the water sets up a typology between Israel at the Red Sea and Christian baptism: " . . . our fathers were all under the cloud, and all passed through the sea, and all were baptized into Moses in the cloud and in the sea" (1 Cor. 10.1–2). Supernatural food and supernatural drink provide the basis for another typology — between the Eucharist, on the one hand, and the food and drink that God gave to Israel in the wilderness, on the other (1 Cor. 10.3). Paul then identifies the rock from which came the supernatural drink with Christ: "For they drank from the supernatural Rock which followed them, and the Rock was Christ" (1 Cor. 10.4). Here, typology is fully realized in metaphoric identity.

The fusion of events from Old and New Testaments creates an affect that distinguishes the language of Christian Scriptures from that of *Tanakh*. There is a concrete realism to the language of *Tanakh* as salvation is for the most part associated with symbols of peace, prosperity, territoriality, and progeny. Scenes in Christian Scriptures are also markedly realistic and concrete, for example, the parable of the seeds, the trial of Jesus, the maid of the high priest conversing with Peter, and the Crucifixion. But that realism is tempered by a rhetorical indirection: crucifixion is a cipher for kingship; planting seed a figure for the kingdom of God. In the words of Erich Auerbach, language turns the reader's attention from "the sensory occurrence and toward its meaning" (Auerbach, *Mimesis* 39, 42). There is a tension — Auerbach even calls it an antagonism — between that concrete language and the meaning transmitted through it. When meaning arises from the fusion of language in Old and New Testaments, as when Christ becomes the rock that Moses struck for water, then both the scenes about the rock in Exodus 17.1–7 and Numbers 20.10–13 and the Christian Messiah become "weak as a sensory impression," since "one's interest is directed toward the context of meanings" that derives from the *relationships* between the rock and Christ rather than toward either individually (see Auerbach, *Mimesis* 42–43). Irony frequently enters into the meaning of texts in this process.

Through typology Old and New Testaments become completely dependent on each other. Novel patterns join Old Testament Scriptures to form a new whole. There is something new "apart from the old," but the new needs the old to "bear witness to it" (see Rom. 3.21). The new myth is seen as completing and fulfilling the old, but the old provides the categories for interpreting the new. As completion and fulfillment, the new claims the greater reality: it is the realization of an earlier *shadow*. In providing the categories for interpretation, the old claims the greater reality: the new is a *copy* of it. For example, the writer of the Fourth Gospel makes the following comment about the Crucifixion: "As Moses lifted up the serpent in the wilderness, so must the Son of man be lifted up" (John 3.14). The lifting up of the Son of man obviously has greater "reality" to that writer than Moses's lifting up the serpent, and yet the saving power of that image of the Son of man depends wholly on the story of Moses in Numbers 21.9. As New Testament and Old Testament are brought together into a new entity, neither can be read without the other. As Paul says, those who try to read the Old Testament without the aid of the Christian message have a veil over their eyes, and "only through Christ is it taken away" (2 Cor. 3.14). Needless to say, when the text of the Old Testament is seen in that way, it takes on a sharply different meaning from what it has when read as *Tanakh*.

Figural interpretation serves to assimilate novel, alien experiences of a person or community into established structures of meaning. Typology has a certain present, existential point of reference as it ranges freely through time. So, in the passage of Corinthians already referred to, Paul writes that the references in the Old Testament to Moses, the cloud, the sea, the spiritual food, and the spiritual drink all become "types or figures of ourselves." Whether it be Paul in the new situation of preaching to the Gentiles, Germanic peoples acquiring novel encounters with Christianity, or early Americans orienting themselves to a new and strange land, figural interpretation serves as a means of comprehending and orienting to ongoing experience (see Auerbach, "Figura" 50–52). In the figural process the novel present is domesticated at the same time as the canon of authoritative memory is modified. Further, the figure that emerges from memory and present-experience shrouds the present. So Auerbach writes, "Thus history, with all its concrete force, remains forever a figure, cloaked and needful of interpretation" ("Figura" 58).

When seen through Christian figures, the present links not only with the past but also with the yet undisclosed future that brings eschatological perfection. In the New Testament, the event of the Christ is disclosed through typological associations with the Old Testament, but the disclosure is not fully given in the present, for "Christ" as "type" looks ahead to future eschatological realities now hidden. Typology brings the past into the present, without losing its reality as past, and the present into a yet undisclosed future, without losing its reality as present. In that way figural interpretation contributes significantly to a Christian understanding of providence, evolution, and teleology that has influenced Western society in many different spheres (see Auerbach, "Figura" 49–60; Frye, *Great Code* 80–81). Thus, in brief, typology is a way of integrating ongoing history, authoritative canons, and models of perfection into a temporal framework of present, past, and future, respectively.

Teaching Tanakh *as Old Testament*

How, then, should one teach a course in which the Hebrew Scriptures are seen as part of Christian Scriptures, that is, as Old Testament? Five recommendations can be offered. (1) At the beginning of the course make clear that there is a difference between *Tanakh* and Old Testament, that the structures of the Christian Scriptures and the Jewish Scriptures differ, and that different religious traditions underly the two Scriptures. (2) Approach the Old Testament sequentially, making a minimal number of allusions to the New Testament. Passages from the Old Testament may sometimes be selected with an eye to their importance in Christian Scriptures, and that principle of selection should be indicated to students. For example, Isaiah 7.14 is much more significant in Christian than in Jewish Scriptures. (3) When analyzing the Old Testament, note especially typologies, homologies, analogies, and other such associations among texts, so that synchronic as well as diachronic elements are recognized in the narrative (see Sternberg, esp. 365–440). For this kind of analysis, traditional rabbinic exegesis offers a rich vein to be mined. (4) When moving to the New Testament, emphasize once again that Hebrew Scriptures are a complete work and do not need the New Testament to complete them. Remember that in the move to the New Testament, novelty is more radical than in any of the changing times in Hebrew Scriptures. (5) Explore typologies between the Old and New Testaments. Through typological analysis, the *literary* structure of Christian Scripture emerges as well as something of the Christian vision of the world that has so shaped Western culture.

Instructors differ widely in what materials they select from the Old and New Testaments. The following suggestions about selections and their organization reflect principles affirmed in this essay.

Students find it helpful to analyze short, self-contained selections before engaging with longer, complex structures. The story of Jonah can provide an entrée into both narrative and poetic aspects of biblical literature. The stories of Ehud, in Judges 3.12–30, and the binding of Isaac, in Genesis 22.1–19, can also be analyzed in isolation from their contexts. Stories of Samson, in Judges 13–16, make a nice transition to more complex narrative units. Psalms 24, 29, 30, 38, 42–43, 45, 68–69, 77, 84, 99, 104–05, 130, Song of Songs, Matthew 6.9–13, and Revelation 15.3–4 illustrate various dynamics in biblical poetry.

The following selections trace the structure of *Tanakh*:

1. Stories of beginnings, from creation to Egypt (Gen. 1–50).
2. The fundamental narrative pattern
    a. Exodus from Egypt (Exod. 1–15)
    b. Covenant and law giving at Sinai in the wilderness (Exod. 16–19, 24, 32–34; Num. 10.11–36, 11–14, 16–17, 20–25)
    c. Conquest (Josh. 1–8, 24; cf. summary statements in Deut. 6.20–25, 26.1–11; 1 Sam. 12.6–8; Neh. 9.6–31)
3. Life in the land
    a. Stories set in the time of the judges (Judg. 4–5, 10.6–12.7; Ruth)
    b. Kingship (1 Sam. 1–10, 15–18, 25; 2 Sam. 1.1–2.7, 5–7, 11–20, 24; 1 Kings 1–11, 12–14, 17–19, 21; 2 Kings 2, 6–11, 17, 18–25; note also Ps. 2, 110, 89)
4. Stories set in exile (Esth.; Dan. 1–6; cf. Joseph in Gen. 37–50)
5. Return (Ezra 1.1–6.18; Neh. 13; 2 Chron. 5–7, Solomon's dedication of the Temple, illustrates Israel's "rest" around the temple of God).

Collections of sayings may be read seriatim or related to appropriate parts of the narrative. For example, legal sayings (Exod. 20–23, 34.10–27; Levi. 17–26; Deut. 16–26) could be read in connection with the wilderness narratives; proverbial sayings or wisdom (Prov. 22.17–24.34, 1–9; Eccles., Job 28, 1–14, 38.1–42.17) in connection with Solomon; prophetic sayings before exile (Amos; Hos. 1–4, 11; Isa. 1–12; Jer. 1–3, 7, 13–20, 25–39) and prophetic sayings in and after exile (Isa. 40–55, 60, 65; Ezek. 1, 8–10, 23, 37, 47–48; Joel; Zech. 1–6, 9, 14; Dan.) in connection with appropriate kings.

For the structure of Christian Scriptures, read Acts 7.1–53, 2.14–42, 3.11–26; 1 Corinthians 15.1–9. For reinterpretation of *Tanakh*, read 2 Corinthians 3.4–18. The fundamental narrative in Christian Scriptures is found in the Gospels. Mark, a short and dramatic rendering of Jesus's life, should be read in its entirety. Mark 14–16 exemplifies the irony of kingship. Other selections from the Gospels could include Jesus's beginnings (Matt. 1–4; Luke 1.1–6.11; John 1–4), the teachings of Jesus (Matt. 5–7, 13, 24–25; Luke 10.25–37, 15), and narratives of Jesus's death and resurrection (Matt. 26–28; Luke 22–24; John 18–21). Stories about the early church (Acts 1–4, 6.1–8.3, 9.1–18.22, 21.15–28.28) and the eschatological finale (Revelation to John) round out the narrative in Christian Scriptures. As with sayings in *Tanakh*, letters and tracts in the New Testament (1 Thess.; 1 Cor.; Gal.; Rom. 1–11; Eph.; Tit.; Heb.; Jas.; 1 Pet.; 1 John) may be read seriatim or correlated with points in the narrative structure of the New Testament.

The Return to *Tanakh*

Barry N. Olshen

> . . . to the Christian the OT is incomplete, its
> major tensions are never really resolved, the time to
> which it points is not realized, its manifold diversities
> are never sufficiently gathered into a unifying center
> . . ., the dynamic quality of the prophetic
> proclamation never reaches a culmination, the
> kingship of God is never radically present. . . .
> James Muilenburg, "Preface to Hermeneutics" 21

In academic and other progressive circles, it has now become acceptable,
even fashionable, to treat *Tanakh* as an independent entity and to refer to
it as the "Hebrew Bible," "Jewish Scripture," or the like. For most people,
however, "Old Testament" still seems the only appropriate title when the context is Western culture or Christian hermeneutics. The ideas expressed in
the epigraph above are fundamental to both approaches. The preceding essay in this volume, Leonard L. Thompson's "From *Tanakh* to Old Testament,"
admirably represents the cultural approach: "It may be lamented, it may be
defied," he writes, "but an appreciation of Hebrew Scriptures in the context
of the humanities and the liberal arts requires that readers wear a Christian
lens and read *Tanakh* as Old Testament." My essay constitutes an alternative
to Thompson and Muilenburg, an approach to reading and teaching the Bible with different standards and different goals.

It is time, I think, to set the historical record straight(er), to right the balance, at least in our classrooms, of the so-called Judeo-Christian tradition,
and to show clearly what misrepresentations and misunderstandings have been
perpetrated and perpetuated along the path from *Tanakh* to Old Testament.
Studying the Bible within the context of the humanities or Western culture
(as most of us understand these terms) is but one approach; we may also study
culture within the context of the Bible. To get at the thing itself, especially
in our own historically oriented era, we can no longer teach the Hebrew Bible within the context of Christian typology. Rather, typology, if it is to be
taught, must be taught within the context of the Bible.

To these and other ends, I have for a number of years been offering a full-
year multidisciplinary course on the Hebrew Bible in translation. One of the
texts I generally use is the Revised Standard Version "containing the Old and
New Testaments" and called "The Holy Bible," a title providing the point
of departure for the course. Concerning the adjective *holy* we briefly discuss
the meaning of the word in English, the Hebrew word *kadosh*, and the concept of holiness à la Rudolph Otto, Mircea Eliade, and the *Interpreter's Dictionary of the Bible* (Buttrick), with at least some reference to Exodus 3 and
Isaiah 6. Regarding the word *bible*, lecture and discussion times are devoted

to its derivation, denotations, and connotations, as well as to the words *testament* and *old* and *new* (as they are commonly understood within this context).

It is in comparing the contents of the Hebrew Bible with the Old Testament that we begin to challenge the generally accepted dictum that, while the meaning dramatically changes, the original text remains the same. Students discover, for one thing, that changing the order of the parts of *Tanakh* affects the structure of the whole and quite radically changes what we call the "text" as well as its "meaning." Students also can be made to see the importance of classifying the individual books of the Bible and the role played by classification in the anticipation and interpretation of meaning. The rearrangement and reclassification of the texts composing *Tanakh* warrant the rechristening "Old Testament." Given the importance of names, naming, and name changes in the Bible, the renaming of the whole can hardly be made to carry too much weight, and we proceed to talk about how loaded a term "Old Testament" actually is.

One clear way to deal with this very complicated subject is by means of a chart indicating the books of the Bible in the Jewish, Catholic (Roman and Orthodox), and Protestant traditions. (Such charts are readily available. See, e.g., B. W. Anderson 4.) The chart should clearly present the fundamental differences in canon as well as title, classification, and arrangement of sections and individual books. Are we to study Ruth as a Festal Scroll (*Megillah*) among the Writings or as a historical book following Judges? Should we group Lamentations with the Festal Scrolls or should it follow Jeremiah? Is Daniel to be read among the Major Prophets or the Writings? These are but three of many questions concerning the order and designation of individual texts. Each reflects the different uses and interpretations of the scriptural work within the Jewish and Christian traditions.

For the purposes of this essay, however, the crucial difference between the Old Testament and the Hebrew Bible lies in their structures as a whole, in the order of their parts and their concluding books. As the acronym *TaNaKH* suggests, the foundation of Hebrew Scripture (and Judaism more generally) is *Torah*, or the Five Books of Moses, and its structural center is *Nebi'im*, or the Former and Latter Prophets. *Kethubim*, or the Writings, is the third division. The Christian Old Testament, however, reclassifies the Former Prophets and (following the order of the Septuagint) transposes the rest of the second and third sections. Thus the Writings take on the central position and the Latter Prophets close the whole, or perhaps more accurately in Christian terms, provide the transition to the New Testament.

The concluding words of the Hebrew Bible (2 Chron. 36) are supposedly those of Cyrus the Great, proclaiming the end of the Babylonian exile, the beginning of the restoration of the remnant of Judah, and the rebuilding of the Temple in Jerusalem. The final word of *Tanakh*, "go up," has the same root in Hebrew as the noun *aliyah*, thus expressing the same vision and yearning as the modern Zionist movement and acting as a cohesive rallying cry for diaspora Jewry for two and a half millennia—"Let him go up."

The transposition of the Prophets and the Writings results in the burial of this promise of return and renewal among the historical books of the Christian Old Testament, which ends instead with the promise of a very different future for Israel. The last book of the Prophets and the Old Testament is Malachi, and Malachi's final lines contain the threat of destruction, the cataclysm of the day of the Lord. "Behold," it concludes, "I will send you Elijah the prophet before the great and terrible day of the LORD comes. And he will turn the hearts of fathers to their children and the hearts of children to their fathers, lest I come and smite the land with a curse [*herem*]" (RSV, Mal. 4.5–6; Hebrew, Mal. 3.23–24). Elijah's sudden and mysterious departure from this world (2 Kings 2.11) gave rise in Jewish tradition to stories about his reappearance on earth. His role is to restore peace and order to the world — in the quotation above, it is specifically to reconcile the generations — and his return is said to herald the coming of the Messiah.

The conclusion of Malachi within the context of this discussion provides an excellent opportunity to introduce the concept of typology. From the very beginning of Christianity, the identification of John the Baptist with Elijah the Prophet has formed a basis for the christological reading of what became the Old Testament. As Elijah is said to precede the Messiah, so the mission of John the Baptist is said to have preceded the coming of Jesus, the Christ. Malachi provides the transition from Old to New Testament. The first words of the New Testament introduce Jesus as "Christ, the son of David, the son of Abraham," in accordance with the Jewish expectation of a savior in the line of David. When John the Baptist is first presented in Matthew 3, he is even dressed like Elijah (cf. Matt. 3.4 and 2 Kings 1.8). Later in the gospel Jesus explicitly identifies the two figures (Matt. 11.13–14, 17.12). It has been my repeated experience that students of all persuasions find this material fascinating. The study of typology is almost certain to captivate them, and so it is especially useful to introduce it early in the course.

If typology becomes an important part of one's course, then the point should be made that this way of thinking begins with the Jewish Scripture, not the Christian. The reinterpretation of older tales or traditions from the perspective of a new salvation event is quite common in the Hebrew Bible from the telling of the Exodus events and after. Hosea 11, Jeremiah 31, and Isaiah 40 and 51 are especially useful for illustrating the process in the prophetic books. Students will thus become aware that the early Church appropriated both the texts and the interpretive approaches of *Tanakh*.

The built-in bias of the term Old Testament does not require much time to expose. That *testament* comes from the Latin, that it is used to translate the Hebrew *brith*, "covenant," and that *old* and *new* refer to more than chronology are easy to explain. The principle of old and new covenants refers specifically to the new covenant of "Christ's blood" superseding the old covenant in either the "flesh of Abraham" (referring to the covenant of circumcision, Gen. 17) or the "stone of Moses" (referring to the Sinai covenant, Exod. 20).

The most famous typological interpretation of Jeremiah is the key text here.

In Jeremiah 31.31–34, the prophet speaks of the dissolution of the old covenant between God and Israel and prophesies a new one—a *brith hadashah*,
for which "new testament" is the translation—in which God's Torah will be
written on the "hearts" of Israel. At least two passages from the New Testament, in which Jeremiah's imagery is transformed, must be read in conjunction with this: 2 Corinthians 3.1–6; Hebrews 8.6–13 and 9.13–15. These passages
make it abundantly clear that the early Church appropriated and reinterpreted
Jeremiah's "new covenant" as well and that the "new" makes the "old" obsolete.

To view accurately the Old Testament in the cultural context of the West
is to trace a two-thousand-year tradition of denigration and misrepresenta-
tion of Judaism and the Jew. What I have been saying is only one aspect of
a far more complex argument against the familiar but spurious contrasts of
the religious cultures of Jew and Christian. The traditional antitheses of tribal-
ism and universalism, retaliation and mercy, (self)righteousness and faith, ha-
tred and love, greed and generosity, and so on have not entirely disappeared
by any means. These oppositions are based on the belief that the Jew is ad-
herent to an "old law" superseded by the new dispensation contained in the
New Testament; that the Jewish religion is narrowly legalistic, based on a tal-
ion of eye for eye and tooth for tooth, as opposed to a Christianity that is based
on mercy and love, tolerance and forgiveness.

These distortions were elaborated in the enormous body of Church literature known as the *Adversus Judaeos* tradition; they entered into the belief
system of the Christian community, and so into its literature and art. Much
of the reason for the force and attraction of *The Merchant of Venice* is that
Shylock so powerfully and so completely embodies the early religious and
cultural stereotypes that compose the negative side of these dichotomies. They
were found nearly everywhere and seem to have been accepted by nearly
everyone. There is, however, no sound reason to perpetuate them in our colleges and universities today. Typology, like other impressive phenomena, may
be studied without passing on its ideology.

In our Bible courses, then, we can discuss the "connection" of the testaments in a literary or historical or even theological way, without conceding
to the silent adoption of the terms "Old" and "New" and without passing on
the biases that most assuredly go with them. After all, the problem of con-
necting the testaments only arose when the second was compiled, and only
after *Tanakh* (the first) was identified as "old." The problem, in a real sense,
is not even applicable to the Hebrew Bible, and, in many ways, its pursuit,
however fascinating culturally and however significant theologically, takes us
further away from *Tanakh* itself—a collection of the law and literature of Israel composed and compiled under certain historical (pre-Christian) conditions. The best place to learn the meaning of "Old Testament" is in the New
Testament course, where the vast scope of its influence and appropriation
can be properly measured.

This approach to teaching Scripture should yield greater respect for the
Hebrew Bible and deeper appreciation of its contents, more tolerance for

an independent Jewish culture, and greater awareness of the roots of Christianity. It represents a kind of "consciousness-raising" for students of Bible and culture alike. It requires that those who already know something of the Old Testament take a more flexible approach to its interpretation, perhaps even change the lens with which they read.

PEDAGOGICAL AND THEORETICAL PERSPECTIVES

A Socioliterary Approach

Norman K. Gottwald

This essay describes the way I orient and structure a course called Introduction to the Hebrew Bible and my rationale for what I call a socioliterary approach. According to my experience and the accounts of other teachers and students, the first-level course is notoriously demanding on the learning skills of students and the curriculum-designing and instructional skills of teachers. Although intended as preparation for more advanced offerings, the introductory course is in fact often the only course in which many college and university students will ever study the Hebrew Bible.

Developments in biblical studies over the last two decades have greatly complicated the task of teaching the Hebrew Bible. In addition to the explosion of new archaeological and textual data, a wealth of new methods has arisen, without replacing valuable older methods, thereby enlarging the scope of what might reasonably be included in a beginning course. Facing an expanding and unsettled field, the teacher must make painful and sometimes confused decisions about what the course will and will not cover. Such curricular choices are usually influenced by the existing traditions of biblical instruction at the college or university in question, by the instructor's understanding of the field and expertise within it, by the available and manageable textbooks, and by the knowledge, expectations, interests, and needs of students.

Three main considerations govern my decisions about the shape and content of the course.

To begin with, the Bible is always studied from a point of view. The number of points of view has increased as new methods of study have developed and as the Bible has been used and interpreted in various religious and cultural contexts over the centuries. In my judgment, it is advisable to acquaint students with the broad phases of the history of biblical interpretation, including divergences in Jewish and Christian views. I do this by a brief overview illustrated with a few texts. In any particular class, students will nearly always express a variety of views, which underscores the crucial role of perspective and presupposition in biblical studies. I point out that my own presuppositions and the role they play in shaping the course are logically and pedagogically distinguishable from those of others in the field and from those of the students.

One aim of the course is to help the student identify presuppositions, recognize how they function, and come to reasoned judgment in holding to or in changing presuppositions as they bear on the content of the course. This orientation runs so much against the grain of notions about education as objectively imparting uninterpreted knowledge that it is not enough merely to state it at the start of the course. Instructor and students need to remind themselves that, while they examine a shared text, they do so from various angles and often with differing assumptions. Thus the course Introduction to Hebrew Bible must examine not only the content of the Bible but the assumptions and interpretive processes of the involved readers.

A second consideration is that the actual study of the Bible is a study of content according to some method or methods. Enough of the content of the Bible must be studied so that students gain firsthand knowledge of what is really in it and, often even more to their surprise, what is not in it. Simultaneously, sufficient methods must be used to bring out the growth of the Bible in its total setting so that students grasp the biblical content as an intelligible multidimensioned whole. This recommendation leaves ample scope for numerous defensible choices of particular contents and methods and of varied ways of articulating them.

In whatever combination and sequence, it is the interplay of content and method that sets the course in motion, gives the study its pace and liveliness, and offers students a way into the text that will have lasting value after the course is ended. In the absence of a fruitful engagement of content and method, biblical instruction tends to drift into one or the other of two deadening patterns: either a reading and summarizing of biblical texts according to an unexamined agenda or a recital of methods and their results disconnected from texts and their sociohistorical settings.

Finally, decisions must be made about content and method. Choices of the biblical contents to be studied require well-considered criteria. My chief criteria are these: (1) regard for the general shape of the Torah, Prophets, and Writings, so that the "story line" (where there is one) is grasped and so that students are exposed to the main literary genres; (2) attention to the likely preunderstandings of students, so that there is a good mix of familiar and unfamiliar materials and so that students can "unlearn" some of the stereotypes they have about the material they "know"; and (3) focus on a smaller group of texts that are useful for demonstrating the fruitfulness of particular methods by actually showing how they work on "model texts."

Decisions about the methods to be employed require equally well-considered criteria. At least every other year, I try to think through carefully the range of methods and their accomplishments, their scope and limits, their interrelationships, and the best way to introduce and illustrate them in a beginning class. My aim is to acquaint students with the major results of the methods, provide them a measure of skill in practicing one or more of the methods, and help them develop criteria for evaluating results that appear to conflict or to be unrelated.

To encourage critical reflection about presuppositions and methods, I structure the course not as a collection of serialized data but as a set of routes (methods) through specified terrain (biblical contents) that provides intelligible and reproducible patterns of movement between and among the wholes and parts of the subject matter. This general movement consists of three specific types of movement that are functionally separate but that must conjointly feed into one another for a satisfactory understanding of the Hebrew Bible. First, there is a literary movement within the stated contents of the Bible between and among its "framing" wholes and its "nesting" parts, together with the process by which the interlocking wholes and parts reached their present form. This is the immediate and obvious object of biblical studies. Second is a sociohistorical movement between the literary contents of the Bible and their wider cultural, historical, social, and religious referents. These referents include direct allusions in the biblical text and broader social and historical phenomena either implied in the text or presupposed by the text. Last, there is a hermeneutical movement between the Bible in its ancient context, as seen by the preceding two movements, and the meanings and uses of the Bible as appropriated and practiced by contemporary readers. This hermeneutical movement reflects on the extent of consonance and dissonance between biblical meanings in their original context and biblical meanings construed as authoritative or suggestive for contemporary life.

Some may object that I have omitted a religious-theological movement. I prefer to treat the religious-theological aspect of the Bible as an integral dimension of the other types of movement. Theological statements are both literary and sociohistorical; they are also hermeneutical since they call for decoding and reinterpretation in the movement back and forth from ancient world to contemporary world. I have no objection to distinguishing a specific religious-theological movement provided it is not regarded as an abstracted realm pulled loose from its literary, sociohistorical, and hermeneutical matrices. Precisely because the theological sphere has so often been either ignored or elevated abstractly above all other biblical considerations, I consciously distribute religious and theological matters throughout the other forms of movement so that they can neither be overlooked nor idealized.

In the organization of my book *The Hebrew Bible: A Socio-Literary Introduction*, each segment of the Bible is treated according to literary and sociohistorical perceptions, while matters deemed theological are frequently discussed in connection with one or the other of these rubrics. In the conclusion, I suggest a graphic format (chart 12) for mapping some of the major interconnections of the literary, social, and theological sectors when viewed chronologically throughout biblical times. Moreover, the hermeneutical movement between "then" and "now" is highlighted at the beginning of the text as at the end, while the influence of the interpreter's stance is brought out at many points in between. The structure of this textbook corresponds fairly closely to the format of the introductory course as I have developed it in recent years.

The older historical-critical methods, which I used exclusively when I began to teach thirty years ago, are well attuned to sharp analysis of the biblical "parts." The newer literary, canonical, and social-scientific methods, which I have added bit by bit to my teaching, are valuable and necessary means for assembling the parts into meaningful "wholes." Nonetheless, most teaching of the Hebrew Bible has yet to find a satisfactory way to bridge the gap between studying the parts and grasping the wholes.

Nowadays I am moving toward a more integral "part-whole" deployment of the various methods, though it is far from smooth and finished in all respects and certainly not yet a synthesis of all the methods. This consolidation has been possible for two reasons: on the one hand, a number of biblical scholars who are practiced in differing methods have begun to take steps toward constructive correlations among them. On the other hand, I have found that students, lacking strong vested interests in any one method, can appreciate the contributions of the various methods and even work out tentative combinations or associations so that the methods do not seem to work against one another. Even when the results of different methods do not readily assimilate into a single grand interpretation, students often find it challenging to live with the ambiguities of this methodological explosion.

In interweaving the literary, sociohistorical, and hermeneutical movements so as to incorporate a range of methods suitable to specific biblical contents, I am now experimenting with the following approach to introducing students to the Hebrew Bible, consisting of a series of closely interlocked and cumulative steps:

1. Identify the Hebrew Bible as a subject matter of study governed by the hermeneutical starting point that the Bible is a cultural classic and a religious scripture. Draw on the history of interpretation to specify some of the ways that the Bible has been and is "seminal" or "authoritative." At this point brief reference may be made to the canon and to enough of the history of biblical translations to orient students to the most widely used contemporary translations.

2. Specify the precise subject matter of the course as that literary whole consisting of Torah, Prophets, and Writings (using literary and canonical criticism), and characterize the contents of the Bible in various ways, including

its topics (what it talks about) and its literary genres (how it says what it says). At this stage, the defining whole is discriminated illustratively according to some of the kinds of parts that compose it so that the whole is recognized to be richly variegated (use results of certain historical-critical methods such as history of religion, form or genre criticism, tradition-historical criticism).

3. Specify the context or surround of the Hebrew Bible as a sociohistorical whole consisting of the communities of Israelites and Jews amid other ancient Near Eastern peoples (use historical criticism and social-scientific criticism). Differentiate "sociohistorical" by referring to all the levels and aspects of community life, such as family, village, tribe, state, social class, cult, religious enclave, and so on. Indicate that this sociohistorical world is sometimes referred to in the Bible (e.g., tribal data in the early books) and at other times only implied or presupposed if we are to make the fullest sense of the text (e.g., nationalist reform and expansion under Josiah as the context of the first edition of the Deuteronomistic history). Geography, archaeology, and ancient Near Eastern history may be judiciously included at this point.

4. Bring together the literary and sociohistorical wholes, viewed as processes, by sketching the literary growth of the Bible from its smaller parts to its final form in interface with the social history (understood as including political, religious, and cultural history). In this way the phases of the literary growth are contextualized with reference to the corresponding phases of social history. At one point or another, such an "interreading" of the literary and the sociohistorical worlds draws on contributions from the entire arsenal of methods.

5. Move to particular segments of biblical literature and characterize or exegete texts. Interrogate these sections of the text by all the historical-critical methods, but, instead of stopping with the historical-critical maneuvers, carry the results of the specific textual studies back to their contexts in the literary and sociohistorical wholes. If, for example, one has exegeted Judges 5, where does it fit in the growth of biblical literature, in the book of Judges, in the Deuteronomistic History, and in the whole canon? With its celebration of peasant warfare against Canaanites, how does the song reflect the society of early Israel, what did it communicate to the society of the time of Josiah when taken into the Deuteronomistic History, and what did it mean for those who canonized Joshua-Judges?

At this stage, one faces opportunities to test the contrary claims of literary critics who insist on taking the text as a self-contained entity and literary critics who admit of the relevance of describing the growth of the text and the text's relation to sociohistorical reality. Having, for example, studied Judges 5 from various angles, students can discuss what is gained and lost when the Book of Judges is treated as self-contained, on the one hand, and when it is treated as an evolved literature with sociohistorical reference points, on the other. Students can also consider whether these two perspectives are in some way compatible (by way of illustration, see my presentation of Joshua and Judges in *The Hebrew Bible*, ch. 6, secs. 23–24, or that of the Moses traditions in ch. 5, secs. 20–21).

6. Complete the full round of study by returning to and evaluating the hermeneutical starting point from which the approach to the Bible began, in step 1. As a result of the orienting maneuvers in steps 1–4 and of the exegetical-contextualizing work of step 5, students will have a solid grasp of some texts that they can apply to their situation as contemporary interpreters. How, for example, do they now view Judges 5 and other "holy war" texts in comparison with their initial understanding when they began the study? How does what they have learned qualify the contemporary cultural and religious understandings of these holy war concepts?

The structured and structuring movement outlined above describes both the overall progression of the course and the typical style of study within the subdivisions of the course. The oscillating part-whole movements on the three levels (or four, if one treats the theological dimension as a separate movement) are undertaken repeatedly with respect to all the contents studied so that they eventually become second nature to students. My description may appear overelaborate and unduly self-conscious, but my experience is that, as the students become practiced, the pedantic specification of each step can be abbreviated or dropped, except as someone raises questions or as the instructor encounters striking or anomalous texts that present special problems.

This socioliterary hermeneutical approach to the Hebrew Bible uncovers its chief structures and dynamics, is instructive concerning modern use and abuse of the Bible, and is congruent with the way we actually learn deeply and lastingly about anything. Finally, the course orientation and structure I have detailed accord with a view of the Hebrew Bible as an open-ended "question-answer book," for we may say of the Bible what Carlos Fuentes has said of the novel:

> The novel is a question that cannot be contained by a single answer, because it is social and society is plural. The novel is an answer that always says: "the world is unfinished and cannot be contained by a single question."

The Multiplication of Similitudes

Ruth apRoberts

Students in Bible-as-literature classes often come in with an assortment of strained attitudes, ranging from that of the "believer" who may be fearful or suspicious to that of the atheist who comes in as a reductionist or scoffer. One may at first ask the whole gamut of them to try to put aside the question Is it true? and look together at what is there. One might refer to Chesterton's idea—and there may be a little shock in this for some—that our myths and legends are the truest thing we have anyway. But from the first, as one accompanies students through selected readings of the historical books, one may invite attention to metaphor. What could be more innocent or more natural for the literature teacher to do? And yet I believe it gently leads into a kind of defusing of the charged attitudes of the students and ultimately to an intellectual enlargement and to a reading of the Bible that is richer and more rewarding—literarily, artistically, and, if one may say so, spiritually.

At the first, it needs to be emphasized that there are two accounts of creation, the six-day account (Gen. 1–2.3) and the Adam and Eve account (Gen. 2.4–3.24). One may ask as a reading assignment that the students be ready to make some observations on the difference in kind between the two accounts. (The term *account* neatly sidesteps the issue of literal truth, where *story* or *myth* might raise hackles.) Students' observations can be gathered into a consensus that the first is comparatively abstract, austere, cosmological, while the second is concrete, homey, full of specificities: the names of Adam and Eve and the geography of Eden, ribs, fig leaves, a serpent, trees, and an anthropomorphic God who walks in the garden in the cool of the day. One can sidestep the difficult doctrinal questions both accounts raise; in fact one must, or be forever embroiled and kept from the syllabus of the course. But one can insist on the two different styles and observe that the Adam and Eve account is composed earlier, and in an imagistic mode that is easier to visualize and grasp, while the six-day creation is on a higher level of abstraction, more philosophical and less imagistic, though the images are bold and magnificent. Borrowing from Kenneth Burke (201–07), one might ask, How would you best present the idea that man is doomed to death, to toiling for bread, and woman to pain in childbirth? Answer: by a narrative such as that in Genesis 2–3. And how would you best present the principle of sublime order and essential good in creation? By a narrative such as Genesis 1.

The murder of Abel supplies us with a stunning isolated analyzable figure: "the voice of thy brother's blood crieth unto me from the ground" (Gen. 4.10). The matter of metaphor can get so enormously subtle that I think it is as well to be utterly simplistic at first when one can be. Is this ordinary speech? What is remarkable about it? It is something *not true*. Is it a valid way to speak? Is it effective? Yes. It is very effective, very strong. Can it be said without the metaphor? Well, you would have to say, The earth, creation, seems to be outraged by this act; murder cannot stay hid but makes itself known to God; and so forth and so on. And it turns out that the metaphor is not only a powerful and engaging way of saying this but also very condensed. Students will consider the differentiation of metaphor and simile, but the distinction is not particularly useful in this course, and "metaphor" is best used in its largest sense, to cover all figurative language. It must be emphasized that metaphor is not a kind of "poetic" beautification or decoration but a mode of thinking indispensable even in science and philosophy, as is being increasingly acknowledged these days (see Lakoff and Johnson).

The development of symbols can be suggested in the Noah material: the dove, the olive branch, the rainbow. One classifies most of Genesis as etiological material, explaining beginnings through metaphor and symbol. The account of the Tower of Babel, for instance, can be so emphasized — a way of thinking about our terrible misunderstandings of one another all over the earth and our consequent loss of power.

As part of a general program of raising metaphor consciousness, one mentions in passing how Jacob complains that Simeon and Levi in the Dinah incident have made his name to "stink" among the local people (Gen. 34.30); how the Midianites feared the presence of the children of Israel, that they should "lick up" the country, "as the ox licketh up the grass of the field" (Num. 22.4); how Moses in bitter black humor complains to God that he has to act as if he were a lactating father to his unruly group: "Have I conceived all this people? have I begotten them, that thou shouldst say unto me, Carry them in thy bosom, as a nursing father beareth the sucking child?" (Num. 11.12). Incidental to the historical account there occurs such a passage as God's reminder to the people in the wilderness, how he brought them up out of Egypt: "I bare you on eagle's wings" (what condensed nobility, strength, and *soaring!*). And then there are the metaphors in actual poems, such as David's comparison of Saul and Jonathan to "weapons of war" in the beautiful lament.

At some time in dealing with the historical books it is well to raise the conventional old medieval idea of the fourfold exegesis, of, for the best example, the escape from Egypt, the wandering in the wilderness, and the conquest of Canaan. First, the historical or literal interpretation: the Israelites did indeed escape from the real historical Egypt under Moses's leadership and did have many trials in the wilderness and did ultimately take possession of Canaan. Second, the allegorical interpretation: the soul, enslaved to sin (the fleshpots of Egypt), in the care of a great leader (Moses), endures many trials and temptations and at last wins through to salvation (the Promised Land). (One might refer to and summarize here other allegories the student might have encountered: the medieval play of *Everyman* and Bunyan's seventeenth-century *Pilgrim's Progress.*) Third, the moral interpretation, which might be simply put as "It matters what you do"; when the Israelites followed God's laws, they found themselves moving on toward the goal; when they backslid, there were terrible punishments and delays. The fourth, the anagogical or mystical interpretation, needs — as a medievalist might say — no less than an angel to explain, but it might be suggested as a vision of darkness into light, or movement from a dangerous and pointless wilderness into meaning, order, the New Jerusalem and the soul's bliss. This review of the old fourfold method constitutes another suggestion of the importance of metaphor or the other than literal: the literal is limiting and misses a variety of possible values in the text.

When we read in Deuteronomy 6.8–9 that the essential Mosaic Commandments are to be bound "for a sign upon thine hand, and they shall be as frontlets between thine eyes. And thou shalt write them upon the posts of thy house, and on thy gates," it might be imagined that this is an exhortation to act *as though* these commandments were marked on our hands, our foreheads, and our doorways. But pious Jews — students should be told — do actually write them on paper and put them in little containers that are then as phylacteries actually bound to the arm and forehead, and as mezuzoth actually attached to the doorpost. The actual practice, or literal interpretation, would not appear to be the essential thing, but is a symbol of the desired state of mind, the perpetual consciousness of the Commandments.

In the poetic parts of the Bible, metaphor becomes the basic mode, and the Book of Psalms has enriched every culture it has touched with a wealth of enduring figures, from the great basic ones, of physical thirst for spiritual need ("As the hart panteth after the water brooks, so panteth my soul after thee, O God" Ps. 42.1), of human life as grass, as the flower of the field (e.g., Ps. 37), to the unique and charming children as arrows ("Happy *is* the man that hath his quiver full of them" Ps. 127.5), to the extravagant cosmic celebrations of nature: the mountains that "skip like rams" and the "little hills, like lambs" (Ps. 114.6), or the "floods" that "clap their hands" (Ps. 98.9). Some metaphors catch the imagination as ever freshly as a figure from Dante or Shakespeare: "We spend our years as a tale *that is told*" (Ps. 90.9) speaks to a modern absurdist consciousness. "The heavens declare the glory of God" (Ps. 19.1) does not lose its meaning: the mute, inexpressibly beautiful expanse of stars above us is *saying* something about the nature of existence. The figure is elegantly developed through the next five verses in suggestive analogy to ensuing verses on the beauty of the law, the nonmute verbalized wonder of the moral consciousness. The Psalm is not naive; it expresses in fact the two wonders of existence as Immanuel Kant saw them: the physical laws of the cosmos without and the moral law within.

The study of metaphor becomes vital in a particular way in the poetic parts of the Bible because of the interplay between metaphor and structural parallelism. Quite habitually, sets of parallels will combine a metaphor in one stich with a discursive statement in the other.

> Who shall ascend into the hill of the LORD?   a
> or who shall stand in his holy place?   a
>
> He that hath clean hands,   b
> and [he that hath] a pure heart   b
>
> Ps. 24.3–4

The pair of questions explain each other as referring to the temple sanctuary; in the pair of answers, the metaphorical "clean hands" is explained as a state of mind by the other metaphor of the "pure heart," which is so common as to have practically lost its metaphorical quality. In Isaiah 9.2:

The people that walked in darkness	a
have seen a great light;	b
they that dwell in the land of the shadow of death,	a
upon them hath the light shined.	b

To "walk in darkness" is mysterious until the darkness is specified in the second stich as the "shadow of death," and from them both together is generated the meaning that the "people" are those who are aware that they will die — and that means the whole of the human race. The two b stichs present both the active and passive reception of light, two ways of perceiving this "enlightening" news. "Arise, shine" (Isa. 60.1). A sublime pair of interglossing parallels occurs where it might seem so commonplace as to be invisible:

The Lord *is* my shepherd;
I shall not want.
Ps. 23.1

The second statement glosses the first: that is what it is to have the Lord for one's shepherd — it is to be in need of nothing.

With the Prophets, it would seem that metaphor is developed with the greatest virtuosity; there is even the conscious challenge of speaking of the Ineffable:

To whom will ye liken me	a
and make *me* equal,	b
and compare me,	b
that we may be like?	a
Isa. 46.5	

This chiasm (abba) makes the issue clear. And Hosea acknowledges metaphor as the definitive prophetic mode:

I have also spoken by the prophets	a
and I have multiplied visions,	b
and used similitudes,	b
by the ministry of the prophets.	a
Hos. 12.10	

And so the understanding of God develops through the Hebrew Bible with military metaphors — a fortress, a rock, a shield; agrarian metaphors — a reaper, a winnower, a burning off of the stubble. He is an architect (Isa. 40.12), and the plumbline itself (Amos 7.7) presumably standing for justice, a potter (Ps. 2.9, Isa. 30.14); and with the new technology of metalwork, he is a smelter (Isa. 1.25), a refiner's fire (Mal. 3.2). As retribution for evil, he is the besom of destruction (Isa. 14.23) or a razor (Isa. 7.20), and, recurrently, fire. God the Father is commonplace; Isaiah has an interesting figure of God as mother, as having born Israel from the belly, from the womb (46.3), and again as a nursing mother whose full breasts keep her conscious of the child (49.15). And out of the sheep-keeping economy come the great and beloved figure of God as "shepherd" (e.g., Ps. 23; Isa. 40.11) and the suffering servant as the slaughtered lamb (Isa. 53.7). These figures run through all Western literature as enabling images, "aids to reflection," ready-made similitudes for poets.

The concept of deity in the Bible is a natural place to bring up the phenomenon of anthropomorphism. The word itself is educative for the student who has not met it before. "Man never knows how anthropomorphic he is," said the wise Goethe. But the topic of metaphor in this course is an occasion to consider just that, how human beings have in all cultures ascribed human characteristics to the forces of nature. "Personification" embraces all such metaphors. The human—all too human—traits of the God of the Hebrew Bible are characteristic: he walks in the cool of the evening, he haggles with Abraham, he is open to the flattery of Moses. But even sophisticated theologians, it might be pointed out, are still anthropomorphizing when they talk of such things as the "will" of God. It turns out to be virtually impossible to think about deity without metaphor.

Whether deity is in question or any other difficult matter—the spiritual, the ethical, the unknown, the new attitude—the metaphorical mode expresses it in terms of the known, the familiar, the visualizable image, the feelable sensation. Amos is a virtuoso. You feel secure, he says, but you are not. It is "[a]s if a man did flee from a lion, and a bear met him; or went into the house and leaned his hand on the wall, and a serpent bit him" (Amos 5.19). You know what physical famine is; there can be a spiritual famine. "Behold, the days come, saith the Lord GOD, that I will send a famine in the land, not a famine of bread, nor a thirst for water, but of hearing the words of the LORD" (8.11). In the historical books, apostasy is sometimes referred to in the figure of adultery, of "whoring after strange gods." In Hosea, this figure becomes the master framing metaphor of the whole book. The marriage of Israel to God is desecrated by the apostasy of Israel—and the metaphor is compellingly developed in the hurt of the husband and his pained but forgiving and enduring love. Suitably enough, Hosea's incidental metaphors are housekeeping ones, of a moth, of food going bad (5.12), of baking—Ephraim is a "cake not turned" (half-baked!—7.8). (Another notably domestic metaphor occurs in an incidental piece of doom prophecy in 2 Kings 21.13: "I will wipe Jerusalem as *a man* wipeth a dish, wiping *it*, and turning *it* upside down.") Agricultural images run through all these Prophets. Hosea develops one at some length:

> Sow to yourselves in righteousness,
> reap in mercy;
> break up your fallow ground:
> for *it is* time to seek the LORD,
> till he come and rain righteousness upon you.
> Ye have plowed wickedness,
> ye have reaped iniquity;
> ye have eaten the fruit of lies:
> because thou didst trust in thy way,
> in the multitude of thy mighty men.
> (10.12–13)

Isaiah is perhaps the richest and most varied. He speaks of "backsliding" (itself a metaphor from cattle raising, Hos. 4.16) as the reversion of vineyard grapes, cultivated (by the Lord), to the sour wild grapes (Isa. 5.2). One of the boldest is that of the huckster:

> Ho, every one that thirsteth
> Come ye to the waters,
> and he that hath no money;
> come ye, buy, and eat;
> yea, come, buy wine and milk
> without money and without price.
> (Isa. 55.1)

At one place he exhorts the people to cast away the molten idols "as a menstruous cloth" (Isa. 30.22). So says the King James Version. The Revision of 1885, the RSV, and the NEB, Luther, and the Jerusalem Bible all fall back on a generalized word for "refuse." But Jerome and the King James translators preserve the specific thing that is, I am told, the sense of the original Hebrew. The fact is worth mentioning, as an example of the bold specificity of Hebrew metaphor, as well as of the strong nerves of King James's committee. It should also be observed that the NEB characteristically slights or defuses or at times even omits the metaphor of the original and that this tendency accounts for what is felt to be the NEB's frequent failure "as literature." But it is really a failure in meaning. The metaphors are, moreover, comparatively translatable devices: father, shepherd, clean hands, dish, moth, light—these have pretty close equivalents in most languages.

I think in a course on the Bible-as-literature one need make no great claim for what many theologians argue for now as the supremacy of metaphor in religious discourse. (See, e.g., Ricoeur, *Rule*, esp. 320–22.) The consistent attention to metaphor simply works by itself to suggest something like that. And if one has students write short essays on metaphor analysis, to try to state in nonmetaphorical language what the meaning or effect of the metaphor is, one need not tell them that what they are doing is anything as radical or heterodox (from some sectarian points of view) as "demythologization." For merely to consider in a fairly disciplined way this remarkable phenomenon of biblical metaphor does by itself induce a much more sophisticated frame of mind than most students start with, a broader, more tolerant attitude to religion, and an immensely heightened appreciation of our great texts, both secular and spiritual.

Textual Juxtaposition and the Comparative Study of Biblical and Ancient Near Eastern Literature

Stephen A. Geller

Early comparative study of biblical and ancient Near Eastern literatures focused on the discovery of parallels: an Assyrian flood story, a Babylonian Job, an Egyptian Book of Proverbs and Song of Songs, and so on. This intense interest in similarities led to the excesses of the *"Bibel und Babel"* school and later the "myth and ritual" and "Pan-Ugaritic" approaches, all of which tried to force Israel into the cultural, and especially cultic, patterns of the ancient world (Hahn, ch. 3). In reaction some scholars like Yehezkel Kaufmann stressed the essential difference between Israel and its neighbors to an exaggerated extent, also forcing meaning on texts.

Recent comparative study has been struggling toward a balance between the poles of similarity and difference (Evans et al.; Hallo et al.). Only such a balance can enable the comparative method to perform what should be its prime goal: uncovering issues of universal human concern in these ancient texts, so remote from us in time and culture and so grudging of their meaning. Instead of imposing meaning on them as earlier scholarship too often tended to do, modern scholarship is gradually learning how to let texts speak in their own voices.

A major tool of recent comparative study is literary analysis. Basic issues do not emerge easily from ancient texts. Often obscure and defective, these texts are accessible to nonspecialists only in translations that usually mask the true difficulties of the texts. Few secondary works offer guidance. But the major problems are internal, involving the manner in which issues are put. The ancients did not formulate them in the kind of logical exposition discovered later by the Greeks. Ancient literature prefers concrete expression to abstract. It is fond of metaphor. Above all, it likes to express meaning indirectly, through allusion, repetition, parallelism, wordplay, the blending of motifs, and even by the physical disposition of the text. Positional features such as juxtaposition, chiasm, *inclusio*, and so on can be crucial to the meaning of an ancient text, a fact appreciated by traditional exegesis but only now being "rediscovered" by modern interpretation. One must attend not only to what is said, as earlier comparative study did, but also to how and where it is said.

The aim of this brief discussion is to show how a method of literary analysis rooted in these insights can help comparative study recover basic meaning in biblical literature. Two examples are presented, both necessarily in sparse outline. They are drawn from the area of comparative study that is probably most popular—and dangerous: myth and mythology. I try to demonstrate in both cases how underlying issues emerge only from careful comparison of biblical and extrabiblical literature and also how the literary device of juxtaposition plays a key role.

The first example is the unexplained juxtaposition of Sabbath and Tabernacle in Exodus. In 31.12–17 an injunction to observe the Sabbath follows detailed instructions concerning the building of the tent shrine in chapters 25–31. In 35.1–3 a briefer Sabbath law precedes the lengthy account of the actual construction of that shrine. Modern criticism has tended to see in this juxtaposition yet another example of the clumsy editing of the Pentateuch. One may, however, gain insight into a possible reason for the arrangement of topics by examining parallel themes elsewhere in the Hebrew Bible and in ancient Near Eastern mythology.

Biblical criticism assigns the Exodus passages to the priestly writer. Also assigned to him is the creation story of Genesis 1.1–2.4, which ends with the Sabbath. Perceptive commentators have noted that the Sabbath is presented positively, as the "work" of the seventh day, a final act of creation (e.g., von Rad, *Old Testament* 147). As such it corresponds to the shrine in a key Babylonian creation myth, the *Enuma Elish* (Sarna, *Exploring* 214). The god Marduk establishes his kingship by killing the primeval sea monster Tiamat, from whose body he creates the world. The acts of creation end with the building of his great palace-shrine Esagila, a "resting place" for the gods (Heidel, *Babylonian Genesis*; Lambert, "New Look").

The common ancient Near Eastern association of temple and creation (Frankfort) suggests that an equation may emerge from the biblical passages. Since the Sabbath is linked to creation in Genesis 2.1–4, and to the shrine in Exodus 31.12–17 and 35.1–3, it is possible, by juxtaposition, to formulate the following schema:

$$\text{creation : Sabbath} = \text{Sabbath : shrine}$$

The priestly writer is forging a connection between creation and shrine through the use of the Sabbath as an intermediary.

This interpretation might seem to represent as foreign an imposition of ancient Near Eastern meaning on the biblical text as any practised by the *"Bibel und Babel"* school. The connection between creation and Tabernacle is undeniably indirect, but it was clearly inconceivable for the priestly author to introduce an actual shrine into Genesis 1-2. Priestly dogma held that the cult originated historically in the Mosaic age. The validity of the shrine, like that of the Aaronic priesthood itself, rested in divine theophany. Only rarely are shrine and creation directly associated in the Hebrew Bible (see Ps. 78.69).

Nevertheless, there were strong mythical and cosmological associations to temples in Israel. The mythical aspects are intimated by the revelation of the form of the tent shrine, the archetypal temple, as a divine "model" *(tabnît)* in Exodus 25.9, quite on the ancient Near Eastern pattern (Frankfort, 256). As the earthly dwelling of God the shrine was the counterpart of the heavenly palace. Also indicative of the mythically rooted aspect of the temple was its location on the "divine mountain" (Clifford). Moreover, many features of its construction and ritual paraphernalia had definite cosmological symbolism:

the brazen "sea," the altar called "mountain of God," and so on (Albright, *Archaeology* 148–55).

Most significant of all, the shrine had essentially the same communal function as in the rest of the ancient Near East. It acted as a channel for divine blessing, a seal of created order. Destruction of the shrine could unleash the forces of primeval chaos, such as war, famine, and plague. Temples were symbols of divinely created stability, eternal and unchanging, "forever" (*lĕʿôlām*), a favorite term of the priestly authors.

For these reasons a purely historical treatment of the shrine's origin would probably have seemed inadequate to the priestly writer in Exodus. On the other hand, the mythical aspects could not be expressed directly. The result is an excellent example of the way the ancients made meaning in texts: the institution of the Sabbath is used as an intermediary between the things the author wants to link. The Sabbath is a "sign" (*ʾot*) linking the shrine in Exodus with creation in Genesis 1–2. This use of a segment of time as a sign rather than as an actual reenactment of the original event in true mythical fashion (Frankfort) is a hallmark of biblical religion.

By this bold association the priestly writer suggests that the building of the Tabernacle is a completion of the acts of creation. The parallel of the end of the work on the shrine in Exodus 40.33 ("and Moses finished the work") to the completion of divine creation in Genesis 2.2 ("and God finished . . . his work") is hardly accidental. In Exodus the divine presence (*kābôd*) descends on the completed Tabernacle. God takes up residence within his creation. The old mythical pattern of divine combat-creation-shrine is, in the Bible, reformulated historically as the splitting of the Red Sea–Sinai theophany–Tabernacle. The priestly conviction that the shrine was the pinnacle and guarantor of the covenant was best expressed by creation.

Implicit in this discussion is the tension, perhaps unconscious, between the historical and mythical-cosmological aspects of the shrine. This tension between myth and history is the underlying issue that may be isolated also in the role of the Sabbath. The essentially abstract, quasi-mythical function given to that institution by the priestly tradition contrasts strongly with the historical explanation given by the Deuteronomic tradition: the Sabbath is a memorial of Egyptian slavery. Abstention from work relives freedom from bondage; contrast Exodus 20.8–11 with Deuteronomy 5.12–15. In one way or another the dialectic of myth and history underlies most aspects of biblical religion.

Earlier comparative study tended to view Israel either entirely within the bounds of ancient Near Eastern mythical categories or, conversely, "free" of myth, rooted only in historical experience. These imbalanced views are ingenuous, as the above example shows. Modern comparative study is coming to understand the complex role played by myth in biblical religion (Childs, *Myth*). Myth is also essential to the biblical view of history, resulting in a sophisticated use of typology. In the example just cited it was specifically the awareness of the role of a literary device, juxtaposition, that allowed meaning to emerge. Juxtaposition plays an even stronger role in my second example.

The flood story is probably the most popular single object of comparative biblical-ancient Near Eastern literary study. The topic has been well studied (Damrosch; Heidel, *Gilgamesh*; Tigay, *Evolution* and *Empirical Models*). The orginal locus of the Mesopotamian story was probably the *Atrahasis* epic of the mid–second millennium. There the flood comes as the culmination of a series of attempts by the gods to limit human population. Human beings had been created to serve the gods but had become so numerous that Enlil, chief god, could get no sleep. Like the pharaoh of the Exodus he decided to do something drastic about this swarm of slaves. But the wise god Enki told his favorite, Atrahasis, to build a boat. The gods themselves were so terrified of the flood and, lacking their servants, so hungry and thirsty that a compromise was reached. Classes of priestesses were instituted who would not be allowed to marry and reproduce, and birth demons were appointed to snatch babies, so human numbers would be controlled (Lambert and Millard).

Clearly, the major theme is the upset of natural balance due to the powers of human reproduction. The ecological aspects of the theme are especially attractive to modern readers. If it is "amoral," that amorality is appropriate to paganism, the gods of which were basically personified natural forces (Frankfort).

The biblical story in Genesis 6–9 is, of course, "moral." Humankind is destroyed for its "corruption," specified as "violence" *(hāmās)*. The flood is part of an extended degenerative moral pattern in the primeval history of Genesis 1–11 whose troughs, so to speak, are Adam's rebellion, Cain's fratricide, Lamech's homicide, the corruption of the flood generation, and the hubris of the builders of the Tower of Babel. Out of this moral morass Abraham-Israel rises in Genesis 11–12. This negative typology is matched by a positive one: Noah, emerging safe from a second watery chaos, is a second Adam. Moses, rescued from the Nile flood in an "ark" is a third. Perhaps Abraham is also a kind of Adam, if the "chaos" of nations in Genesis 11 can be viewed typologically. The biblical story, like the Mesopotamian, is exceptionally well rooted in its literary context. The contrast of the tales in terms of morality is expected.

A comparative analysis that remained on this level would be incomplete. Careful examination of the two stories reveals an interesting development. The theme of sexual increase in the Mesopotamian version has been transmuted in the Bible into an increase of wickedness; but the sexual aspects of the Mesopotamian story appear in heightened form in two brief narratives juxtaposed to the beginning and end of the flood story, bracketing it, as it were. Both deal with shocking sexual aberrations.

Genesis 6.1–4, a famously enigmatic fragment, describes the intercourse between divine beings ("sons of God") and human women, producing a race of hybrid heroes. God is angry and in an (admittedly obscure) verse limits human life span to 120 (!) years, thus denying the hybrids the divine aspects of their patrimony.

In Genesis 9.20–27 Noah gets drunk and "uncovers himself" in his tent. His "nakedness" is "seen" by his younger son Ham, whose own son Canaan Noah curses upon awakening. Canaan shall be a slave forever. There is a shudder in this story. Nothing could be more unsettling to patriarchal Hebrews than an intimation of homosexual incest with a father.

These striking juxtapositions are no more accidental than the one studied above. It is reasonable to suggest that the first is intended to make the point that the corruption of the flood generation was sexual as well as homicidal; after all, the people of the flood generation were, in fact, the hybrids in question. The complex of sex and violence in relation to the flood generation is fully developed in the later Enoch tradition. In the Bible, the author, or editor, reinforces the point by using the "leading word" (*Leitwort*) *rbb*, "increase," both in 6.1 and 6.5: "when man began to increase in the land . . ." and "God saw that man's wickedness had increased on the earth. . . ."

The point of the second fragment is absolutely clear: it foreshadows the later Israelite conquest of Canaan, the fulfillment of the curse. But the real meaning of the double juxtaposition lies in the superimposition, so to speak, of both narratives on the main flood story itself. What emerges, in allusory fashion, is the forceful suggestion that the later Canaanites are to be viewed in the light of the corrupt generation of the flood. There is a special link between the latter and the people of Sodom and Gomorrah, also destroyed for collective wickedness: violence and especially sexual perversions. The Sodomites are evidently intended to represent archetypal Canaanites. It was for their unnatural sins that the land "vomited out" the Canaanites (Lev. 18.28, after a list of sexual crimes).

The sexual theme implicit in the Mesopotamian story has not been dropped by the Bible but developed in an inimitable way into a mythical-historical complex of great depth and richness. From this complex of themes one can discern what seems to be the dominant underlying issue of both flood stories. Despite their differences, both seem to be attempting a definition of "natural," which, in ancient fashion, they express indirectly, through examples of what they consider "unnatural."

"Unnatural" in Mesopotamia means "imbalanced, violating created order." Human increase was unnatural because it upset the divine ecology. In Israel it means "sexual perversions and bloodshed." Both are presented as physically intolerable to nature, a metaphorical way of making the point. Shed blood "cries out" from the earth (Gen. 4.10), and, as noted, the land "vomited out" the Canaanites—it couldn't bear them in its system. The perverse flood generation also had to be wiped off the earth for, like matter and antimatter, it could not coexist with created order. The sense of physical aversion makes the moral crime more repugnant.

Similarly, illicit contact with the divine is "unnatural" in the Hebrew Bible. It need not be sexual as in Genesis 6.1–4. Hubris, the human attempt to appropriate divine characteristics, is equally revolting. The generation of the flood, half-divine in its perversion, forms part of a triad of hubris in the primeval history, along with Adam's theft of divine knowledge and the attack on heaven by the builders of Babel.

No claim is made that the ancient world achieved a concept of "nature" in the Greek, let alone the modern, sense. But palpable in the flood stories is an intuition of "natural law" ancestral to that achieved later by the rabbinic concept of the "Noahide Commandments" obligatory on all humankind.

Both examples presented here reveal how wrong it is to view ancient Israel as "free" from myth. On the contrary, Israel used ancient myth with great freedom in order to animate history with profound typological associations. The examples also demonstrate that, to understand this essential meaning, comparative method must be informed by literary analysis that is attuned to the ancient means of expression.

When this general literary approach is applied to the practical problems of teaching, there can of course be no substitute for detailed textual analysis and deep immersion in historical and cultural background. I would stress the importance of careful outlining of the texts to be studied. Because much ancient literature is fragmentary and obscure, interpreters often work only from part of a text, with no overview of total content and structure. Even biblical exegetes frequently display ignorance of the overall pattern of the books they are studying. Emphasis on simple outlining of the text is therefore not banal but essential to total interpretation.

Outlining has great pedagogical value, in my experience. If a teacher begins literary analysis by outlining texts together with students, the cooperative effort helps neutralize the difference in training. In this task at least, students and teachers stand more or less on the same level, and the sense of equality seems to excite the former as much as it challenges the latter.

Much more than a preliminary step, outlining can carry one far along the road of interpretation. Particularly for those dealing with difficult ancient texts, an outline represents a kind of working hypothesis, a grappling with the essential structure of form and meaning in the text. Successive revisions mark progressive stages in literary understanding. The outline highlights repetitions, digressions, non sequiturs. The sorts of questions asked in the above sketch leap almost unbidden into view; above all is the key question of juxtaposition: why is X next to Y?

Recurrence and Sublimation: Toward a Psychoanalytic Approach to Biblical Narrative

Yael S. Feldman

There is something ironic in the undertaking of this volume, inasmuch as it foregrounds the literature of the Hebrew Bible just when *post*biblical literature has been declared the model of contemporary literary theory (see Handelman). This irony notwithstanding, there is, no doubt, a pedagogical need (not to say a critical one) to sharpen our definitions and draw clear demarcation lines between the terms *Bible* and *Midrash* (or *Kabbalah*), for they are sometimes used indiscriminately in poststructuralist hermeneutics. This need seems particularly pressing in view of the "anxiety of theory" I have recently sensed among my upper-level and graduate students. I will even argue that it is precisely this anxiety, or rather the conceptual mystification that has bred it, that draws these students to such courses as Literary Approaches to the Bible and Bible and Literary Theory.

One approach that I have found helpful in simultaneously demonstrating and demystifying poststructuralist theory is that of applied psychoanalysis. While on the one hand my class exercise sheds light on some of the central imprecisions that underlie the contemporary hermeneutical debate, on the other hand it highlights the "originary" role that Freud's ideas have played in creating this very climate.

To begin with, I present my students with an aphorism I heard from the son of Protestant missionaries as an "explanation" for his unflagging interest in Judaism: "Catholicism is the Unconscious of Protestantism, while Judaism is the Unconscious of Catholicism." As a rule, students' responses point in two directions. Some want to know what was, for that scholar, the Unconscious of Judaism; others question the validity of viewing Judaism as the Unconscious of another system of thought. In either case, I help them narrow down the question to the biblical text and its precarious position within the dichotomy of "Judaism as the Unconscious" versus "the Unconscious of Judaism." I point out the relative paucity of psychoanalytic readings currently used in college classes on the Hebrew Bible (a fact clearly substantiated by the responses to the questionnaire initiating this project). I further observe that, stylistically, the Hebrew Bible is ideal for phenomenologically oriented readings, which are, in turn, either consciously or unconsciously inspired by Freud (see Kermode). However, while technical "gap filling" and other Freudian interpretive strategies are in evidence in recent readings of biblical narrative (see esp. Alter; Greenstein, "Riddle"; Sternberg), thematic Freudian analysis is rather rare.

Why should this be so? Why shouldn't the recent renaissance in the literary study of the Bible benefit from the concurrent "return to Freud" of literary criticism? (And why should the position of Scripture be any different from that of Midrash or Kabbalah or Jewish mysticism in contemporary theoretical discourse?) Can we believe that Freud's notorious censure of religion (*Future*) still renders his teachings unacceptable even today, when Scripture is read as literature? Possibly, to some extent, but not in all cases. Or perhaps the religious aura of Scripture is still too forbidding to allow the probing of its unconscious? Probably so in some quarters, but not in all. Or, and this is the most provocative option, is there some basic lack of fit between the "treatment" and the "patient"? Could we say, figuratively speaking, that, in the Bible, the workings of textual repressions are too successful to allow a meaningful psychoanalytic interpretation? And wouldn't such a hypothesis explain Freud's own meager use of biblical material (with the exception, of course, of *Moses and Monotheism*, which deserves a separate discussion) and his preference for Greek and other mythological sources? But with this sort of reasoning, wouldn't we be describing the psychological matrix against which Freud rebelled rather than explaining the inapplicability of his theory for the interpretation of this matrix?

I suppose we would. Moreover, we may inadvertently wander into the much debated issue of Freud's Jewish identification. This digression, however, would not be completely out of order, because the first problem to surface in any Freudian reading of the Bible is the disparity between the foci of the two cultural systems—Oedipus and Isaac (see Wellisch; Bakan; Shoham; Lyotard). There can be no doubt that Freud could not identify with Isaac. Nor could he identify with Abraham in that famous episode, for he was just as "bound" by his heavenly father as Isaac was. Does this mean, then, that Freud's insight into the psychosexual dynamic of the family has no bearing on biblical narrative? I would doubt it. We can argue that Sara's conspicuous absence from the crucial moment in the life of her son and husband is compensated for by Rebecca's plotting with her son and against her husband. We can also claim that Jacob's filial behavior is more clearly "oedipal" than Isaac's and that the stories of the David cycle are replete with similar displacements. One would have to admit, then, that despite some major differences—notably the shift of focus from filial to sibling rivalry—at least some of the psychic structures represented in the Bible are amenable to "classical" Freudian interpretation. (On the broader implications of this shift, see particularly Ruether, *Faith*.)

At this point in the class discussion I introduce the only work that I know of which is totally devoted to such analysis, Dorothy Zeligs's *Psychoanalysis and the Bible* (recently reinforced by a book-length study of *Moses*).

This book is precisely what its subtitle tells us, "A Study in Depth of Seven Leaders," beginning with Abraham and ending with Solomon. Although very useful and often on target as a collection of "case histories," this study illustrates the conceptual blurring of boundaries mentioned above. As happens in many a study of biblical narrative, particularly of Genesis, the scholar nonchalantly moves, in a kind of free association, from the text being studied to either or both of two adjacent systems: the ancient, often prebiblical and non-Hebraic, mythology and the Hebraic oral "tradition," the Midrash, more popularly known as "Jewish legends." This is what Zeligs does when she declares, "While the Bible tells us little about the relationship between Abraham and his father Terah, tradition in the form of extra-biblical legend is more expansive . . . " (4). Summing up this extra-biblical material, which is, typically, conducive to the analysis of oedipal and preoedipal conflicts, she says:

> It is not the intent here to attribute to Abraham the actual content of these legends which may have evolved at a much *later* time. The feelings and motivations that prompted them may be in response to the *underlying* attitudes *hidden* in the biblical text. Legends and myths arise in the popular mind in unconscious identification with the hero.
> (8; emphasis added)

Here I call students' attention to Zeligs's awareness that her use of extrabiblical materials is problematic. But what precisely is the problem? On the face of it, chronology. Zeligs does not feel at ease using legends that evolved at a later time, unless she claims that these later readings are the readers' "responses" to latent repressed content, absent from the biblical text itself. What Zeligs's interpretive procedures reveal is that very often biblical narrative by itself is too cryptic to be amenable to psychoanalytic interpretation. Had she no recourse to "legendary" material, she would have had no access to the underlying fantasy, to the Unconscious of the manifest text. Furthermore, since the problem with which she consciously grapples in this passage is perceived as one of chronology, could her solution be interpreted as an unconsciously displaced chronology? In other words, can we say that what is structurally hidden or latent is also temporally earlier? Wouldn't the material have to "have already been there" in order to be suppressed?

An affirmation of this suggestion will agree, of course, with Freud's archeological perception of the unconscious and his notion of the "return of the repressed." But it also brings to mind Gershom Scholem's perception that "to a certain degree, mysticism signifies a revival of mythical thought" (*Major Trends* 8). Since mythical thought is the earliest stage in the development of human consciousness, one can detect in Scholem's historical scheme a trace of, or an analogue to, Freudian psychic structures.

It should come as no surprise, then, that psychoanalytically inspired studies of the Bible, to the extent that they are concerned with classically Freudian "id psychology," namely, unconscious conflicts and fantasies, cannot make do with the biblical narrative per se. Rather, they analyze precisely that mythical material that, after being denied, rejected, or suppressed by the Bible, found its way into Midrash and Kabbalah. (That this textual Unconscious represents the typically female Other should also come as no surprise to anyone familiar with the Midrash and Kabbalah, on the one hand, and with the matriarchal substratum of biblical literature, on the other; see Reik, *Crea-*

tion; Schlossman; Maccoby; cf. also Roheim; Schneidau; Kristeva.)

There is no rule, of course, against this kind of analysis, or against the blurring of the boundaries between the Bible and its adjacent textual systems. After all, students of the Jewish tradition have been doing something similar in European *yeshivoth* for hundreds of years. But they do not delude themselves that they are studying the Bible. They are studying Rabbinic Judaism, as some contemporary poststructuralists currently do.

This is not the place to go into my view of the cultural meaning of this revival of interest in both the textuality and intertextuality of rabbinic tradition. My plea to restore to biblical narrative its right to textual independence is not meant as a call for precision for its own sake. Rather, it is meant as a precaution against losing sight of the specificity of biblical narrative, both aesthetically and psychoanalytically. For what this text may lose in drive psychology and fantasy content, it gains in super-ego psychology and therapeutic effects. (For recent summaries of the various psychoanalytic models available for literary and artistic interpretations, see Skura; Wright; Spitz.) Unlike its mythical precursors and successors, biblical narrative dramatizes not the unconscious play of instinctual drives but rather the conscious process of harnessing them. Genesis and Exodus in particular unfold the drama of the creation of Freud's "Civilization"—surely not without its Discontents, but with a greater share of its potential for sublimation than Freud was capable of recognizing (for a similar approach, though from different angles, see Reik, "Discovery"; Chasseguet-Smirgel).

In this context students readily perceive biblical "knowledge" as carnal, cognitive, and moral—and in this very order. It is therefore no accident that the domestication of the sexual drive is a major theme throughout Genesis, rivaled only by the analogous gradual sublimation of the aggressive drive. (In more advanced classes, one may bring into the discussion the rabbinic debate over the closing of the biblical canon and the ensuing resolution to include both Song of Songs and Ecclesiastes—the epitomes of Eros and Thanatos, respectively—thereby repeating the action of domestication of these drives on a higher order.) The sublimation of the aggressive drive, as students are quick to recognize, is represented not by filial rebellion, as in the Greek (or Shakespearean) world, but by sibling rivalry. Significantly, the aggressive drive moves from the first, realized murder, through different mitigated representations of the same impulse, up to the total reversal of a potential murder, as in the Joseph episode. Predictably, it is in this account that a conscious representation of the unconscious appears for the first time. Joseph, the dream interpreter, is also the first human being to recognize and verbalize the interdependence between past and future. Finally, it is here that the moral implications of this recognition are explicitly stated, only to be further developed and orchestrated on a collective level in the next book, Exodus. The journey from Cain to Joseph, and later to Moses, is the earliest literary representation of a move from blind aggression to reasoned insight, from acting out to remembering and knowing.

But isn't this what the psychoanalytic process is all about? And wouldn't this insight lend a new meaning to the most prominent feature of biblical poetics, namely, narrative recurrence, known more popularly as repetition? Yes and no. Here we run into an intriguing paradox. For Freud, the compulsion to repeat is equated with the death drive—the impulse to resist change, progress, and life (Freud, "Beyond"). In the psychoanalytic process, repetition replaces memory; only by breaking this vicious circle can the subject allow the re-membering of alienated experiences, thereby achieving a new integration of the self (Freud, "Remembering"). In this scheme, memory and repetition are enemies. Not so in the Bible. Here, they are allies. It is through recall and recurrence that change is slowly brought about. But notice the slight lexical difference I've introduced. "Repetition" is almost a misnomer in discussions of biblical narrative. In all the scholarly compendiums recently written on biblical poetics the emphasis is on "theme and variations." While verbatim repetition, Meir Sternberg says, marked the literary representation of the ancient prebiblical myths, repetition with a difference was the innovation and contribution of the Hebrew Bible. It is for the sake of this poetic distinction that I propose to substitute "narrative recurrence" for repetition. Yet by this substitution I gain something else—for it is this view of the psychoanalytic process that is currently being developed.

Following Paul Ricoeur's phenomenological critique of psychoanalysis (*Freud*) and his highlighting of both the verbal and narrative nature of the "clinical fact" ("Question" 836–43), "narrative psychology" has been gaining ground, as in the theories of Roy Schafer ("Narration"), Merton M. Gill, Adolf Grünbaum, and Donald P. Spence ("Narrative Recursion"). Most recently, the emphasis on the function of metaphor (Ricoeur, *Rule*), multiple histories (Schafer, "Appreciative"), and narrative truth (Spence, *Narrative Truth*) in the psychoanalytic process has led to a new understanding of "narrative recursion." "[T]he original conflict or fantasy or early experience," Spence says, "is almost never literally repeated in the transference; rather, what we see is a series of variations on a single theme." It is this specific clinical recursion (i.e., "in variation") that "cuts down on the senseless repetition which would make the pattern seem mechanical and unnatural," thereby effecting the transition from language to action ("Narrative Recursion" 191, 195).

The parameters of this "action" (e.g., change, growth, adaptation, sublimation) and the socioethical norms they imply are currently being fiercely debated within the psychoanalytic community. (In upper-level classes one may here introduce Lacan's critique of American ego psychology and particularly his interpretation of the repetition compulsion, including his rather enigmatic statement that "repetition demands the new" [61].) And it is perhaps in this respect that the spiral movement of biblical narrative is most instructive. Paradoxically, contemporary psychoanalytic theory is only now catching up with the secret behind the sublimatory power of this earliest representation of civilization and its discontents.

Between the Bible and Torah

Francis Landy

For many of my students, the notion of a Hebrew Bible, as distinct from the
Old Testament, is strange, quite apart from the different order of books. Some
are discouraged from taking the course because they assume they have to
know Hebrew. In a sense they do, for I explain untranslatable ambiguities,
alliterations; I read in Hebrew. They lose confidence in their familiar text and
thus begin, in the traditional Jewish sense, to learn Torah.

Torah is not a book. It is a teaching, with two aspects that always correspond:
the Written and the Oral Torah, the text and the tradition. Our words are
as intrinsic a part of the Torah as is its script: its duality is expressed in the
rabbinic pun that on the two tablets of stone was engraved (_harut_) freedom
(_herut_) (cf. Babylonian Talmud, Erubin 54a; see also Roitman). The pupil is
equal to the master, according to the Midrash (Lauterbach 2: 166); the rabbi
is equal to God and assumes his authority (Babylonian Talmud, Baba Metsia
59a); and we in our turn reveal fresh faces of the Torah (Scholem, _On the
Kabbalah_ 65). Like the angels, who utter a word of divine song and die (Babylonian Talmud, Hagigah 14a), we turn the language of the universe into our
evanescent speech. As Torah, then, the Bible loses its distance; it is not simply a historical document and an ecclesiastical authority. We have to be aware
of its time, its truth claims, its limitations. But it speaks for the human quest
for knowledge and redemption — from death and chaos — and hence is part
of our language.

The loss of distance may have other disturbing consequences. The Bible
can no longer be seen as the Good Book; its God is totally compromised.
This is perhaps the most difficult but exhilarating of discoveries, that God
is implicated in the ambivalence of his creation. The horror of the Hebrew
Bible, its ultimate tragedy, its failure to satisfy narrative expectations, is one
consequence of this implication (Crenshaw; Davidson). Another is the Bible's refusal to answer questions, at least not without begging more questions.
Thus instead of giving the answer to the world, the Hebrew Bible makes the
world more imponderable, because of the intensity of its investigation. Instead of the unanimity of the corpus, we have a dialogue in which every book
of the Hebrew Bible interacts with every other.

The task, then, is to become part of this language and questioning, to invite the original author into the classroom, through sharing in his or her work.
If, in some sense, the author is God, and the book like the world is the medium
of his own self-understanding and questioning through his human image, then
our investigation puts us in touch with that which is ultimately validating.

The author will only come if interested. We become aware of an extraordinary subtlety and humanity, an ability, for example, to bring a character to
life in a few words and the impartiality that grants even the wicked their due
and their moments of dignity, as part of creation. Another aspect of this sub-

tlety is the undercurrent of humor, which biblical readers have tried to suppress in the interest of decorum. Recognition of this humor reveals underlying tensions but also love.

In teaching the Hebrew Bible I divide the class into groups to discuss texts or revise lectures; this arrangement palely reflects the yeshivah practice of pairing students and letting them read, argue, tease; intimacy with the text coincides with friendship. Or I write questions on the blackboard, as the focus of discussion. On a talkative day, I embark on lectures I can never end, the product of multiple readings and the text's recalcitrance. My inherent frustration as a university teacher—lack of time, exhaustion, and so on—and the chronic sense of failure themselves suggest openness, possibility, that no lecture can end, that no subject can be concluded. I divagate down whatever blind alley looks interesting, for all is Torah. The irrepressible joke—both hubris and communion—indicates a refusal to make allowances for the text's age and an ultimate respect for its authority. In the gaps and fumblings for words, one becomes aware of a presence. More than facts and interpretations, the way that which is beyond words communicates in difficult and indirect language is what I hope to show my students, to have them recall even when all details are forgotten. Having the "original" text always present, even though the meaning is not always understood by most of the class, has a positive function, since it focuses attention on the text as sound, as incantation, whose true meaning transcends the signification of its words. On the other hand, it may be a way of maintaining a hermeneutic privilege, an access to an arcane language, and hence be the object of suspicion.

My practice is generally called literary-critical, a term I do not wish to embrace too readily. The primary questions I ask are of the text as we have it, rather than how it developed or what historical information may be inferred from it. The label *literary-critical* polarizes too much; it substitutes an aggressive academic institution for a somewhat faded one. Within the community of world literature, the Bible risks being treated as a book among books instead of as a teaching that tells us of our ancestors and hence of our very selves, as part of a divine language (see Kugel 303–04).

To illustrate my approach, I turn to the story of the burning bush. In this story, which is itself the subtlest form of Torah, God indirectly awakens the curiosity of his pupil, Moses, and proceeds to provoke questions, whose answers elicit more questions that Moses does not ask. God's instruction of Moses is constantly under strain because of the conflict between resistance and desire and because the relationship between God and Moses itself is part of what has to be learned. The text is as follows:

> Now Moses was shepherding the flock of Jethro his father-in-law, the priest of Midian; and he led the flock behind the wilderness; and he came to the mountain of God, Horeb. (Exod. 3.1)

Now Moses was leading his flock in the wilderness: we can note in passing the proleptic function of the image of the shepherd (Greenberg, *Understanding* 67–68). We enter storytime, the narrative enchantment on which critical thinking reflects; paradoxically, a second naïveté (Ricoeur, *Symbolism* 351–52), absorption in the text through interpretation, is precondition and abiding context for exegesis. We are enveloped in a story, which in the Bible is a universal history. Hence no part of the text, not even a verse, can be treated in isolation from the whole. We bring to our understanding of Exodus 3.1 all that we know about Moses's past life, the romance of his infancy, his initial encounter with his life's work, his traumatic flight into the pastoral world. He is a person with a double identity, who escapes into exile from both his adopted home and his real self; unknowingly, he there reenacts the lives of his ancestors.

Not only does Moses go into exile; he goes further, "behind the wilderness," to the back of beyond. In the desert, where there is no life, where he is entirely anonymous, something recognizes him and calls him. Mysteriously, he comes to the "mountain of God." He has left behind estranged personae: Egyptian prince, revolted by and identified with the slave society he cannot join; shepherd and son-in-law of the priest of Midian, with its clannish desert spirituality. The far side of the world is symbolically, as in any quest narrative, the other side of the self; he discovers what is missing in himself, what his destiny is, whose partner he will be. More crucially, he discovers his memory.

The mountain of God is a surprising designation. In Canaanite mythology, the home of the gods was in a mountain in the far north, not one in the southern desert, in the hinterland of Midian. The anachronistic intrusion of the name by which the mountain was known to the narrator's audience many centuries later, alerts their sense of symbolic geography, alluding possibly to Elijah's journey "to the mountain of God, Horeb" in 1 Kings 19.8 and to his listening to the still, small voice. The name, however, also serves to introduce God into the text.

Just as we attach to Moses a considerable biographical background, so the reader of the Bible has, by this point, accumulated many impressions of God that are brought to bear on the text. We may expect that, for Moses, chancing upon God's place is a prelude to revelation, and this correlates him with other figures, such as the patriarchs, to whom God revealed himself at sacred sites. We may also suspect a subtle divine will that drew Moses there. Since in Genesis each theophany decisively affects the narrative, we can now expect a new turn. We know of God's care and ultimate manipulation, even when he is being totally self-effacing, such as in the story of Joseph (Gen. 45.8). Ironically, then, God is both completely implicated in the narrative — so that his mystery is equivalent to the mystery of life — and yet withdrawn from it. We cannot know his ultimate intention; we do know that he is ambivalent toward creation and that the world's autonomy is possible because of divine reticence (see Cohn, "Narrative Structure"). Further, God transcends all categories, and the biblical narrative itself is a parable (see Williams). This awareness is of special pertinence here, since in Exodus 3 God struggles to define himself in human language, to the mystification of all interpreters.

The name *Horeb*, which means the "dry" or "desolate" one, may raise the question, What is its relation to *Sinai*? The two names possibly represent different traditions (Clifford 121–22) and in any case correspond to a common phenomenon in the Hebrew Bible, whereby different aspects of a thing are linguistically distinguished. "Sinai" may refer to the bush, *sene* (Greenberg, *Understanding* 69); this manifestation is referred to in Moses's last song (Deut. 33.16), thus completing a circle: Moses's first experience of God recurs in his final blessing.

God has been absent from the narrative for a long time; in the Joseph story, for example, he only appears once, in a vision to Jacob (Gen. 46.2–4). In the two chapters preceding Exodus 3 his absence has been especially pronounced; he is silent and seemingly impotent in the face of Pharaoh's challenge to Israel's future. These chapters contain echoes of the creation story, which, like the note that God-fearing midwives were rewarded with houses (1.21), reassure us of the continuity of divine blessing (see Ackerman). Only in Exodus 2.23–25 does God reemerge powerfully and repeatedly as the active subject:

> And it was, in those many days, that the king of Egypt died, and the children of Israel sighed from their bondage, and cried out; and their plea rose up to God from their bondage. And *God heard* their groaning, and *God remembered* his covenant with Abraham, with Isaac, and with Jacob. And *God saw* the children of Israel, and *God knew*.   (emphasis added)

In addition to our general knowledge of God, derived from the story so far, we have a particular context with which to relate the specification of the "mountain of God" in Exodus 3.1. A consequence of God's "seeing" Israel and "hearing" their cry is Moses's unwitting arrival at the mountain immediately thereafter. This would modify the theory of separate sources for these passages; the whole is greater than the parts (Childs, *Exodus* 28, 51). Another feature of Exodus 2.23–25 to be pointed out is the reenactment of the Flood story. God remembers his covenant with the patriarchs just as he remembered his covenant with Noah (Gen. 8.1); this act of remembering culminates a whole series of echoes in Exodus (e.g., genocide by drowning in 1.22, the ark in 2.3). It is most important, however, to take the verbs seriously. God hears, remembers, sees, and knows. What is represented is a coming to consciousness that corresponds to that of Moses. The two protagonists reflect each other; their convergence is thus spiritual as well as spatial. The forgetfulness and ignorance of God, before he knew and remembered, is the counterpart of the enslavement and alienation of Israel, and hence the world, to false gods and masters.

Reading as Empowerment:
The Bible from a Feminist Perspective

Mieke Bal

Feminism's most valuable contribution to modern scholarship consists of the systematic emphasis on the ideological position of the scholar. The basic assumption of feminism is that the asymmetrical position of female members of our society is overwhelming, harmful to both women and men, and amenable to change through feminist analysis. So far, so good; but then the question arises, How does one work that assumption into a course on reading the Bible? The answer to that question is the subject of this essay.

Three attitudes predominate feminist analyses of the Bible: taking the Bible as inspiration for feminism today and continuing to use it as a guide for life; blaming the Bible for its sexism and rejecting it; and admitting that the Bible is ambivalent, that it has aspects of both a positive and a negative view of women.

The first attitude implies idealization of the Bible, blindness to its negative aspects, and ultimately obedience to a noncritical view of the authoritarian text. Such a stance makes it easy to remain a faithful believer and to continue accepting the worldview implied in the religion. Despite many illuminating insights, Phyllis Trible's *God and the Rhetoric of Sexuality* is characteristic of this attitude.

The second attitude implies idealization of the present and a lack of historical awareness. It may eventually lead to attitudes close to anti-Semitism: the Jews did it all. It reassuringly excludes the self from the problematic issue under consideration. It can, however, be very illuminating, especially as an initial breach in the first attitude, which is more general. Esther Fuchs's forthcoming *Sexual Politics in Biblical Narrative* exemplifies the positive, and sometimes the negative, aspects of this approach.

The third attitude prevails in Trible's new book, *Texts of Terror*. This book is, however, still basically uncritical since it adopts the underlying assumption of the other two attitudes: namely, that the text has a truth to be revealed. In a search for the "right" message, *Texts of Terror* is profoundly ahistorical.

The most promising attempt to overcome the problems in these three attitudes is to change the presuppositions rather than the outcome. Because the concept of *truth* presupposes that historical change can be transcended, it can no more be used to change the present. Instead, the idea of *relevance* posits the dependence of text on context. If we step over from "truth" to "relevance" as a basis for understanding, four consequences ensue that can help us to overcome the problems.

First, there is no "objective" inherent meaning, value, or message. The text is seen as a cultural object that works on people because people work with it. The latter process becomes the new object of analysis. Within the feminist perspective, the questions to be examined are, How has the Bible been used and how is it now used against women or for the promotion of asymmetrical relations between women and men?

Second, the analyst will account for the historical position of her or his procedures. The uncritical use of concepts that are taken for granted in modern times must be challenged; when confronted with a description of a gender position, the analyst will attempt to place it in its institutional context.

Third, the use of tools of modern critical theory, especially narratology, will not promote more certainty or truth; rather, it should help in finding gaps, problems, contradictions that point to problematic aspects of the text.

Finally, the results of the third consequence will be used for comparative analysis of both the text and its readings. This procedure helps in determining gender-related preoccupations of modern readers.

It is possible, and indeed fruitful, to approach biblical texts with the help of these presuppositions. Assignments should encourage a careful and empowering reading that will leave room for both technical accuracy and personal commitment. In the following pages, I outline a course based on the Book of Judges.

Ideostories

The feminist approach will be most interested in popular biblical stories that concern women. These stories feature in popular culture—films, pop songs, children's Bibles, novels, comic strips—and they have been represented in painting, drama, and music. An obvious example is the Samson and Delilah story. As it has become popular, however, the story arguably differs from the biblical text of Judges 13–16. The process of popularization has selected the episode of Delilah, repressing the questionable birth, the role of the mother, and, significantly, the disturbing death of Samson's first wife. Moreover, the Delilah episode has been thoroughly distorted, combining secrecy, lying, and betrayal while the text has only betrayal. The text seems to appeal to large numbers of readers and to promote a process of distortion that I call ideological action. The case becomes even more interesting when we remember that Delilah is often compared to Yael, Judith, and Esther. We can question the similarity as well as the repression of other instances of the shrewd seduction of an enemy. Delilah is clearly used as the example because she is a woman and is on the side of the enemy, while Yael and Judith are on the "right" side. Yet Yael's murder of Sisera, in Judges 4, is in many respects comparable to Ehud's murder of Eglon, in Judges 3. This comparison is strikingly rare, however. Esther's story seems only to have shrewdness in common with the others. Since Delilah is usually blamed for her seduction rather than admired for the quality of her wit, the similarity becomes more and more doubtful.

Stories that seem to trigger this sort of distortion, and subsequently distorted comparisons, can be labeled *ideostories*. The term indicates narrative texts that seem to attract ideological abuse. Their structure lends itself to investment with ideological values sometimes reversed and mostly twisted, while the story appears unchanged. These stories have clearly opposed characters, easily seen as goodies and baddies, and they are easy to remember. Fixed as images (Greek: *eidon*, the root of ideology), they can be used against women without reference to the stories' precise content. The comparisons and distortions are based on the form of the text rather than on a detailed analysis of its substance.

The story of Samson and Delilah can be assigned as a feminist exercise in various ways. Students can be asked to bring copies of drawings, etchings, paintings, children's books, or tabloid newspapers where the story appears. Using simple tools from narratology (see Bal, *Narratology*), they may analyze the story and answer the question Who does what? systematically, on the basis of the text, not of their own interpretations. They may be asked to write down, beforehand, their remembered version of the story and then to forget it, in order to assess the difference later. In the same way, they might analyze different translations, visual material, and popular written material, assessing the differences from a feminist perspective. The analysis of a scholarly commentary can be a useful part of this exercise because it spurs students to question the authority of both scholarship and the text. Some statements the students cannot check, but others are so obviously ill-founded that they promote an experience of the empowerment of criticism. The entire exercise shows students that their bias is neither unique nor unconscious but comparable to the obvious bias of the rewriters.

Feminist Thematics

A related approach is the analysis of themes that are of interest for a feminist perspective. If we confine ourselves to Judges a number of themes become relevant.

Virginity is a value whose status may have changed in modern times but whose meaning has an illusory stability. Conceived of as the bodily integrity of a nubile girl, it indicates social "marriageability": a value on the market. It would be worthwhile to question the general validity of this interpretation. The episode of the sacrifice of Jephthah's daughter brings up this concept (Judges 11). On the one hand, the sacrifice is worded as the object of meditation, mourning, or lament: the girl's request to go to the mountains for two months before her death in order to prepare for it. The word *virginity* is here used in a future-oriented sense, implying ripeness rather than sexual purity and meaning that the woman is ready for a new phase of life. The passage has been interpreted as referring to a rite of passage common before marriage. On the other hand, the narrator represents a different perspective when he says, "she had known no man," a phrase that is perhaps too easily taken as synonymous with virginity. This concern with bodily integrity may well be a male perspective: that a woman has had no previous sexual experience is important for the husband, not for the woman. The exclusive ownership of the female body, expressed, for example in Freud's essay "The Taboo of Virginity," is not what Jephthah's daughter seems to be thinking of. Her request to spend two months with her female friends in the mountains, in the wilderness that is all over the world the symbolic space of the rite of transition, matches with the fact that should "normally" have awaited her as the chief's daughter: to be given in marriage to the victor, as Achsah was in Judges 1.

Sacrifice is another thematic concept that the feminist reader cannot help but question. Although Jephthah's daughter is the only character in the Bible that is actually and explicitly sacrificed, we may wonder whether the case stands alone. First, a comparison between the precise phrasing of her sacrifice and that of the near sacrifice of Isaac is crucial. In arguing that the Genesis phrase "the one you love" applies also to the "parallel" case of Jephthah, A. Slotki notes, "The Hebrew *yahid*, feminine *yehidah*, denotes 'a favorite child.' . . . It is applied to Isaac (Gen. 22.2) although Abraham had Ishmael at the time" (Cohen, *Joshua* 257). This conflation of the two texts supports two ideological biases: it ignores the problematic side of Abraham's rejection of Ishmael and the racism of Abraham's subsequent actions; and it obliterates the scandal of the difference between the rescuing of Isaac the son and the killing of the daughter, with its likely connection to gender.

When we turn to two other murders of young women, the uniqueness of the daughter's sacrifice becomes questionable. Like the daughter, Samson's bride is murdered by fire, and both murders are similarly motivated. If we take it that "normally" Jephthah would have had to give his daughter to the victor, his appeal to Yahweh rather than to another hero can be seen as fatherly possessiveness. In like manner, Samson's father-in-law refuses to let his daughter go. The rape and murder of the "concubine" in Judges 19 receives an explicitly ritual aftermath that suggests sacrificial aspects.

A third theme of interest is that of hospitality and the house (*bayit*). The victimization of the three young women just mentioned takes place in, or in front of, the house of the (or a) father. An analysis of the word *house*, including its incorporation in the city name Bethlehem and its spatial and familial meaning within the stories, displays a dialectic between safety and danger, chastity and rape, ownership and giving away. A feminist thematics can focus on the concepts that indicate female status throughout the book. The common assumption that the word translated as "concubine" means "female of lowly status" or "secondary wife" is not warranted by the story in Judges 19. The enigma of the father's cheerful reception of the son-in-law, as well as the luxury of the father's hospitality, has surprised many critics. The impression of wealth makes the lowly status generally attributed to "concubines" less than plausible. The welcome in the father's house argues against the woman's being a concubine in the current sense.

A consideration of Samson's first marriage might further illuminate the situation of the woman in Judges 19. Samson's is a type of marriage where the daughter remains in the house of the father, which explains the daughter's seemingly autonomous actions. This sort of marriage, which we can call father-local or patrilocal, is pointed out as early as 1929 by Julian Morgenstern (*"Beena"*; see also his "Additional Notes"), though under the slightly misleading term of "matriarchy." The same arrangement is apparent in the confrontation between Jacob and Laban. An awareness of this practice helps students to understand the institution of marriage in the biblical context and see that ancient and modern marriages differ. It also points up that our form of marriage is not the only one. The blurring of historical difference inevitably leads to sexist readings. The woman of Judges 19, for example, is said to "have played the harlot against him [the husband]." The assumption is, then, that leaving him is playing the harlot. The text has, "she was unfaithful to him" and *then* went away. The very fact that the man comes back to her father's house to fetch her makes it implausible that such an important issue as sexual unfaithfulness is at stake. Given the rest of the story, it is more plausible to take it that the "unfaithfulness" in verse 2 refers to her leaving her father, being unfaithful within the framework of the patrilocal marriage, and that she afterwards goes back. There is, then, a struggle between the father and the husband, between two types of marriage, as there was in Samson's story. This interpretation explains why the woman is absent from the hospitality scenes.

The Politics of Coherence

The most basic problem of a feminist interpretation of the Bible is the fallacy of coherence: in dealing with the books, we assume that they are "about" something, that they have a unified theme we can label. Judges is assumed to be about the conquest of the land of Canaan (historical theme) and the learning of monotheism (theological theme). Scholars acknowledge that it is difficult, even impossible, to establish a chronology of the historical events of the book, yet that is the first thing each commentator tries to do. This focus, however, obliterates a possible geographic or thematic composition of the book. The composition of the final section, Judges 17–21, is clearly geographic and thematic. In 17–18, a Levite from Bethlehem comes to Ephraim; in 19, a Levite from Ephraim comes to Bethlehem. Judges 17–18 dramatize one form of "going astray" that was pictured in the beginning of the book: the worship of idols. Chapters 19 through 21 represent the other form, intermarriage, as the danger to be avoided. The relations between Ephraim and Bethlehem/Judah are usually seen within the history of the conquest; thus, they are not connected to the problems of marriage. Yet, a feminist analysis enhances the latter problems and sees as the book's most relevant theme the competition in the finale between the two different institutions of marriage, the virilocal and the patrilocal.

Discussing coherence and the hierarchy of themes is a useful way to end a course that has started with the concept of the ideostory. The commonly adopted principle of coherence is shown to serve particular interests. The coincidence between history and theology, the conquest of the land and of the religion, is significant. Monotheism and monoethnism, as well as monogamy, are related issues. Each of the stories of Judges that deal with female characters holds some disturbing statement that is invariably ignored or exiled to footnotes. When students understand the underlying interests, they will feel more capable of choosing their own attitudes toward the ideology implied. This new awareness need not lead to rejection; it may lead to commitment to some aspects and criticism of others.

The adoption of an alternative principle of coherence is only seemingly a relapse into the fallacy that is criticized. First, the principle is adopted in full awareness of its content and its motivations. Second, it is not attributed any truth status but is seen as a political option. One need not, but one can, focus on aspects discussed. Third, the new coherence is historically anchored. The concern with marital institutions that it brought to the fore enhances the historical otherness of the narrative. It reflects the feminist motivation to show the changeability of statuses and institutions. It also serves the interest of biblical scholarship, with which it shares many concerns.

One should assess the contribution of narrative theory to feminist analysis. The tools that can be used, and have been implicitly used in this brief outline, are the questions of the subjects. Who speaks? was the question that brought out the difference between the daughter's and the narrator's expression of virginity/nubility. Who sees? or Whose view is expressed? is the one that solves problems in the Samson story (see Bal, *Lethal Love*). It helps us see that Samson is not a full participant in the exchange or, in other words, that Delilah expresses his own view. That is why he gives himself up. Who acts? is the question that shows the evolution, within chapter 19, of the status of the woman: active in the beginning, she ends up as the absolute object, of rape, torture, murder. The final question, then, becomes, Is there a relation between the growth of violence and the growing disempowerment of the female characters in the final part of the book (see Bal, *Death*)?

Teaching the Bible with the help of these considerations is a useful contribution, not only to feminist analysis, but to biblical scholarship as well. The approach empowers readers by helping them understand and criticize, while the display of its dynamics undermines the ahistorical "eternity" of modern patriarchy. Last but not least, biblical texts become more interesting, in both the common and the specific sense.

Rereading Eve and Other Women: The Bible in a Women's Studies Course

Ruth Adler

Before teaching the Bible as part of a women's studies course, I, like most teachers of the Bible, had touched only tangentially on biblical women. Therefore I was pleased to have the opportunity to map out a journey with my students through the pages of the Bible, seeking out the female characters and the female perspectives, challenging prevailing assumptions, and identifying previously unnoticed problems in the text.

At the outset, I confronted a problem common to teachers of the Bible: students came to my course with many preconceived and some erroneous ideas. Both the religiously oriented students who read the Bible frequently and heard it cited from the pulpit and the nonreligious ones, who knew it from hearsay or feminist readings, were convinced that they knew about the Bible's portrayal of women. In the beginning, some of them even resisted doing the assigned readings because they felt they knew the subject so well. My task was to teach them to address the seemingly familiar text afresh. To give them a new perspective, I helped them acquire an understanding of biblical style: its conciseness, nuance, allusion, purposeful repetition, and play on words. I assigned readings from the works of Robert Alter and Phyllis Trible and required careful and critical evaluation of all that we studied.

From inquiries I made at the outset, I learned that students were better acquainted with the negative female figures than with the positive ones. Most assumed that the Bible depicts women as passive and subservient, or as evil and seductive. I stressed that the Bible, with its many books of varied genres and periods, does not paint a monochromatic picture of women. The portrayal of women in the laws, for instance, differs greatly from that in the narrative and prophetic sections. While most women in the Bible occupy subordinate positions and are generally cast in the roles of wife and mother, some play main characters in their stories and hold key positions in the community of Israel. In fact, it is difficult to generalize about biblical women because almost every literary archetype appears in one or another biblical book, ranging from Deborah, a kind of Joan of Arc, to courtesans such as Rahab and seductresses such as Delilah.

Since I wanted the class to sample as many different scriptural genres and character types as possible, I gave students many outside reading assignments, such as the legalistic portions of the Pentateuch. Others, such as the creation of woman in Genesis, Achsah's request for more land from Caleb in Judges, and the Book of Ruth, were read closely in class. Two principles guided my teaching: I insisted that students be familiar with specific texts and not speak in vague generalities, and I constantly endeavored to engage students intellectually and emotionally in the learning process, inviting them to make discoveries on their own and welcoming personal responses.

I would like to elaborate on the manner in which I taught the creation and the fall because they are pivotal to the study of women in the Bible. Theologians still invoke these first chapters in Genesis to justify woman's subservience. Feminists, such as Kate Millet and Elizabeth Gould Davis, claim that the creation story has an "antifeminist objective" and refer to the story of the fall as the "central myth of our cultural heritage." Even the *Instructors' Guide* to the *Norton Anthology of World Masterpieces* cautions that the subordinate role of Eve and her responsibility for the fall are difficult subjects that should be taught in the light of the patriarchal society they reflect.

Bible critics differentiate between the apparently conflicting accounts of the creation in Genesis 1 and 2 and interpret them as parts of different traditions. The first purportedly portrays the equality of the sexes ("male and female created He them"), while the second, which depicts Eve's creation from Adam's rib, is said to bespeak woman's inferiority. For the analysis that follows, I am indebted to Alter (*Biblical Narrative*), Joseph B. Soloveitchik, and Trible (*God*), who show that, from a literary point of view, the two accounts mesh and complement each other. The first chapter presents the creation of the universe in a general biological progression with the human being as the last creature to emerge, whereas the second chapter offers a detailed anthropocentric account of the process. This interpretation not only refutes woman's subservience to man at creation but also contributes to a literary perspective, since it illuminates otherwise unnoted stylistic nuances. From this perspective, for instance, the introductory verses in Genesis 2, sometimes deemed superfluous or repetitious, may be viewed as an appropriate poetic expression of an anthropocentric universe: the earth is depicted as waiting with bated breath for the appearance of its central character to till the soil and interact with the environment.

Students were asked to observe the differences between the first and second account of woman's creation. They perceived immediately that one depicts a simultaneous creation, while the other puts woman's creation subsequent to man's. When asked to differentiate further, they noted that it was "as if a different lens was used" in each—a panoramic lens focused on the cosmos versus a close-up lens focused on the human being. After rereading the two accounts, they easily correlated the specific descriptions with the differing perspectives. They noted, for instance, that the commandment to be fruitful and multiply is proffered to the natural biological being of chapter 1, whereas the second chapter speaks of the soul (*Nefesh*, 2.7). The first account mentions biological needs such as food for physical sustenance and portrays humankind as a part of the animal kingdom. The second account consistently refers to cognitive, emotional, and spiritual aspects. Thus in chapter 2 Adam demonstrates his intellectual prowess by categorizing the animal species. As an emotional-spiritual man, he experiences intense loneliness without a spouse and responds poetically and joyously to the appearance of a partner, exclaiming, "This is truly bone from my bone and flesh from my flesh!" Relationships to parents and attachment to spouse also occur in chapter 2, as does the moral imperative to abstain from eating from the Tree of Knowledge.

Whenever I teach the Bible, I am aware of how many misconceptions arise from mistranslations of the original Hebrew. The Hebrew expression *'ezer k'negdo* is usually translated as "helpmate" or "helper" (2.18) and thought to denote inferiority. Yet the Hebrew word *k'negdo* actually means "opposite him" and connotes equality. Similarly, the word *tsela*, translated as "rib," can also be translated, in accordance with biblical usage elsewhere (e.g., Exod. 26.27), as "side." Thus Adam and Eve may be seen to have been created simultaneously as an androgynous being that was later separated. It puzzles me that this explanation—consistent with both creation accounts, in line with biblical usage, and also supportive of the idea of woman's equality—is not better known, though it is cited by the most popular Jewish exegete, Rashi. Even omitting this alternative explanation, the creation story, without its usual stereotyped interpretations, provides a remarkable expression of sexual equality in an otherwise male-centered world: when the human being is created, mention is made at once of the female together with the male; both man and woman are blessed and commanded to master the environment; in Genesis 2.18 God seeks a companion for Adam rather than a sexual partner, a mate who will be "opposite," that is, equal, to him.

As crucial as the creation story is for the understanding of women in the Bible, the story of the first disobedience and explusion has wider ramifications for the Judeo-Christian tradition. Like most of us, my students were brought up with the image of Eve as a gullible temptress who was easily swayed by the serpent and then used all her cunning to seduce Adam. She was thus deserving of the punishment meted out to her and rightfully made subservient to man. A close reading of the text, however, imparts an entirely different picture of Eve.

The Bible dwells at length on the discourse between Eve and the serpent about the nature of the prohibition and the theological consequences that would ensue from its transgression. Eve does not succumb readily to temptation but engages in intellectual inquiry beforehand. Only when the serpent assures her that there will be spiritual reward, that she and Adam will be godlike in their knowledge of good and evil, is Eve convinced. Nor does she then take action hastily. The text does not simply state that she took the fruit and ate it. Rather, a series of clauses appears in Genesis 3.6 to demonstrate stages of deliberation and careful consideration: "The woman saw that the tree was good for food, and that it was pleasant to the eyes, and that the tree was desirable for gaining wisdom, and she took of the fruit and she ate, and she gave her husband with her and he ate." It is noteworthy that Eve's decision to partake of the fruit is finally made after she perceives that "the tree was desirable for gaining wisdom." In fact, what is truly surprising is that a close reading of the passage reveals Adam to be gullible and easily seduced. The text juxtaposes Eve's inquiry and deliberation with Adam's naive and obedient complicity: "and she gave her husband with her and he ate." Yet the

image of Eve as easy prey for the serpent is so imbedded in traditional thinking that most students found it hard to accept this interpretation. Only because they had learned to recognize the nuances and allusions of biblical style
were they at all prepared to consider a different reading. At the end of the
semester many students confessed that the deepest impact of the course came
from this reevaluation of Eve.

In explaining the supposed curse on Eve, "He shall rule over you," I made
the further point that the future tense in the Hebrew word *yimshol*, usually
translated as "he shall rule," does not necessarily convey this definiteness and
can be taken as a statement of future possibility, as "he *may* rule over you."
A passage in John Steinbeck's *East of Eden* turns on the significance of this
translation for Genesis 4.7. Steinbeck notes that when God says *timshol* to
Cain, the correct translation is "thou mayest," making it "the most important
word in the world. . . . For if 'Thou mayest'—it is also true that 'Thou mayest
not'" (398). Similarly, pertaining to the relationship between the sexes, Genesis 3.16 may be taken not as an injunction to Adam but, rather, as a statement about the natural consequences of the primal couple's actions and broken
trust. In lieu of the previous harmony, sin and the shifting of responsibility
ushered in mistrust and its concommitant power struggle.

The beginning of Genesis did not, of course, take up the whole of the course.
In discussing the legalistic writings, I noted that one can infer, as Raphael
Patai does, that woman's position in biblical times was analogous to her position in contemporary Arab tribes where polygamy, patriarchy, and patriliny
are the norms. But I taught the legal aspects of the Bible more in the context
of other ancient Near Eastern law codes, such as the Code of Hammurabi
and the Middle Assyrian law code. One unique biblical feature is the rever-
ence for the mother, who is accorded equal authority with the father in the
Ten Commandments and other places in the Torah (e.g., Lev. 19.3 and Deut.
21.18). The Book of Proverbs repeatedly exhorts against the wiles of the
"strange woman" but also extols the woman of valor (31.10) and, even more
important, enjoins offspring to adhere to the teachings of father and mother.
Furthermore, the words of wisdom cited in Proverbs 31 are spoken by a
woman, and wisdom is personified as a woman. A wealth of feminine imagery
for God exists in the Bible and has been aptly documented by Trible. Other
especially interesting and pertinent passages are Jeremiah's promise of a time
when a woman would assert herself freely with a man (31.22), Hosea's remon-
strance against the double standard (4.14), and Hosea's images of the ideal
relationship (2.18 [Hebrew]).

In teaching the Book of Judges, I was surprised to discover that, except
for Delilah, students were unacquainted with its wide array of female figures.
Even Deborah was unknown to most of them. Oddly enough, when asked
to write their reactions to the various women in Judges, they indicated their
admiration not for the charismatic Deborah but for the unknown Jephthah's
daughter, who, as one student put it, "just did what she had to without com-
plaining." A book purportedly of the same historical milieu as Judges and

one that deserves attention is Ruth, unique in its female centeredness. The touching friendship between mother-in-law and daughter-in-law provides a useful alternative to the usual stereotyped view of this relationship.

In all, the course reclaimed many of the overlooked women in the Bible. The wise women of Tekoah and Abel (2 Sam. 14.2–21 and 20.16–22) are examples of those not generally given their due. They were apparently readily accepted as political advisers in their male-centered society. Viewed in relationship to Lemuel's mother, whose words are cited in Proverbs 31, they may indicate the official presence of women as sages and advisers in biblical times, as Claudia V. Camp argues. So too the mention of Noadiah (Neh. 6.14) suggests that there were probably more women acting as prophets in ancient Israel than Miriam, Deborah, and Huldah.

Throughout the term, I encouraged discussion and disagreement and did not foist my views on the students. One discussion about Sarah and Hagar was especially interesting. Because Sarah sends Hagar away, students tended to perceive Hagar as a hero and Sarah as a villain. I pointed out that the Hebrew Bible delights in depicting human foibles, and although Sarah is not correct in sending Hagar away, neither is Hagar justified in her arrogance. I suggested that Sarah may be seen as a concerned mother when she sends Ishmael away but that Hagar's abandonment of her dying son is unconscionable.

The course gave us a new perspective on the past and the present. Both the men and the women in the class emerged with a clearer understanding of women's roles in the Bible, and the women left with an added pride in their ability to empathize with biblical role models. We all learned that in biblical times women fared better than we had previously imagined. At the same time, students began more seriously to question accepted patriarchal elements in contemporary society, such as a woman's adoption of her husband's surname, the use of "he" when "she" is meant as well, and men's predominance as chief actors in the world.

Why I Don't Begin with Genesis

Herbert N. Schneidau

Beginning a study of the Bible with Genesis is likely to stir up all the stereotyped assumptions, religious (and antireligious) prejudices, and stock ideas that can impede or even paralyze students' attempts to read the Bible critically and heuristically. Who comes to the Bible free of presuppositions? I prefer to sidestep these as much as possible at first.

I open with a selection or sampler called "Oldest Texts?", which includes the references to the Book of the Wars of Yahweh and the Book of Jashar, the "credo" of Deuteronomy 26.5–10 (with a very brief description of the von Rad hypothesis and of source criticism in general), and the Songs of Deborah and Miriam. Pausing only slightly over the many issues in these texts, I go on to a hypothesis of my own about the Divine Warrior as fundamental to the earliest conceptions of Yahweh: the texts in Exodus, Numbers, and Joshua that speak of one or another mysterious agency going in front of the people are for me garbled testimonies to the archaic tradition of Yahweh as king, that is, battle leader (see 1 Sam. 8.20). Only half jokingly, I propose that a traveling forge (Moses as sorcerer, as in the Midianite/Kenite hypothesis) was the original form of the column of fire and smoke and that the other hypostases — hornets, angel, "panic," and eventually the Ark — are metonymic fragments left over from a belief that Yahweh himself once led a guerrilla horde. To this tradition, the charismatic leadership of the so-called judges would have been the natural successor: the militia bands of these deliverers fought against the chariot armies of Canaanite city kings, dominating in the mountains but (except at Megiddo) losing in the plains: see Judges 1.19, 1 Kings 20.23, 28, as well as the pervasive symbolism of "cities of the plain" versus the mountains "from whence cometh my help." In this period, the recurrent temptation must have been to ask for a human king, with a standing army, and Gideon's reputed insistence (Judg. 8.23) that Yahweh must be the king testifies to the survival of the old tradition, as does the whole legend of the three hundred against Midian. In short, charismatic leadership was not merely a forerunner of dynastic leadership but was actively hostile to it, and opposition to the monarchy (1 Sam. 8, 12) was not only conservative and traditionalist but implied a well-founded fear of what the standing army would do when enlisted in the service of human pride. We must remember what "kings" meant in the stories of Joshua and Judges and how this opposition revived among the prophets.

I often remind my students that this whole hypothesis is rather speculative, intended more to set up frameworks for reading the saga of kingship than to solve historical problems. But I do try to bring in the theses of George Mendenhall and Norman Gottwald (*Tribes*) where appropriate, comparing their views on the clash between "Israelite" or "Hebrew" peasant elements and "Canaanite" monarchical power structures. I also proffer my belief that the military tradition of guerrilla fighters versus kings and chariots bespeaks the same opposition (note that not until well into David's reign was the chariot accepted as a Hebrew weapon). The laws of holy war in Deuteronomy 20 still remember the militia principle, with the further implication that their genocidal rules foreclosed the possibility of any warrior caste's making a livelihood from raiding.

At this point I try to frame the issue of sociohistorical research versus literary criticism. To me, whether the rise of Israel was due to conquest or revolutionary retribalization or theocracy is interesting, but not the main question. I am concerned with what the text has meant over the centuries (subordinating the religious orthodoxies, which are easily available elsewhere). For me, the most neglected kind of interpretation is one that studies literary effects, which perforce have been fateful in determining the role the Bible has played in our culture, transcending sectarian dogmas. Is this just an English professor's chauvinism? I suggest that the positivist discourse of the social sciences blunts awareness of these effects. Neither Mendenhall nor Gottwald is particularly sensitive to symbolism, for example; they are so concerned to refute the "nineteenth-century idea" of the Hebrews as pastoral nomads that they neglect the force of the Bible's pastoral symbolism, from the patriarchs to the Psalms and beyond. I suggest that pastoralism was a totemic badge for the Hebrews, however few of them ever made a living from it, and that it expressed better than any other images the opposition to cities, courts, mythological syncretism, and imperialism that we can all find in the text. The monumental ambivalence of the Hebrews toward earthly rulers, dynasties, temples, and cultic establishments is plain enough, but positivist critics neglect its major consequences. If a culture does not fully trust its own institutions, it can only trust a book that records both institutions and censures of them. So these stresses and strains resulted in the text-centeredness that is the mark, in spite of recurrent perturbations, of the Western tradition. In other words, not only are the social scientists seeking different answers, but they may be ignoring the distinctive question, which is that of the text rather than of the events behind it. Their quest by its nature reduces Hebrew history to a minor if illustrative episode of the ancient world. Right now, a powerful trend in their studies finds many parallels to Hebrew attitudes in the surrounding cultures. But for us, the Bible has subsumed all the parallels from the ancient world, and the question is not whether it is unique but exactly how it achieves its signifying powers.

I do not mean to dismiss history, which after all was the Hebrew answer (if not invention) to the problem of how Yahweh could be God of Israel and also Lord of the universe. The tension between the historical and the symbolic claims of the Bible cannot be simply resolved, for the historical claims must be taken symbolically and vice versa. Just as, for Christians, the Kingdom in a sense really did come, so all the historical claims are in a figural way validated by their very force among us, embodied in the book. Similarly, all symbolic claims are best understood as historically conditioned. We should try to erase neither the scandal nor the particularity.

The saga of kingship is the real focus of my course, because it brings up all these issues. Historically, it manifests the identity crisis of ancient Israel, whether to have a king "like the other peoples" or to retain the old system. Literarily, it may well be a prose rebuke to the poetic epics so well known in the Mediterranean world: certainly the centrality of the David-Goliath episode provides a satiric perspective on the warrior ethic usually implied in those. As David slays the mighty champion with a shepherd's weapons, we think back to the taunt song in which Jael nails Sisera (Judg. 5; note the tent and bowl of milk), or the other in which Pharaoh's chariots are drowned (Exod. 15); or we think of the parable of Jotham and the shameful end of Abimelech (Judg. 9–10); and we should think ahead, to the prophets' denunciations of those who trust in their own strength. Even the problem that the accounts of David's wars against the Philistines are missing may reflect this pattern: only in a few crude passages does the Bible celebrate warrior prowess without qualification. The Bathsheba story might seem to open with implicit warrior values (2 Sam. 11): it was the spring of the year, not the time for young men's fancies but rather when kings go forth to battle, after the winter rains. David, however, lolls at Jerusalem and falls into sexual envy, then into murder. And how is his sin made manifest to him? Through a pastoral, antimonarchic parable. When Agamemnon takes Achilles's woman, it becomes a matter of insult and honor (after all, with Patroclus around, Achilles didn't have that much use for her—see Philip Slater's *Glory of Hera*). For Nathan the violation of warrior ethic is not important. But he chooses to symbolize grievous sin by the theft of a lamb (2 Sam. 12). Nor does the force of the David-Absalom story lie in the latter's misuse of his prowess and his chariots (2 Sam. 15). Rather it is in David's lament, disheartening to his whole army because it asserts familial ties in the face of the need to celebrate victory (2 Sam. 19). Whereas the warriors of other cultures fight against threatening outsiders, the Bible knows that the most terrible wars are those in which a man's enemies are those of his own household (Micah 7.6).

In chapter 4 of my *Sacred Discontent* I sketch out a theory of how the Saul stories figure in this questioning and undermining of warrior values of "might makes right." David too can be used: history validated him not so much as a victor (though in reality he must have been one) but as a man with genuine humility and the power of self-abasement: he hides in caves; begs Saul's favor, comparing himself to a dead dog, a flea; serves his country's enemies; lets his spittle run down his beard; dances immodestly before the Ark; accepts the rebukes of Nathan and Shimei; and so on (1 Sam. 22–2 Sam. 16). Whereas Saul offended religious custom and wiped out religious leaders, meanwhile raising monuments to himself and showing other signs of the pride that might well characterize one who came from Benjamin, the only tribe that ever showed aspirations to become a warrior caste, David subordinated himself to religious leaders, brought the Ark to his capital, and made his sons priests. These traits make David far more than the Hebrew warrior-hero.

At the same time, the story subtly asserts that rigid adherence to the old order will not do either. In the brilliant opening scenes of Eli and Samuel, powerful symbolism culminates in the image of the old, heavy, blind priest falling over like Humpty Dumpty when he hears of the Ark's capture. Thus, when the Israelites try to coerce Yahweh into aiding them (cf. the later misuse of the "Day of Yahweh" idea), the glory departs, and the failure of the petrified and corrupted old order is figured in Eli's fall. Eli's perverse and troublesome sons also prefigure a recurrent theme, on which variations are played by the sons of Samuel, Saul, and David: even Solomon, after all, falls prey to syncretizing sin, and his Temple has many pagan overtones. So the acceptance of the dynastic principle is hedged around with cautionary tales and texts (see Deut. 17.14–17). Perhaps Jonathan's is the most poignant story, especially the legendary scene in which he bids farewell to David (1 Sam. 20.24–42). For all his success as a warrior, Jonathan knows the kingdom is not for him, and he helps David to escape, though it means his own ruin. The last scene is historically incredible — why did they need the arrow shots for signals if they fell on each other's necks afterward? — but as an image it is potent. David goes off weeping, to exile, humiliation, and triumph, while Jonathan returns to "the city" — to his father's court, prosperity, and ignominious death.

As Erich Auerbach put it, the Bible's claim to exclusive truth is what forces it into constant reinterpretation of itself (*Mimesis*, ch. 1). The birth of revisionism is in the Bible, and the text's continuing dynamic force makes Western tradition what it is, for better and worse.

TEACHING GENRES AND INDIVIDUAL TEXTS

Genealogy as a Code in Genesis

Edward L. Greenstein

Genesis is one of those books of the Bible in which narrative gives way to what seems to many like lists of dry information, the genealogies. One may skim them or skip them, following what Roland Barthes calls the "rhythm" of reading:

> [W]e do not read everything with the same intensity of reading; a rhythm is established, casual, unconcerned with the *integrity* of the text. . . . We boldly skip (no one is watching) descriptions, explanations, analyses, conversations. . . . And yet, it is the very rhythm of what is read and what is not read that creates the pleasure of the great narratives"
> (Barthes 10–11)

Alternatively, one may read or analyze genealogical lists, doing so with the same intensity one feels for the story. Both within biblical narratives and in the lists themselves genealogy may be interpreted as a code of meaning that bears widely on the background and significance of the narratives. In what follows I outline an analytical approach to genealogy that may be used as a model for classroom presentation (see Wilson, *Genealogy*, and Scolnic for further study).

Four passages in the Book of Genesis refer to Abraham's place of birth. Two locate it in Ur of the Chaldees, in southern Mesopotamia; two others place it in Aram Naharaim (or Paddan Aram), in northwestern Mesopotamia. Before reaching any conclusions, let us examine the passages more closely.

Genesis 11.27–32 relates that Abraham (or Abram, as he was still called) was one of three sons born to Terah in Ur of the Chaldees. Verses 28 and 31 refer explicitly to Ur. The passage tells that Terah took his family to Haran, which is in Aram Naharaim.

We are therefore surprised when in the very next verse, Genesis 12.1, YHWH (the name of the Hebrew God) commands Abraham to leave his birthplace and go to Canaan. Reading the narrative as a chronologically ordered sequence, we had assumed that Abraham was born in Ur, moved to Haran, and set off from there to Canaan. Was Abraham born in Ur or in Haran? In the ensuing narratives about Abraham, we encounter two further references to his place of birth. In Genesis 15.7 YHWH tells Abraham, "I am YHWH who has had you go out from Ur of the Chaldees. . . . " This verse seems to know nothing of the Haran connection. In Genesis 24.4 Abraham orders his servant to travel to Abraham's "land" and "birthplace." The servant heads straight for Aram Naharaim (verse 10). Knowing that a person cannot have been born in two different places, what are we to make of the apparent contradiction?

The answer depends on whether we approach this question as a matter of history or as a broader issue of reading texts. A historian, or a reader who reads like a historian, can abide only a single solution: Abraham was born in Ur, or he was born in Haran. Perhaps we have here two traditions. If so, one is wrong. There are no references to Abraham, this Abraham, outside the Hebrew Bible, and so there is no way to corroborate either tradition. Ancient Near Eastern scholars can adduce material to associate Abraham with southern or northern Mesopotamia, but partisans of one view cannot convince adherents of the contrary position. In any event, a historian must choose between the two traditions or try to reconcile them. How can one reconcile them?

One can selectively reinterpret the evidence. One can argue, as Cyrus Gordon does, that Ur was meant to refer to a northwest Mesopotamian Ur, not the southern Ur of the Chaldees. As an approach to reading, this tack differs little from the one that chooses traditions. It claims that at some point the transmission of the tradition went wrong and Ur was misidentified.

Alternatively, one can attempt to revise the sequence of events. Citing the ancient rabbinic principle that "there is no early or late in the Torah" (i.e., the Pentateuchal narrative does not follow a strict chronological order), certain medieval Jewish commentators say that God commanded Abraham to leave his home in Ur before the family moved to Haran. That resolves the contradiction between Genesis 11 and 12 but not the discord with chapter 24. In verse 7 there, Abraham tells his servant, "YHWH, the God of heaven, who took me from my father's house, and from the land of my birth . . . , he will send his messenger [i.e., angel] ahead of you, and you shall take a wife for my son from there." There is no way to reconcile this verse with Genesis 15.7, cited above, in which YHWH says he took Abraham out of Ur of the Chaldees. The historically oriented reader must choose between traditions or seek an alternative approach to reading the text.

The historical reading rests on the premise that what one finds in the text must conform to some outside reality or be rejected as unhistorical or wrong. One has the option of assuming a different and conflicting premise: the text represents its own reality, which may in turn reflect the ideas of those who composed or transmitted the text. Rather than try to match the text's references to Abraham's birthplace with points on a map, one can interpret the contrary references as reflexes of different yet mutually acceptable ideas. One can, in the tradition of Hermann Gunkel, read the genealogical associations in Genesis as a code representing the relations that ancient Israel bore toward the various nations among whom the Israelites lived.

One can support such an approach by noting that many of the personal names listed in Genesis can be identified with the names of nations or places. Nearly the entire text of Genesis 10, for example, refers to geography and ethnology in terms of genealogy. The spread of Greek control to the Aegean and Asia Minor is expressed in verse 4 as the spawning of Elisha, Tarshish, the Kittim, and the Dodanim (read: Rodanim—people of Rhodes, on the basis of 1 Chronicles 1.7 and the Septuagint) by Yavan (Ionia). The regions of the Egyptian empire—"Cush, Egypt, Put, and Canaan" (Ethiopia, Egypt, Nubia, Canaan)—are depicted as the progeny of Ham (verse 6). Verse 11 portrays Assyria as a person and verses 15–18 represent the various peoples of Canaan as its offspring. Any ancient Israelite would understand this. Genesis 34 personifies the Canaanite town of Shechem, which later came into Israelite hands, as an aggressive, then submissive, man who raped a daughter of Jacob. Jacob's brother Esau is identified as "Edom," that is, the people of Edom, and Jacob himself, "father" of the Israelite tribes, is called "Israel." According to the genealogical code of Genesis, Edom and Israel are brothers. We may decipher this as a reflex of the affinity or rivalry between nations of equal standing or power that Israel felt vis-à-vis the Edomites. The stories about Jacob and Esau, or Israel and Edom, deal in many human matters on many levels other than that of international relations. But in the context of Genesis, the eponymous ancestors of peoples forebode the history of those peoples in their own stories (see further Greenstein, "Riddle," and Geller, "Struggle").

Consider the narrative about Lot and his daughters (Gen. 19.30–38). Following the catastrophe that befell Sodom and Gomorrah, Lot's daughters are bereft of bridegrooms and desperate for sons. They intoxicate their father and rape him. Out of this incest, Moab and Ammon are born. That both Moab and Ammon are identified explicitly as the "fathers" of the nations that bear their names—the Moabites and the Ammonites—beckons the audience to hear the tale on a symbolic level. The Ammonites and Moabites are "cousins" of Israel, as Lot was Abraham's nephew. But Israel is pure and deserving while its eastern neighbors are illegitimate. The episode surely underpins the injunction in Deuteronomy 23.3 that excludes Ammon and Moab from "the assembly of YHWH." The genealogy of Moab and Ammon marks the predetermined inferiority of those nations to Israel, the people of impeccable lineage.

Within the Israelite tribes, genealogy can be interpreted as a key to relative strength or status. Jacob, "Israel," married two sisters, Leah, whom he received through stealth, and Rachel, whom he loved. Each wife had a handmaid with whom Jacob sired two sons. Leah had six sons and Rachel two. The lineage of each son/tribe signifies the position of that tribe within the Israelite tribal scheme. Family position "explains" the political balance of tribes. Sons of the beloved wife are ensured a high status. In an extraordinary transformation, sons of the elder son (Joseph) of that wife (Rachel)—Ephraim and Manasseh—achieve the status of tribes in their own right. The concubines' sons lie on the fringes of Israel, in terms of both geography and power, while Rachel's brood occupies a central position. We may take Jacob's family, then, as a code of internal Israelite political relations, just as we interpreted the genealogical connections of the patriarchs as an Israelite mapping of the moral, if not actual, standing of the Middle Eastern peoples.

Analogously, the contradictory tracings of Abram's (Abraham's) birthplace can, and I would say should, be read as two codes, each bearing a different message. The two birthplaces carry vertical and horizontal significance. First, by linking Abram, the first definitive Israelite ancestor, to Ur of the Chaldees, in southern Mesopotamia, Genesis loops the Hebrew lineage back to the origins of civilization, to Noah, the world's first *tzaddik*, "righteous man" (Gen. 6.9). Horizontally, Abram's connection with Aram Naharaim expresses a contemporary feeling of kinship with the Arameans. Jacob, for example, suffers some exploitation at the hands of his Aramaic-speaking father-in-law, Laban. In the end, though, they make a pact of peace (Gen. 31.44–48). The site of the peace-making Laban names in Aramaic, Jacob in Hebrew. The unity in diversity that the pact represents is reflected aboriginally in the placing of Abram's birth in the heart of Aram.

As history, the narratives about Abram's birth do not read coherently; as coded stories, or myths, they do. Each geographical assignation tells a different piece of the biblical worldview.

The Flood Story: Four Literary Approaches

John Maier

With enough time for discussion, the same text—the Flood in Genesis 6.5–9.17—could be used to illustrate four different approaches to a literary work of art: literary history, rhetorical criticism, structuralism, and symbolism. Together, and in the sequence suggested here, the four approaches illustrate the problems and possibilities of a hermeneutics that will engage the biblical scholar and the student of literature. Just as "literary criticism" often means one thing to the biblical scholar and quite another to the student of, say, Dickens, hermeneutics is sometimes advanced as if interpretation theory for biblical texts is worlds apart from hermeneutics advocated by modern literary critics (Tollers and Maier 1–4). Historically, the two were closely related, as Lynn Poland explains (1–7). Hermeneutics arose from the otherness of the biblical text—the need to explain what was no longer common ground—from the sense of alienation the modern felt in the presence of an ancient text.

One might begin, then, with the apparent opposition between two very different ideas of "literary criticism" of the Bible. The best place to start is with literary history, which includes textual and philological work and the attempt to distinguish different documents behind the biblical texts. Norman Habel's *Literary Criticism of the Old Testament* finds two different stories fused into one. For him, as a critic in a tradition that stretches back to the eighteenth century, literary criticism is "the task of analyzing the literary features of a given document to determine its literary character, origins, and states of written composition" (6). Close examination of the Flood reveals an early Yahwist narrative and a later Priestly narrative. What may seem like a straightforward account turns out to be far from seamless: two introductions, two accounts of the nature of the problem that has given rise to the Flood, two statements of the extent of the problem, two different reactions by God to the problem, two verdicts, two roles for Noah, two sets of distinctive terms, two different styles (18–42). Seldom has the case for the "documentary hypothesis" been stated so clearly and persuasively.

Once that has been said, though, one might challenge the approach by a "rhetorical" criticism of the same text. Isaac M. Kikawada and Arthur Quinn, in *Before Abraham Was*, question the "documentary hypothesis." The same Flood story Habel had so carefully separated into Yahwist and Priestly versions provides Kikawada and Quinn with their most persuasive chapter, "One Noah, One Flood: The Coherence of the Genesis Version" (83–106). In an analysis that is somewhat akin to New Criticism, Kikawada and Quinn attempt to show that the literary patterning of the Flood and of Genesis 1–11 as a whole so crosses through the Yahwist-Priestly division of the text that the documentary hypothesis collapses. In place of bits and fragments of traditions, they offer a well-designed artistic whole. The unity of the flood narrative is shown by the larger rhetorical patterns or narrative designs in the text.

Chiasm, in which motifs are balanced on either side of a central episode or statement, is one such narrative design. The authors' outline of the Flood (104), taken from an earlier article by Gordon J. Wenham (388), provides an excellent teaching tool to illustrate rhetorical criticism and chiasm. Both pieces draw heavily on the earlier work of Umberto Cassuto (*Commentary*).

Concepts of a "new literary history" can then be illustrated with the same text. What I have labeled (very inadequately) structuralism consists of a whole range of theoretical approaches to the text (including poststructuralism) that have come, in recent years, to challenge earlier assumptions about literary history and the "new" criticism of literature. One might consider, as just two of many approaches, certain underlying structural oppositions in the Flood story, on the one hand, and canon formation, on the other.

It is not always possible to distinguish formalist criticism of literature— like rhetorical criticism—from structuralist analysis, although in theory at least they should be distinct. Formalist criticism studies the surface of the text to point out its texture. Structuralism (in some guises) seeks underlying principles, precisely what the surface of the text hides. Kikawada and Quinn manage in two ways to reveal certain underlying structural principles in the stories of Genesis 1–11: once the shape of the surface is made explicit, they look at certain thematic patterns, and they contrast biblical and Mesopotamian versions of the same story. In the second approach, they follow earlier attempts by Nahum M. Sarna (*Understanding* 39–59) and, even more, E. A. Speiser (47–73).

Important but hidden thematic concerns that can be seen in the Flood story are, to mention just two, an anticity bias, and the need to increase and multiply the population of the earth. The first, the anticity bias, is hardly visible in the biblical text; the second is visible enough (Gen. 9.1), but not obviously connected with the city.

The interconnections are clarified through comparison with Mesopotamian texts. While the old source-and-influence approach to literary history has given way to the problems of intertextuality and canon formation in the new, the very differences between the biblical account of the Flood and, say, the flood story in the Akkadian *Gilgamesh* 11 allow certain structural oppositions in the text to become visible. The city culture of Mesopotamia appears to be closely linked to the danger of overpopulation, and although this is nowhere stated in such terms, the flood stories preserved in the Mesopotamian "stream of tradition" may all be linked by the overpopulation of cities. (Mesopotamian cities did experience a sharp increase in population at about the same time that the earliest Sumerian literature arose, in the Early Dynastic period at the beginning of the third millennium.) Anne Daffkorn Kilmer's very bold interpretation of the Sumerian tales "Enki and Ninmaḫ" and "The Deluge" and the Akkadian *Atraḫasīs* and *Gilgamesh* accounts of the flood sees in all of them anxiety that the gods will not allow limitless fertility (172). The most powerful of the gods, Enlil, demands that the population of the earth be cut back—by famine, drought, salinization of the soil, starvation, and, finally, when the other schemes are thwarted by the god Enki, by flood. Humankind is saved, again through the mediation of Enki, but at a price. Kilmer thinks the stories give theological justification to barrenness among women, cloistered women, and infant mortality as divinely sanctioned means of population control.

The closest parallels with the biblical flood are to be found in *Gilgamesh* 11. There is a reconciliation between human beings and gods at the end of the *Gilgamesh* 11 account, but nothing like the biblical injunction to "be fertile and increase and fill the earth." Quite the contrary. The Noah-like Utnapishtim is the agent through which humankind is saved, but there is yet a grim reminder for him that nature is ever there to keep the population low: lions, the wolf, famine and plague (Gardner and Maier 240).

Setting one of the Mesopotamian flood stories next to the biblical account may also suggest a way in which the Flood and the other narratives that precede the patriarchs in Genesis found their way into the Torah, as what may be called countertexts. In retelling the story, countertexts recognize other, earlier versions only to subvert them.

Although most scholars are inclined to think that the stories making up Genesis 1–11 appeared early in the history of the Hebrew people, there is little internal evidence that the Flood, Adam and Eve, Cain and Abel, and the Tower of Babel were known before the period of the exile. The enormous interest in just these stories in later Hebrew, Apocryphal, Gnostic, and New Testament writings suggests that the stories of Genesis 1–11 — the most popular stories in the Western tradition — may have become important precisely as countertexts to Babylonian accounts at just the time when contact between the chosen people and the Babylonians was forced on the Israelites.

The Flood may also be used as a basis for considering an old topic in literary studies, symbolism, in the somewhat newer guise of literary hermeneutics. Take the term assigned in some Mesopotamian accounts as the reason for ordering the flood in the first place: the *rigmu*, or "noise," human beings make, thereby disturbing the sleep of the gods. It is a difficult symbol to grasp. Noise may be a symbol of rebelliousness. It could, then, parallel that puzzling term in Genesis 6.13 that is given as the cause of God's decision to bring on the Flood, translated sometimes as "lawlessness," sometimes as "violence" (*hms*; see Speiser 51, 117; Frymer-Kensky 153–54). Kilmer thinks that the "noise" of humankind is the natural consequence of the great increase in population, a striking poetic image and not a symbol of, say, rebellion. The term in the Mesopotamian accounts would, then, not be similar to biblical *hms* but, rather, be its opposite. In one tradition, the destruction of human life is somehow necessary; in the other, the taking of life violates the most basic command of all, to increase and multiply. While the Akkadian terms and the Hebrew term require exact philological work to establish their usual meanings in ordinary contexts, that effort cannot be completed without knowing how the words are used in complex texts.

Understanding a powerful symbol like *rigmu* or interpreting the *hms* with which the "earth" is filled is not, then, merely a matter of settling on the "correct" lexical definition. It is, much more, a reading of the text and an understanding of the larger narrative design. Still, these are but preliminary steps toward interpretation.

The hermeneutics of complex metaphors, myths, and symbols in the Bible has been, from the start, a measure of our alienation from the text. In this enterprise biblical scholarship in the last 150 years and literary theory (as a part of a more general hermeneutics) face each other as partners, though critics have seldom acknowledged that historical fact. Philosophers like Paul Ricoeur, who has also studied the symbols of archaic human life (Maier 34–35), are now posing the questions that at a certain stage in our classroom discussion we should be asking of the Flood story. To take but one example, in *The Symbolism of Evil*, Ricoeur distinguishes four basic "second-degree" symbols or myths and sees the flood in terms of what he calls the drama of creation and the "ritual" vision of the world. He points out that unlike the biblical Flood, where human sin is the motive of the terrible devastation, the Mesopotamian versions see the flood as part of the chaos that has been the lot of the universe since its beginnings. "The flood is precisely not connected with human faults, since it proceeds from an excess of wrath on the part of a god who, instead of sending the flood, could have warned men by calamities commensurate with their faults" (186).

Today is a particularly good time in which to teach narratives like the Genesis Flood story. Students are likely to be shocked at the complexity of a story known to them from childhood yet rarely "read" as literature is supposed to be read. The hostility between biblical scholar and student of literature, even disagreeing as they had over the term *literary criticism*, has largely disappeared. Biblical scholars are receptive today to literary theories and critical strategies; and students of literature have called earlier pat assumptions about literature into question. The Flood provides a particularly useful illustration of literary-critical concepts and of the tools scholars have used to analyze the text. Profound philosophical questions prompted by a reading of the Genesis Flood story are facilitated by the four approaches sketched here. Indeed, they can hardly be considered without first discussing the story as a literary work of art.

The Narrative Mirror of Exodus 32:
A Critique of the Philosophers' God

Herbert J. Levine

Many students come to the study of the Bible as literature with preconceptions that adversely affect their reading. Yet one such set of preconceptions, the philosophers' description of the immutable nature of God, can be used against itself to teach students to approach God as a literary character rather than as a subject of doctrinal propositions. We can be guided in this deconstruction of the philosophers' God by Moses Maimonides (1135–1204), himself a proponent of a propositional, a priori approach to divinity. Applying Maimonides's principles for reading scriptural statements about God can show students how far from the spirit of the text one must go in order to satisfy the philosopher's penchant for an abstract God. This wrong turn must produce a counterturn, until we arrive at a theory and practice of reading more in consonance with the biblical text. In this latter part of the argument, an anti-Maimonidean theologian, Abraham Joshua Heschel (1907–72), will be our literary mentor.

Maimonides's *Guide of the Perplexed* (1200) was written to reconcile the conflicts between the then dominant Aristotelian description of God as unchanged and unchangeable prime mover and the emotional, anthropomorphic idiom through which God is revealed in the Hebrew Bible. Maimonides understood that such biblical descriptions of God were filtered through and for the common, corporeal intellect. He would show those who sought a philosophical apprehension of God's incorporeal and immutable nature how to decode the anthropomorphisms of Scripture.

Thus, Maimonides claimed that in Scripture we are presented only with human analogies for the incomparable divine nature: "Whenever one of His actions is apprehended, the attribute from which this action proceeds is predicated of Him, may He be exalted, and the name deriving from that action is applied to Him" (125). God is said to be merciful because similar actions, when performed by us, are motivated by that quality. When God's actions toward humankind include great calamities and God is said by Scripture to be angry or vengeful, such actions take place "because of the deserts of those who are punished, and not because of any passion whatever, may He be exalted above every deficiency" (126). For Maimonides, emotions in all their changeableness are a defect that human beings must learn to control through their higher reason; how much more, he argued, are emotions incommensurable with the perfection of the divine being.

Since many students bring with them a simplified version of the Maimonidean God, it is particularly difficult for them to assimilate the many biblical scenes that depict God's anger. I want to focus attention on the text of Exodus 32, God's and Moses's angry reactions to the idolatrous episode of the golden calf. Because divine and human emotions are portrayed so similarly here, the scene forces us to consider the usefulness of Maimonides's analogical principles in reading Scripture.

Exodus 32 presents God and Moses as alternately countering and mirroring each other's emotions. God narrates the people's apostasy to Moses and then concludes: "I see that this is a stiffnecked people. Now, let Me be, that My anger may blaze forth against them and that I may destroy them, and make of you a great nation" (vv. 9–10, New JPS). Moses, however, does not let God be. Appealing to God's reputation and past promises, Moses counters divine anger with human conciliation and succeeds in persuading God to renounce "the punishment He had planned to bring upon His people" (14).

At this juncture, the text portrays a fascinating reversal of roles. What God threatened to do, Moses himself does. In the second half of the chapter, instead of countering God's anger, Moses mirrors it. Enraged, he smashes the tablets of the law, destroys and dissolves the molten calf, making the Israelites drink it, and, finally, calls the Levites to his side and charges them in God's name to "slay brother, neighbor, and kin" (27). After this outburst, which causes the death of three thousand people, Moses reascends to God, telling the people that he will now try to win forgiveness for them. Earlier, an angry God had wanted to destroy the people and begin again with Moses. Now, a conciliatory Moses implores God either to forgive the people or to erase *him* from God's record. God displays no further desire for uncontrollable anger but, echoing Moses's conciliatory tones, answers Moses, "He who has sinned against Me, him only will I erase from My record" (33). The text reports that erasure as the next order of business: "Then the Lord sent a plague upon the people, for what they did with the calf that Aaron made" (35). God's initial blazing anger against the whole people has been tempered; only those who actually sinned are destroyed.

Maimonides's principle of reading, we recall, was that representations of divine emotion are made by analogy to human emotion. Maimonides's God cannot really be angry at all: Moses is the sole angry one in the scene, and his anger is simply projected onto the perfection that is the Maimonidean God. If we extend this Maimonidean principle of reading, Moses becomes the sole actor in the scene. Is there a God in this text? No, not if we take Maimonides at his word.

To what sort of reading does this extrapolation from Maimonides lead? Where the text shows God as initially wanting to destroy the whole people, not simply the transgressors, the Maimonidean reader can say that this expresses the extent of Moses's anger on learning of the people's apostasy. Where the text portrays God as capable of being mollified by Moses's appeal to the divine reputation, the Maimonidean reader can argue that Moses is concerned for his own reputation as leader of his people. Where the text shows God's final settling of the score by extending Moses's initial punishment to all the transgressors, the Maimonidean reader can claim that this reflects Moses's need to rationalize and justify the consequences of his own destructive anger.

I have pursued this antithetical reading to suggest that the philosophers' claim for an emotionless God strips this scene of its complex interplay between human and divine agents, mirroring each other's motives, emotions, and actions. In this scene, we do not simply have one being, conveniently divided into the alter egos of Moses and God. Maimonides would have us believe in an immutable divine will, yet the drama of this scene depends on showing that God's will does change in response to human mediation and, furthermore, that human beings and God intimately affect one another, moment by moment. Moses's partial punishment of the people follows immediately on God's renunciation of total punishment. God's completion of the people's punishment follows immediately on Moses's request for total forgiveness. God's anger is all-consuming, but Moses's can be discharged only with the help of a band of zealous Levites. God's justice demands the punishment of all the transgressors, but Moses, eager to heal the breaches between the people and God and the people and himself, approaches God to talk about forgiveness rather than justice. In offering himself in atonement, he may even be acknowledging some guilt in having arrogated God's anger to himself; but in ignoring that offer, God reaffirms Moses's special relationship as agent of God's will.

At this juncture, we are indeed far from the Maimonidean way of reading. Heschel's theology of pathos can provide students with a useful corrective, which confirms their experience as readers: namely, that the God involved with the human characters of the text feels for and with them and that they likewise feel for and with God. What Heschel calls "the divine pathos" is communicated through the urgency of God's encounters with Moses and the other prophets. The mutuality of feeling in such encounters is what characterizes the biblical God's relatedness to human beings. From God's passion for justice, human beings learn to emulate the divine response. For Heschel, then, the medieval rationalization of biblical anthropomorphisms was based on a weak misreading. The divine pathos should be viewed not as a personification but, rather, as a uniquely theological category. "It is perhaps more proper," he writes, "to describe a prophetic passion as theomorphic than to regard the divine pathos as anthropomorphic" in the manner of Maimonides (260).

Two comments that Heschel makes about Exodus 32.10 show how he saw God's primary role in our text: to teach Moses how to react to the idolatry of the people by involving him in God's response and by showing him God's own involvement. "Now, let Me be," God says, "that My anger may blaze forth against them. . . ." Why should God turn to Moses with the phrase, "let me be"? For Heschel, this signals that "without Moses' consent, God's anger would not turn against the people" (283). God is freely, voluntarily choosing to be angry, just as human beings can choose to pursue a course of righteous indignation. Heschel goes on to imagine how we would respond to God's anger if the text had come down to us without the phrase, "that my anger may turn against them," but simply as "Now let me alone that I may consume them." We have here, he claims, a God personally involved through his anger, not "an unfeeling, stony-hearted God Who, without personal involvement, is about to consume a whole people" (293–94).

Maimonides's theology virtually erases God from the text, while Heschel's restores God to the text as its real prime mover. Since these theologies each imply a theory of reading, they are easily adapted by the literary teacher of the Bible. Using them, a teacher can help students recognize that the notion of God as a perfect being is not of biblical origin and that therefore it can only be a hindrance to appreciating the character of God in the Hebrew Bible. Heschel offers a telling example to illustrate this point: "In the Decalogue, God does not speak of His perfection, but of His having made free men out of slaves" (274). In freeing students from their constricting preconceptions about God, we perform the invaluable act of empowering them as readers.

The Prophetic Literature of the Hebrew Bible

Adele Berlin

Biblical prophecy has been examined from the vantage point of many disciplines, but what clearly distinguishes the classical prophets from all other comparable phenomena is the literary quality of their work. When we read the classical biblical prophets—Isaiah, Jeremiah, Ezekiel, and the Twelve Minor Prophets—we are reading mainly speeches, moving rhetoric designed to affect the behavior of live audiences. Thus it is through a literary approach—through an analysis of themes, motifs, and rhetorical strategies—leavened with some knowledge of the historical background, that we can best begin to grasp the power of the prophets' message.

The preexilic prophets (those who lived before the Babylonian exile in 586 BCE) were most concerned with destruction. The eighth-century prophets of the northern kingdom (e.g., Amos, Hosea) warned of the destruction of Israel (which occurred in 721 BCE); those in the southern kingdom, from Isaiah and Micah in the eighth century to Jeremiah and Ezekiel in the sixth century, predicted the destruction of Judah (which occurred in 586 BCE). To the people of Israel and Judah, such a thing was nearly inconceivable, for psychological as well as religious reasons. Psychologically, it is extremely difficult to convince people that the future of their country is in danger. Do we in America really believe that the Russians could conquer and enslave us? It may happen to others, but it could never happen to us. In ancient Israel there was, in addition to this psychological aspect, a religious dimension. The God of Israel protected his land and people. A defeat of his people would mean a defeat of his power. How could the most powerful God allow his land to be conquered, allow his Temple, the place where his presence was most manifest, to be destroyed. A prophet who suggested such things, thought the Israelites and the Judeans, must surely be crazy and perhaps also dangerous. But to the preexilic prophets, the downfall of the kingdom was certain and imminent. Only large-scale repentence could avert the awful inevitability. When we understand this, we can understand the urgency and hyperbole of the prophet's words. For words are the prophets' primary tool and weapon; by force of words they must rouse the masses to action, change government policies, and ward off danger from their opponents. The prophets were a real-life attempt to demonstrate, with mixed success, that the pen, or, for them, the spoken word, is mightier than the sword.

Prophetic rhetoric is skillfully wrought; like any good poetry, it blends sound with sound, word with word, image with image in an intricate verbal texture. But the goal is not mere aesthetic pleasure; these words pack a punch when it comes to content. The first chapter of Isaiah is a good example of prophetic rhetoric in action.

Isaiah begins with an address to the heavens and earth. That is, the prophet does not address the people directly but lets them overhear, as it were, what

God has to say about them to the world at large. What he has to say is far from complimentary. In chapter 1 Israel is first described as an ungrateful and rebellious child, an adolescent, if you will (v. 2), and then degraded even further in a devastatingly effective pair of parallelisms that "proves" Israel to be more stupid than an ass (3). The stupidity is ignorance of God, the root of the sinfulness with which the nation is laden. Isaiah turns now to address the people directly, in his own voice (before, it was God speaking through the prophet), reasoning with them about the folly of their self-defeating sinfulness that has led to beatings and woundings, metaphors for the devastated land of Judah (5–8). It is likely that this speech was delivered during Sennacherib's siege of Jerusalem in 701 BCE, after many Judean towns had already fallen to the enemy, so that the picture that Isaiah evokes correlates with reality. He describes Jerusalem through three images signifying aloneness amid desolation: "like a hut in a vineyard, like a shed in a cucumber patch, like a city beleaguered" (8). Finally, to emphasize how close they had come to destruction, he says, "Had the Lord of Hosts not left us a remnant, barely, we would be like Sodom, we would resemble Gomorrah" (9). Sodom and Gomorrah being the Bible's archetype of catastrophic devastation (see Gen. 18–19), the comparison is effective. Moreover, although the actual naming of the two cities comes at the climax of the first section of the speech, Isaiah has been subtly alluding to them earlier, through the use of terms that also occur in the Genesis narrative ("laden," "heavy with sin" in v. 4 — cf. Gen. 18.20; "overthrown" in v. 7 — cf. Gen. 19.25, 29).

Then, with a clever twist, Isaiah switches from the evocation of destruction to the evocation of corruption: "Hear the words of the Lord, you captains of Sodom . . . " (10). Before, Jerusalem was likened, in its potential destruction, to Sodom and Gomorrah; now the people of Jerusalem are likened, in their corruption, to the people of those infamous cities. Moving to a conventional motif, the chapter notes that ritual acts (sacrifices, festival observances) cannot compensate for the moral and religious decay in society. It is important to stress that the prophet is not opposed to cultic practices per se but is only trying to show that God finds them ludicrous in the light of the people's behavior. (For more on this idea see 1 Samuel 15.22–23; Amos 5.21–25; Micah 6.6–8.) Social injustice, another prophetic motif (see also Hosea 4.2; Amos 2.6–8, 4.1–2, 8.4–7; Micah 3.1), is decried in verses 16–17. Another turning point occurs at verse 18. God, who has just expressed contempt for empty rituals, is eager to come to an understanding with his people. He wishes them to remove the stain of their sins, wash away their blood guilt, become white and pure again. The color imagery is vivid crimson versus snow-white, red-dyed wool versus undyed fleece. There is also wordplay: "If you agree and give heed, you will *eat* the good things of the earth; But if you refuse and disobey, you will *be eaten* by the sword" (19–20).

This chapter of Isaiah contains many of the stylistic techniques found throughout the prophetic writings and, indeed, throughout biblical poetry: parallelism, metaphor, paronomasia, allusion, and personification. Did the prophets speak in poetry? To a large extent they did. Certainly theirs is a special use of language, an elevated and elegant use. Even when they resort to prose, the poetic function, in the Jakobsonian sense, predominates in their speeches, focusing attention on the message for its own sake. This special use of language may be found, more or less, throughout the Bible, but nowhere do we get a stronger sense of it than in the prophetic literature, where the medium is an essential part of the message.

The prophets' medium is, by and large, words, but these are sometimes reinforced by symbolic actions: Isaiah goes naked and barefoot (Isa. 20.2), Jeremiah wears a yoke (Jer. 27), Ezekiel acts out the siege of Jerusalem (Ezek. 4–5), Hosea's marriage (Hos. 1–3) symbolizes the relationship between God and Israel. These examples underline again that prophetic words are not abstractions, not private musings, but real speeches meant for real audiences.

If the need in preexilic times was for chastisement and warning, the need after the exile was for comfort and hope. They are beautifully provided in deutero-Isaiah (Isa. 40–66) and in the later parts of Ezekiel. Perhaps the most moving example is found in Isaiah 40. It starts without introduction and without making clear who is being addressed (except that the addressee is plural). But the message is clear: "Comfort my people; Speak tenderly to Jerusalem; Tell her that she has paid more than enough for her sins." Although the Judeans are in exile in Babylonia, the prophet portrays the return from the perspective of the land of Judah. The herald (or perhaps a personification of Jerusalem herself) spies the Lord leading his people home, as a shepherd leads his flock, and announces this to the other towns of Judah (9–11). This episode can be compared with that of the weeping mother, Rachel, who is told that her children will return to her (Jer. 31.15–17). Compare also the very different situation in which Ezekiel is taken on an imaginary tour of the rebuilt Temple in Jerusalem (Ezek. 40–48).

Deutero-Isaiah's most difficult problem is to convince the conquered Judeans that their God is still powerful. To do this, he pictures God as creator of the world, larger and stronger than anything in it. God measures oceans by the handful, the sky in a handsbreadth (40.12). The nations of the world are, on this scale of measurement, mere specks of dust and no match for God. He can arrange and rearrange them as he pleases. Rhetorical questions make the argument even more convincing: "Who measured the waters . . .? Whom did God consult . . .? To whom can you liken God?" Rhetorical questions do not request information; they provide the setting for eliciting the desired information from the listener. That is, they program the listener to give the correct answer, and, having given it, the listener is made an accomplice in the speaker's purpose. By the end of the speech in Isaiah 40, who is not convinced?

Although prophecies of consolation are the mainstay of exilic prophets, they are present in earlier prophets as well. Comfort is always a part of the prophetic message because no prophet, even one predicting punishment and destruction, believes in a permanent termination of the relationship between God and Israel. After the punishment will come a renewal of the people and their land. The image of renewal often contains the element of reunification of the divided kingdom (Israel and Judah) and a reversion to the golden age of the Davidic monarchy, along with the motifs of prosperity and peace. Amos 9.11–15 expresses these ideas: "I will set up again the fallen booth of David. . . . The plowman shall meet the reaper [the harvest will be so plentiful that it will continue until the next planting season] . . . the mountains shall drip wine [the luxuriant grape harvest]. . . . [T]hey shall rebuild ruined cities . . . they shall plant vineyards. . . . [A]nd I will plant them upon their soil, nevermore to be uprooted. . . ."

In a similar vein Isaiah envisions a time of justice and harmony when "the wolf shall dwell with the lamb . . . and the lion, like the ox, shall eat straw" (11.6–7). At that time of natural harmony, Israel and Judah shall mend their quarrels, and God shall lead them out of captivity as he led them out of Egypt to their homeland.

Jeremiah, like Amos and Isaiah, speaks of Israel's march homeward, planting vineyards in Samaria, gathering in the dispersed people, easing the path back, with God leading his people like a shepherd (31).

Ezekiel's famous chapter of comfort (37), like much of the book of Ezekiel, is different from the other prophets but no less vivid. Ezekiel sees, in a vision, a valley of dry bones that are brought back to life. In later interpretations this chapter took on connotations of individual resurrection after death, but originally it was purely symbolic of the new life that would be breathed into Israel. The people will spring to life and be returned to their land. Immediately following this vision is a symbolic action in which Ezekiel is told to take two sticks of wood, one marked "of Judah," representing the southern kingdom, and the other marked "of Joseph," representing the northern kingdom. The prophet is to join the two together, forming one stick — symbolizing the reunification of the two kingdoms.

While I have pointed out thematic similarities, each prophet, indeed, each passage, develops its theme somewhat differently. It is interesting, for instance, to compare variations on familial relationships (husband-wife, father-son), signifying the relationship between God and Israel. Some of them stem from the historical context; others reflect stylistic or poetic choices that individual prophets have made. A host of other questions might also be put to the text. Why do some passages contain rural imagery and others urban imagery? Why are some sections rich in unusual vocabulary or complicated syntax while others are more simply expressed? What do names and other specific references connote? How is God portrayed? How much of the prophetic persona emerges? In short, the same kinds of questions that one addresses to any literary text are appropriate to pose to prophetic texts.

And, above all, there is the language. It is a language of great beauty and resonance, with the power to move all who hear it, no matter how distant they may be from the original context of prophecy. A large part of the effect comes from parallelism, the combining of linguistic equivalences that is characteristic of most ancient Near Eastern poetry. Through parallelism a poet can develop and intensify ideas and provide links and symmetries between seemingly disparate events. "You were sold for no price; and you shall be redeemed without money" (Isa. 52.3). Note the terse symmetry brimming with significance, which makes the future restoration seem as certain as the past exile: just as you were sold, so you shall be redeemed. But beyond the superficial identity of the two lines, other shades of meaning creep in. Since God/Israel derived no benefit from being sold (see 52.5), so, owing nothing to the buyer, with no further payment God can repossess his people. In fact, it is only fair that he should do so. Moreover, by elevating everyday business terminology to the level of metaphor, the exchange of national destiny is raised from the human plane to the divine. There is a power higher than that of Judah and Babylonia who will make this parallelism come true.

The exception to most of what has been said above about classical prophecy is the Book of Jonah. Unlike the others, it contains no long rhetorical addresses (Jonah's only words are "In another forty days Nineveh will be overturned"). It is, rather, a story—a highly structured, carefully worded narrative. Nevertheless, it is included among the prophetic books and concerns a prophet and his mission. Jonah is best understood in relation to the problem of true and false prophecy, a problem that occupied Jeremiah (27–28) and Ezekiel (3, 33) as well. But, whereas these prophets deal with it in their own historical contexts, the Book of Jonah raises the discussion to an abstract level. Jonah is (most probably) a fictional prophet, sent on a fictitious mission to Nineveh. (No other Israelite prophet was sent to speak to a foreign people; some prophets speak of foreign peoples, but they do so for the benefit of their Israelite audience.) In the course of the story the reader, as well as, one hopes, Jonah, comes to understand that the real task of a prophet is not to make accurate predictions but to cause the people to repent. Jonah, knowing that God is merciful, tried to avoid delivering his message of destruction, fearing that the people would repent and be spared. When they were spared, Jonah was greatly upset, viewing his mission as a failure. But Jonah did not fail. He achieved what all the preexilic prophets sought in vain: repentance of the people and the consequent cancellation of their decreed destruction. A prophet's stock-in-trade is his words, but the last thing a prophet of doom wants is that his words should come true.

Suggested Reading

Most studies of biblical prophecy are too technical and not literary enough for use in courses on the Bible as literature; however, several are worth using as references for the historical background and for analyzing individual prophetic books. They also provide an entrée into the various approaches that biblicists employ in the study of prophecy. Among such works are Joseph Blenkinsopp, *A History of Prophecy in Israel* and Klaus Koch, *The Prophets.*

Older classics are Johannes Lindblom, *Prophecy in Ancient Israel* and Abraham Joshua Heschel, *The Prophets*. For recent discussions and commentaries on individual books that are sensitive to literary concerns see Francis I. Andersen and David Noel Freedman, *Hosea*; Yehoshua Gitay, *Prophecy and Persuasion: A Study of Isaiah 40–48*; Moshe Greenberg, *Ezekiel 1–20*; Jonathan Magonet, *Form and Meaning: Studies in Literary Techniques in the Book of Jonah*; and J. A. Thompson, *The Book of Jeremiah*. See also the articles on Ezekiel in *Interpretation*: Michael Fishbane, "Sin and Judgement in the Prophecies of Ezekiel"; Moshe Greenberg, "The Design and Themes of Ezekiel's Program of Restoration"; Werner E. Lemke, "Life in the Present and Hope for the Future"; Carol A. Newsome, "A Maker of Metaphors: Ezekiel's Oracles against Tyre"; and Robert Wilson, "Prophecy in Crisis: The Call of Ezekiel." General surveys of prophetic style and content that are useful in introductory courses are Robert Alter, "Poetry and Prophecy," in *The Art of Biblical Poetry*, and Samuel Sandmel, "The Literary Prophets," in *The Enjoyment of Scripture*.

Teaching Psalm 23

Raymond-Jean Frontain

Poetry, Robert Frost remarked, is what disappears in translation. When teaching the literature of the Hebrew Bible, one must early on make students aware that, if in translation poetry is often what unfortunately disappears, sectarian theology is just as often what magically appears. Students rarely question the authority of the translation they are most familiar with, presuming that it has somehow been "revealed" or "delivered" just as surely as the tablets of the law reportedly were to Moses. Before beginning a serious study of the Hebrew Bible, students must be asked to recognize their dependence on the power of the translator. Students whose response to the Bible is faith-oriented need not be distraught: the Roman Catholic Church long asserted the divine inspiration of Jerome in making his Vulgate, and believers may make a similar accommodation as they please.

In an upper-division course open to undergraduate and graduate students, I try to meet this problem by spending the second class of the term comparing four translations of a psalm familiar to most readers in the King James Version. During the introductory session, I describe the writing and assembling of the canon, distinguishing between a book or scroll's "authorial intelligence," the person(s) responsible for the words that have come to appear on the page in the original language, and the "editorial intelligence," the person(s) responsible for organizing the discrete units or scrolls into a single volume, the arrangement of which intentionally or unintentionally influences the reader's interpretation of any particular book or scroll. My example is the Book of Ruth, which reads as a hauntingly beautiful tale of friendship and devotion when considered in isolation but which shrinks to a minor pastoral interlude when seen in the larger scheme of Israel's epic history as narrated in Judges and Samuel, the books between which it traditionally appears. I stress the need to read each text both within and without the context created for it by the Bible proper, and I introduce the problem of yet a third "intelligence" at work in any biblical text: the translator's. At the end of the class, I distribute a reprint of four Renaissance translations of Psalm 23, asking students to consider for next session the ways in which each translator's use of English controls our response to the text while possibly asserting a theological bias that a reader often cannot identify, much less refute. (I reprint the translations as they appear in Rollins and Baker 131–41, but any university library will contain many others.)

In our second meeting, I draw four columns on the blackboard so that we can place significant variations side by side. We eventually produce a chart that looks like table 1. The discussion of these differences, which is invariably animated, generally focuses on four concerns:

1. *Simplicity of language*. Psalm 23 asserts a simple and joyous trust in God's providence; it is a moving declaration of absolute faith. Such calm assurance

Table 1.

GREAT BIBLE (GR) (1539)	GENEVA BIBLE (GN) (1560)	BISHOPS' BIBLE (BP) (1572)	RHEIMS-DOUAI (RD) (1582)
The Lord is my shepherd;	The Lord is my shepherd;	God is my sheepherd;	Our Lord ruleth me,
therefore can I lack nothing.	I shall not want.	therefore I can lack nothing.	and nothing shall be wanting in me;
He shall feed me in a green pasture	He maketh me to rest in green pasture	He will cause me to repose myself in pasture full of grass,	in place of pasture there he hath placed me.
and lead me forth beside the waters of comfort.	and leadeth me by the still waters.	and he will lead me unto calm waters.	Upon the water of reflection he hath brought me up;
He shall convert my soul	He restoreth my soul	He will convert my soul;	he hath converted my soul;
and bring me forth in the paths of righteousness for his name's sake.	and leadeth me in the paths of righteousness for his name's sake.	he will bring me forth into the paths of righteousness for his name sake.	he hath conducted me upon the paths of justice for his name.
Yea, though I walk thorow the valley of the shadow of death	Yea, though I should walk through the valley of the shadow of death	Yea, though I walk through the valley of the shadow of death	For although I shall walk in the middes of the shadow of death
I will fear no evil, for thou art with me;	I will fear no evil, for thou art with me;	I will fear no evil, for thou art with me;	I will not fear evils, because thou art with me;
thy rod and thy staff comfort me.	thy rod and thy staff they comfort me.	thy rod and thy staff be the things that do comfort me.	thy rod and thy staff they have comforted me.
Thou shalt prepare a table before me	Thou dost prepare a table before me	Thou wilt prepare a table before me	Thou hast prepared in my sight a table
against them that trouble me;	in the sight of mine adversaries;	in the presence of mine adversaries;	against them that trouble me.
thou hast anointed my head with oil,	thou dost anoint mine head with oil,	thou hast anointed my head with oil,	Thou hast fatted my head with oil,
and my cup shall be full.	and my cup runneth over.	and my cup shall be brimful.	and my chalice inebriating, how goodly it is!
But thy loving kindness and mercy shall follow me all the days of my life,	Doubtless kindness and mercy shall follow me all the days of my life,	Truly, felicity and mercy shall follow me all the days of my life,	And thy mercy shall follow me all the days of my life,
and I will dwell in the house of the Lord forever.	and I shall remain a long season in the house of the Lord.	and I will dwell in the house of God for a long time.	and that I may dwell in the house of our Lord in longitude of days.

is best rendered in verse 1 by GN's "I shall not want." While communicating the speaker's total passivity, RD's "and nothing shall be wanting in me" is less powerful an assertion of faith, while BP's "therefore I can lack nothing" is too reasoned a conclusion, making the psalm more an expression of careful ratiocination and less an outpouring of spiritual exuberance. Likewise, GR's rendering of verse 4, "thy rod and thy staff comfort me," is weakened in GN by the insertion of the appositive pronoun "they," while BP's flabby "thy rod and thy staff be the things that do comfort me" diffuses most of the idea's emotional force. Finally, the psalm's concluding assertion of the Lord's continuing hospitality and providence is made vague by GN's estimate of "a long season," BP's "for a long time," and RD's "in longitude of days"; GR's "for ever" alone communicates the speaker's quiet firmness of faith.

2. *Dramatic immediacy of images.* Old Testament poetry, as Ruth apRoberts and others point out, is built on concrete, specific images. Psalm 23 is structured around the complementary images of the Lord as a shepherd providing the helpless soul with food, water, rest, and guidance and as a host hospitably entertaining his guest as well as protecting the guest from enemies. The rod and the staff in verse 4 are symbols of comfort and support rather than of chastisement and correction as they are elsewhere in the Psalms.

Our translations differ, however, in the dramatic immediacy of the images. For example, while RD's "Our Lord ruleth me" correctly communicates the sense of verse 1, it fails to establish the poem's governing pastoral motif. And in verse 2, GR's image of "the waters of comfort" explains the emotional complex behind GN's choice of "the still waters" and BP's "calm waters," but for that very reason it seems more emotionally removed from the experience than the other two. RD's "the water of reflection" suggests an emotionally distanced, meditative stance on the speaker's part, undercutting the psalm's spiritual exuberance. Perhaps the most glaring discrepancy in this regard is contained in GN's rendering of verse 5 as "my cup runneth over," which beautifully suggests the overflowing of divine providence and grace that the speaker is celebrating, and BP's "my cup shall be brimful," which both postpones the speaker's satisfaction to some indeterminate future and suggests fullness, but not loving, gratuitous overabundance. The problem of word choice is underscored by the radical discrepancy among renderings of the simple action reported in verse 2: is the speaker fed in the green pasture (GR), encouraged to rest (GN, BP), or simply placed there (RD)? Students must recognize that the text they are reading often relies not simply on the translator's limitations but on editorial conjecture as well.

3. *Understanding of temporal sequence.* What is the action of divine providence within time? Curiously, our four translators do not agree. Has it been done already, is it occurring now, or will it happen at some unspecified future date? Has the Lord led the speaker (RD), is he leading the speaker now (GR, GN), or will he lead the speaker (BP) by the still waters? Has the Lord prepared a table for the speaker to discourage enemies deliberately (RD), will he do it sometime later (GR, BP), or is he in the act of doing it now (GN)?

Even individual translations are not consistent, GN and BP reporting the one action in the present and the other in the future tense. Classroom discussion of the implications of each translator's choice inevitably approximates the Renaissance debate over justification by faith alone: is the speaker willing to depend entirely on the future providence of God or is the speaker encouraged to do so by some past sign of election or favor? Each translation concludes with the speaker's quiet confidence in the future, but GN's use of the present tense throughout most effectively prepares the reader, suggesting as it does an eternal present of beneficence, comfort, well-being.

4. *Subtlety of theological subtext.* Martin Luther insisted that the Bible translator be a theologian first, and the role that each of our four translations played in Reformation and Counter-Reformation debate allows them particular purchase for making students aware of the general problem of a translator's theological bias. Students can intelligently discuss the difference in religious experience suggested by GN's rendering of verse 3 as "He restoreth my soul" and GR's (but also BP's and RD's) "He shall convert my soul." Some historical background information may be required, however, before they can appreciate RD's use of "chalice" in verse 5, as opposed to "cup" in the three Protestant translations, a distinction that approximates the sixteenth- and seventeenth-century conflict between the Roman Catholic altar and the Protestant communion table. It was while studying the Psalms that Luther formulated his doctrine of justification by faith alone; he undertook his translation of the Psalms, which he called "the Bible in miniature," to make explicit the revelation that he felt was only implicit in Jerome's Vulgate. Clearly, texts other than Psalm 23 may depend even more heavily on the translator's theological bias.

Should class time allow, I conclude the session by distributing copies of the translation of Psalm 23 that most people are familiar with, the King James, and we discuss its particular poetic excellence. On occasion I have also handed out copies of the translations in the Standard Version, the Revised Standard Version, and the New English Bible and asked students to comment on the problems of attempting a modern idiom. The first formal paper of the term is a three-to-five-page comparison of three translators' renderings of any seven-to-ten-verse passage in the Bible.

A Way of Teaching Job

Robert E. Simmons

My suggestion for teaching Job is to use William Blake as a guest instructor. His reading of Job is given in final form as a set of twenty-one illustrations (plus a title page), each containing around its edges quotations from Job and other books of the Christian Bible. Engraved late in Blake's life (1823–26), the designs represent the best of his artistic and interpretive abilities. The engravings are readily available and can easily be copied or made into slides. Bo Lindberg's *William Blake's Illustrations to the Book of Job* provides the necessary background information.

Studying this visual form of Job provides welcome variety in the traditional Bible course. Intrinsically interesting, the designs are highly detailed, yet set in a structure so firm as to demonstrate the integrity of Blake's thought. Their analysis parallels that of the Bible in terms of complexity, importance of detail, and symbolic and allegorical meaning. The simultaneous study of pictorial and literary texts brings out the similarities and differences between the two media. Blake's interpretation always sparks debate and suggests new directions for discussion of the problem of suffering, the relationship of the physical world to God, and the nature of both God and Satan.

To understand Blake's interpretation, we must realize that Blake, like other Christians of his day, saw Job as repeating the story of the Christian Bible, the story of the fall and the Resurrection. There is a major difference, however, between Blake's reading and that of the orthodox Christian: for Blake the fall begins with the creation of the physical world. It follows that the creator is not God, but an imposter. It also follows that the resurrection will consist of a repudiation of this false god and his work.

Blake's set of designs follows a chiasmic structure, not dissimilar in this respect to the biblical text. The first half (plates 1–10) portrays the shaking of Job's faith in the false god as a consequence of Satan's attacks. The second half (12–21) portrays the revelation of the true God and Job's restoration. The central plate 11 (described below) divides the two halves. Each half may be halved again. In the first quarter (1–5) Satan attacks Job's family, but Job retains his faith in the false god. In the second quarter (6–10) Satan attacks Job himself, and Job's faith is shaken, despite the arguments of his friends for the false god. In the third quarter (12–16) Elihu proposes a different idea of God, and God appears and explains why the creation of the physical world represents the fall. This constitutes Job's main insight. In the fourth quarter (17–21) Job accepts God and is restored. The relations between chapters and designs, as suggested by Lindberg (110), are illustrated in table 1.

A key point in Blake's interpretation, of course, is the nature of the false god, for whom Blake gives us one consistent symbol: a book, presumably a Bible (plates 2, 5, 16). The title-page design is actually a picture of a book floating in clouds. The false god, then, is identified as a "book" god. A quota-

Table 1.

Chapter in Job	Blake's Design	Thematic Movement
1	1–4	
2	5–7	
3	8	Shaking of Job's faith
4	9	
12, 14	10	
7, 19	11	Nature of false god
32–37	12	
38	13–14	
40–41	15–16	Job's faith restored
42	17–21	

tion beneath the design on plate 1 suggests what is meant by this symbol: "The Letter Killeth / The Spirit giveth Life" (2 Cor. 3.6). The contrast between the first and last plates of the designs also hints at Blake's meaning. On plate 1 Job and his wife are seated beneath a tree on which hang musical instruments; they have Bibles on their laps and seem to be leading their kneeling children in worship. A Gothic cathedral rises anachronistically in the background. On plate 21 Job and his entire family are standing, playing the musical instruments that formerly hung untouched. No Bibles or cathedral can be seen, though otherwise the foreground and background remain the same. Perhaps this is Blake's way of symbolizing the movement from exile to redemption, calling to mind, for example, Psalm 137. 1–2: "By the rivers of Babylon, there we sat down, yea, we wept, when we remembered Zion. We hanged our harps upon the willows in the midst thereof" (KJV).

The meaning of the book as a symbol and the nature of the false god are revealed in the central plate 11. There Job is shown in the throes of a nightmare, as devils reach for him from below, while the false god, above, equipped with a single cloven hoof and wrapped in a serpent, points to the twin tablets of the law. The devils, like Satan, represent the pains of the physical world, which the false god relates to moral behavior. This relation between moral behavior and physical punishment is the essence of the book god, the traditional god of institutional religion. Since Job is a just man, and yet suffers in the physical world, this god must be unjust. This is Job's crisis of conscience, the dark night of the soul preceding illumination. Both god and devils are his tormentors. After plate 11, Job has rejected this false god.

But the nature of the true God remains a mystery to him. He knows only that he cannot accept the superstitious link between morality and events in the physical world. It is Elihu (plate 12) who suggests that the friends are mistaken, that God does not exist in the physical world. Immediately Job perceives God (plate 13), and Elihu disappears, confirming his function as God's announcer. Remarkably, God looks exactly like Job, and when we review the other plates we see that he looks exactly like the false god as well. The explanation of this resemblance is that God dwells and has always dwelled in Job's mind. As God explains in the following three plates, it is Job himself who, by believing in a god of corporeal punishment, created the physical world and made himself a victim of suffering.

At the beginning of the fourth quarter (plate 17), God is shown for the first time come down to earth, blessing Job and his wife face-to-face while the friends cringe and cover their eyes, too superstitious yet to see the truth. Job accepts that God dwells within his own mind, and in the next plate the new power this knowledge gives him is vividly shown as Job prays for his friends. The energy of existence is now seen to flow from Job into the world, instead of being seen as coming (in destructive form) from the world.

Satan is also a product of the mind. When Job believed in a moral God and thought human actions were rewarded and punished in the physical world, Satan became God's agent in that world. But when Job realizes that God dwells in his own mind and that the corporeal world does not exist, Satan disappears, as he does in the biblical text.

The difference between knowing God through tradition and faith and knowing him through personal experience is expressed by the biblical Job through a metaphor of perception: "I have heard of thee by the hearing of the ear: but now mine eye seeth thee" (42.5, KJV; qtd. on plate 17). In Blake's terms, this distinction consists in replacing a god of corporeal punishment with a god of forgiveness of sins. Sin can only occur in the physical world. In the mental world, sin is merely error, which is driven away by truth. In the mental world there is no judgment, no punishment, only the flux of error and truth. To recognize a wrong one has done is to be saved and honored. Hence, all recognition of error leads to joy and reunion with God, who is truth. But in the physical, moral world, recognition of sin leads to punishment and separation from God. Since we can never be free from error, in the physical, moral world we will be forever punished. But if we live in the mental world, we will be forever rewarded with truth.

Discussion of Blake's designs raises many points to debate, most especially the nature of the Jewish and Christian views of God and Satan. The details of the designs, as well as the accompanying quotations from both testaments, lead the reader always back to the biblical Job, but with a fresh angle of vision: just what is needed toward the end of a long course.

Folktale Form and National Theme, with Particular Reference to Ruth

Alexander Globe

The biblical narratives concerning Jacob, Joseph, Samson, Ruth, Esther, Daniel, and others share a number of problematic traits. Like several of these texts, the Book of Daniel contains serious errors of fact about the period of history in which it claims to be set: Belshazzar, son of Nabonidus (not of Nebuchadnezzar, as in Dan. 5.18), was defeated by Cyrus of Persia (not Darius the Mede as in Dan. 5.31). Divergences from actual events usually bring these narratives closer to widespread literary motifs. As early as the fourth century, Eusebius of Caesarea commented on the striking similarities between the feats of Samson and Hercules (Moore 364–65); the story of Potiphar's wife in Genesis 29.6–20 recalls the Egyptian "Tale of Two Brothers" (Pritchard, *Ancient Near Eastern Texts* 23–25); various tales, including *Ahiqar*, provide parallels to Daniel (Hartman and Di Lella 55–61); and so on. Consequently, these biblical narratives have been variously classified as legends, sagas, fictionalized histories, historical romances, novels, novellas, short stories, idylls, folktales, or other genres with a strong fictional or nonhistorical element. If conservative scholars prefer to ignore such difficulties, liberal critics discover the disunifying specter of interpolation. The genealogy at the end of Ruth and the entire thirty-eighth chapter of Genesis, to name only two examples, are often stigmatized as late editorial insertions. The student who has read little but modern fictions, with their emphasis on original plots and characters, can find folktale plots too predictable and the characters superficial or improbable. Samson capitulates to Delilah an inconceivable four times in Judges 16.4–22; Jacob's goat-skin disguise in Genesis 27.15–23 and Laban's substitution of Leah for Rachel in Genesis 29.21–26 seem unlikely deceptions to twentieth-century readers; and commentaries abound with strictures on the inadequate motivation of characters (on Ruth 1.1–5, see E. F. Campbell 58–59).

These narratives make more coherent sense when read and taught as folktales, which follow quite different conventions from those of either historical chronicles or psychologically realistic modern fiction. In his often-quoted *Morphology of the Folktale* Vladimir Propp describes the "parts of speech" and "syntax," as it were, of the Russian fairy tale. For Propp, folktale characters assume one of a number of stereotype roles: the hero (who may be either a quester like St. George or a victim like Cinderella), the false hero (who fails to achieve the hero's goal), the villain (who attempts to destroy the hero), the donor (e.g., the fairy godmother in Cinderella), and the helper (e.g., the finery that gets Cinderella to the ball and the slipper that identifies her afterward). Folktale characters are not motivated psychologically but are instruments of the 32 functions Propp finds in the folktale plot (table 1) or of the

Table 1.   Plot and Character Functions in Vladimir Propp's *Morphology of the Folk Tale*

Part I.   Introduction of Hero and Villain

a   *Initial situation:* time and place of story, composition of family, birth of hero, argument of brothers over primacy.

Preparatory Section

1   *Absentation:* family member dies or leaves home.
2   *Interdiction:* prohibition or command is given to hero.
3   *Interdiction violated:* hero violates prohibition or obeys command.
4   *Villain's first reconnaissance:* villain tries to find out about hero.
5   *Villain receives information.*
6   *Villain's deception:* villain attempts to possess hero or his belongings.
7   *Victim submits to villain:* hero is deceived, unwittingly helping villain.

Part 2.   The Hero Triumphs over the Villain

Complication

8   *Villainy (victim heroes):* villain harms family member.
8a   *Lack (questing heroes):* family member either lacks or desires something.
9   *Connective incident (victims):* hero is transported or freed.
9a   *Connective incident (questers):* hero is called, sent, allowed to leave.
10   *Consent to counteraction (questers):* hero agrees to act on the request.
11   *Departure or dispatch of the hero:* hero leaves home.

A Donor Gives the Hero a Helper

12   *Donor:* donor tests or attacks hero to transfer a helper.
13   *Hero's reaction to donor:* hero reacts positively or negatively.
14   *Helper:* helper or magic agent is given to hero by donor.

The Hero Uses the Helper to Defeat the Villain

15   *Guidance:* hero goes to find what he is searching for.
16   *Struggle:* hero and villain join in direct combat.
17   *Marking:* hero is branded or marked.
18   *Victory:* hero defeats villain.
19   *Liquidation of villainy or lack:* villainy or lack (8, 8a) is reversed.

Part 3.   Return and Recognition of the Hero, Punishment of the Villain

20   *Return:* hero returns home or goes to land of princess.
21   *Pursuit:* hero is pursued by villain.
22   *Rescue:* hero is rescued from pursuit.
23   *Unrecognized arrival:* unrecognized hero arrives home or elsewhere.
24   *False hero's claims:* false hero presents unfounded claims on hero's belongings.
25   *Difficult task:* task set for hero or false hero.
26   *Solution of task:* hero succeeds or false hero fails.
27   *Recognition of hero.*
29   *Transfiguration of hero:* hero is given new clothes, palace, etc.
28   *Exposure of false hero or villain.*
30   *Punishment of false hero or villain.*
31   *Hero is married and ascends to the throne.*

extended list of 151 characteristics in his first appendix. Thus the often improbable or unexplained actions of characters, such as the apparently unmotivated deaths near the beginning of many stories, turn out to be standard features of the genre. More than one role may be assumed by any character, and any number of new episodes, called "moves," may be introduced by returning to an earlier point in the morphology and tracing a new series of functions, in roughly the same order as Propp's lists. Different themes are usually treated in different moves, instead of being woven together as in modern fiction. Not every function need appear in every tale, but at least one act of villainy or one lack and its resolution must be present (functions 8 or 8a, and 19).

While some scholars have incorporated certain of these observations into general theories of narrative structure (see the survey in Meletinsky), it is significant that the specific details of Propp's morphology have been found in both oral and written works ranging from the biblical Book of Ruth and the *Odyssey* to modern European tales and games (Sasson; Dundes 61–72, 80–87). That such conventions can be passed on orally even in literate societies can be shown by having a class of students, most of whom will not have heard of Propp, define the basic plot of a descendant of the folktale, such as a Western or a childhood game. Whatever its origin, the widespread dissemination of the folktale form suggests that Indo-European and Semitic storytellers found it useful for organizing audience response. Indeed it proved so successful that the conventions tend to dominate whatever historical events lie behind the tales, burying purely factual data in stereotypical plots, characters, and imagery (see Gizelis; Hoffman). In the Bible, the reader finds religious interpretation also coloring historical events (see Widengren).

The morphological structure of a folktale is hidden as deeply under the surface as grammatical structures lie beneath the surface of a sentence. The arrangement of episodes in a folktale does not always mirror the underlying morphology, just as the arrangement of words in a sentence (e.g., parallelism) need not mirror the grammatical structure of that sentence. Many biblical texts are arranged in the ring structures common in Mesopotamian, Ugaritic, Greek, and Latin texts (Fishbane, *Text*; Fokkelman, *Narrative Art in Genesis, Narrative Art in Samuel*; Trible, *God*; Welch). In a ring structure, the last episode offers a contrast to or fulfillment of the first episode, the second-to-last episode contrasts with or fulfills the second episode, and so on, the episodes forming pairs of concentric rings or frames until the center is reached (see table 2 for the device in Ruth). The central section contains an important theme or event that illuminates the rest of the narrative, particularly the beginning and end. Propp did not notice that his functions form a ring structure (see table 1), the birth of the hero being balanced by his or her integration into adult society as symbolized by marriage (function a // 31), the expulsion of the immature hero contrasting with her or his successful return to society as an adult (1–7 // 20–30), and the villainy or lack contrasting with its liquidation (8–11 // 15–19). At the center lies the hero's response to the donor, who provides the means of defeating the villain or lack (12–14). Here the hero's identity is revealed through a symbolic helper. The folktale thus functions both as a charter for personal maturation and as an encoding of the cultural values of the hero's society. Its popularity owes a great deal to an almost invariably comic ending that leaves the listener (or reader) with a secure sense that the social status quo remains unaltered.

The Book of Ruth consists of two Proppian moves, where the opening crises of childlessness and famine so common in folktales are reversed (see the elaborate analysis in Sasson 203–12). In the initial situation, Naomi and her daughter-in-law, Ruth, are left as defenseless widows. As in many folktales at this point, no reason is given for their husbands' deaths (function 1; Ruth 1.1–5). The two victims become questing heroines in search of food and family (9a–11; Ruth 1.6–22). Predictably, the two problems are treated in separate moves, the first ensuring sustenance (Ruth 1.23–2.23) and the second securing a husband for Ruth (3.1–4.10). In both moves, Boaz, the kinsman of Naomi's dead husband, is the donor; the nearer kinsman who refuses to marry Ruth plays the false hero unwilling to solve the task that Boaz sets (functions 12, 24–26). The book ends with the recognition of Ruth as heroine, her wedding, and the prayer that God will make the couple like ancestors of the twelve tribes of Israel, particularly the chosen Judah. Appropriately, Ruth is the great-grandmother of David, king of Judah and Israel (functions 27, 29, 31).

On its rhetorical surface, the Book of Ruth is organized in a series of rings or frames that highlight the theme of personal and national reward for righteousness (table 2; see the extensive analysis in Radday, "Chiasmus in Hebrew" 71–76). The initial famine and deaths (sec. A) are reversed at the end by Ruth's marriage, which ensures both her family's sustenance and the continuance of the line of Israel from Judah to David (A'). Ruth's faithfulness to Naomi and her mother-in-law's God (B) is rewarded when Boaz redeems her and the elders bless her as an Israelite (B'). Naomi's emptiness is dispelled by the ample barley harvest and the prospect of Boaz's redeeming Ruth (C, D // C', D'). As a donor, Boaz welcomes Ruth twice, first as she gleans for food (E), then as she approaches him on the threshing floor asking for marriage (E'). Given the fact that the important national festivals of Passover and First-fruits are celebrated at the start and end of the barley harvest, it is fitting that two important meals form the last frame (F // F'). At the center stands Naomi's advice about visiting Boaz at night to claim the levirate rights that will integrate Ruth into Israelite society (G). Ruth's assent to the plan rewards her loyalty, reverses the original catastrophes, makes a foreigner the ancestor of David, and prepares for the extraordinary role of women at the end (see the feminist reading of Trible, *God* 166–99). Not only is Ruth's son miraculously nursed by a woman past the age of childbearing, but he is named by the townswomen instead of by his parents. Given this feminine and non-Israelite focus, juxtaposed with a genealogy of David in a work sharing stylistic affinity with early biblical books (E. F. Campbell 23–28), Ruth may have had a part in the legitimization of the Davidic dynasty, particularly of Solomon, whose

Table 2.   Ring Structure (Antimetabole) in the Book of Ruth

A   Famine forces Elimelech to Moab, where his wife, Naomi, and her daughters-in-law, Ruth and Orpah, all become widows (1.1–5).

B   When Naomi returns to Bethlehem, (1) Orpah refuses to leave Moab, (2) Ruth follows Naomi, and (3) Ruth accepts Naomi's God as hers (1.6–18).

C   Naomi calls herself Mara, "bitter," because she left full and returned empty (1.19–21).

D   Naomi and Ruth arrive at the barley harvest, i.e. close to Passover (1.22).

E   Ruth gleans grain in the fields of Boaz, a kinsman who welcomes her (2.1–15).

F   Boaz has Ruth eat with him, lets her glean, sends Naomi barley (2.16–23).

G   Naomi instructs Ruth to visit Boaz and claim levirate rights (3.1–6).

F'   Boaz falls asleep on a heap of grain after eating and drinking (3.7a).

E'   When Boaz wakes, Ruth asks him to redeem her. He tells her he must first ask a nearer kinsman (3.7b–14).

D'   Boaz gives Ruth six measures of barley to give to Naomi (3.15).

C'   Ruth says Boaz told her she would not return empty to Naomi, who now knows that Boaz will settle the matter quickly (3.16–18).

B'   During the legal hearing, (1) the closer kinsman refuses to redeem Ruth, (2) Boaz redeems her, and (3) the witnesses pray to God that Ruth and Boaz will be as fertile as Rachel, Leah, and Judah's son (4.1–12).

A'   Ruth and Boaz marry. Their first son, nursed by Naomi and named by the women of the town, is the grandfather of King David (4.13–22).

mother was originally wed to a non-Israelite and had a prominent role in securing her son's succession (1 Kings 1.15–31).

The ring structure shows not only how the Israelite incarnation of the folktale moves from personal archetypes to the theology of national history but also how the genealogy forms an integral part of the book. Both the first four and the last four verses contain ten names falling into two national groups. In Ruth 1.1–4, seven of the names are Israelite (four being personal names and three geographical), and three are Moabite (two being personal). In the genealogy, the names of seven Israelites from Perez to Boaz are continued with three names from the son of the Moabite woman to David. A similar structure thus underlies the book's start and end, ensuring that the genealogy is not merely an editorial afterthought.

The list of names in the first four verses of the book provides more than just a dramatis personae. Even as folktale characters' actions mirror plot functions, so their names often have an allegorical cast alerting the listener or reader to their narrative roles. The sons of Elimelech are fated to die young: Chilion literally means "failing" (Deut. 28.65), and Mahlon ("sickly") puns on the verb "to pollute," "to defile" (Gen. 49.4; Exod. 31.14; Lev. 21.4). Naomi means "beautiful" or "delightful" (2 Sam. 1.23; Cant. 1.16), while Orpah, literally "back of the neck" (signifying rejection in Josh. 7.8), predictably turns her back on her mother-in-law. Ruth's name offers a complex pun on the words "woman friend" (Exod. 11.2); "female companion" (Cant. 1.9); "to pasture," "to tend" (Gen. 30.31); and "shepherdess" (Gen. 29.9, applied to the same Rachel who is named as a model for Ruth in ch. 4.11). Ruth's faithful companionship becomes the pasturing of her adoptive nation, whose preeminent shepherd is David. Finally, the family of Elimelech, literally "My God is King," fittingly provides the tribe of Judah with "praise" (see Gen. 29.35, 49.8) by making the clan of Ephrath "fruitful" (see Gen. 41.52) in producing the ancestor of David. Thus the beginning of the book hints at the national focus of the concluding genealogy.

Ruth can be read and taught as a sophisticated folktale. It follows a narrative pattern that has been transmitted with remarkable stability in Indo-European and Semitic folk literature from antiquity to the present. This pattern illustrates the passage from youth to adult life, reinforcing the social status quo with its comic ending. In this book the faithful Ruth (and, by extension, Naomi) is rewarded with the security that only marriage can bring a woman in traditional patriarchal societies. The folktale genre, with its personal focus, is ideally suited to the Bible, where so much national history is figured in specific individuals' lives. It is almost as if the personal model legitimizes national aspirations, and vice versa. In characteristic Israelite fashion, the individual is placed in the larger context of national religious history. The Moabite Ruth is the great-grandmother of David, and the book may originally have had a role in legitimizing the Davidic dynasty. As in the folktale genre generally, the plot, characters, and symbolism of Ruth become aspects of one another, being more closely intertwined than in modern fiction. Just as the deep structure of the prototypical folktale plot consists of a series of frames or rings, so the rhetorical structure of Ruth, like many other biblical narratives, consists of a series of frames. They not only attest to the integrity of the opening and closing of the book but also highlight the theme of the central episode. There the foreign Ruth's legal claims on Israelite society unexpectedly ensure the continuation of Judah's line through to David.

Sensual or Sublime:
On Teaching the Song of Songs

Marc Brettler

"It is like a lock whose key is lost or a diamond too expensive to purchase."
This simile of Sa'adya Gaon, the Jewish exegete and philosopher active in the
early tenth century, aptly describes the paradox of the Song of Songs; no reader
can complete this work without being moved by its beauty, though that very
same reader would be hard-pressed to claim an understanding of the text.
How can this paradox be constructively conveyed to the student?

The problems involved in teaching the Song of Songs are so complex and
require such sophistication to understand that I save the Song for my penul-
timate class. By then, the contrast between the Song and "typical" biblical
texts is particularly obvious, heightening the interpretive issues. An examination of Job has sensitized students to the difficulties of interpretation. (The
essays in *Semeia* 7 [1977] are useful for this purpose and are very accessible.)
Proverbs and Ecclesiastes have provided a preliminary exploration of the tension between religious and secular biblical writings. The Song's attitude toward
love allows an interesting contrast to Genesis 2–3 (Trible, *God* 144–65), bring-
ing the course full circle. Furthermore, my final class considers the issue of
canonization, how the Hebrew Bible became a book; this topic follows naturally from a discussion of the Song of Songs, which raises issues concerning
secular versus religious writings, reinterpretation, and the Bible as authority.

It is impossible to cover the entire range of interpretation for the complete
Song in a single class. Instead, I describe the book's interpretation in broad
terms: as allegory, both religious (e.g., God and Israel, Christ and the Church
or the individual) and secular (e.g., Luther's state and the individual); as a
drama, either secular or religious (related to the so-called sacred-marriage
rites, known best from Mesopotamia); as a cycle of wedding songs; as a cycle
of love songs or a unified love song. (A complete survey of interpretations
is in Marvin Pope's *Song of Songs* 89–229.) The reason for this diversity may
be illustrated with a quick comparison of verses: Do the similar 2.7, 3.5, and
5.8 indicate a compositional unity, are they a dramatic refrain, or do they represent a common motif used by different poets? Similarly, do the narrative
and verbal similarities between 3.1–5 and 5.2–8 imply thematic development
within one song or differing treatments of a theme by multiple authors? Once
the class becomes aware of these general issues, one can focus more narrowly,
first on the conflict between secular and sacred interpretation, then on a small
pericope that illustrates the problems of the book's richness.

I teach a rather traditional introductory course, which stresses the need
for understanding biblical works within their ancient Israelite contexts. This
approach gives rise to two questions concerning the Song: Did poets in the
ancient Near East speak of love and sexuality? Could a poet in ancient Israel,

a largely aniconic culture, speak of God as a lover in such graphic terms?

Students immersed in the Bible for a semester should be aware of texts that suggest an affirmative answer to the second question. These include Hosea 1–3, which proclaims that Israel's harlotry with Baʿal (a deity, but also Hebrew for "husband") will be replaced with a proper relationship with God, Israel's *ish* (husband); the sexually explicit Ezekiel 16, in which Israel "is God's" (v. 8), probably in the sexual sense; Isaiah 62.4, which depicts a ménage à trois consisting of the people Israel, the land Israel, and God. These texts point strongly to an allegorical reading of the Song. To explore allegorical readings of the Song, I distribute a handout that includes an English translation of the Targum (in Pope, s.v. each verse), which is an Aramaic "translation" in the form of historical allegory dating from the early Islamic period, and a selection from Richard Littledale, *A Commentary on the Song of Songs from Ancient and Mediaeval Sources*, which incorporates a large number of Christian allegorical interpretations. I encourage students to discuss strictures that might be placed on the allegorical method. In conclusion I note the early rabbinic traditions concerning the sacredness of the Song as allegory, especially in the school of Rabbi Akiba (c. 50–135 CE), where the Song seems to have been connected to early mystical speculation (see Scholem, *Jewish Gnosticism* 36–42). Akiba's claim that "[t]he whole world is not worth the day on which the Song of Songs was given to Israel, for all the Scriptures are holy, but the Song of Songs is the Holy of Holies" (Pope 19) indicates how strongly entrenched the sacred interpretation of the Song was already in the second century CE.

This position is immediately compared with Jewish traditions that firmly prohibit the secular use of the Song, such as the statement "He who trills his voice in chanting the Song of Songs in the banquet house and treats it as a sort of song has no part in the world to come" (Pope 19; rabbinic statements like this one suggest that in the early first millennium CE the Song was read secularly as part of the wedding festivities). Not only Jews read the Song as a secular work; the Christian exegete Theodore of Mopsuestia (d. 428), an important representative of the Antiochene school, insisted on a nonallegorical interpretation of the Song, for which his work was later banned (Pope 119). The soundness of literal interpretations is reinforced by a brief exploration of sexuality and love poetry in ancient Near Eastern literature. I include Mesopotamian heterosexual and homosexual erotic (cultic?) statuary; Mesopotamian potency incantations (both described in Biggs); readings from an Akkadian poem of unfulfilled love that ends, "I am telling you how I really feel; / Your love means no more to me than / Trouble and vexation" (Pope 79); an Egyptian poem whose imagery is remarkably close to the Song (Lichtheim 182; on this imagery in general, see Falk 80–87); and a short stirring Egyptian poem describing a man's brave efforts to reach his distant lover, which ends, "O night, be mine forever, / Now that my queen has come!" (Lichtheim 193). These sources cumulatively suggest that eroticism and love were concerns in the ancient Near East in much the same way that they are in our society.

I then examine the possibilities presented by the nonallegorical interpretation through a detailed analysis of 5.2–16, especially 2–8. The students have a handout with three modern translations of this passage (Ginsberg et al.; Pope; Falk) to heighten their awareness of the ambiguity and beauty of the Song. I explore ambiguities in the unit: Verse 2 — Is it a dream? When does the lover awake? Verse 3 — Is the woman simply saying that she won't arise, or is she fantasizing about being with her lover for eternity? Verse 4 — Is this a keyhole? a sexual reference? Is the lover penetrating or turning away? Are the woman's innards seething from anxiety or lust? I note possible sexual allusions: knocking, opening, hands and holes and moisture. I try to sensitize the students to the rapid changes in pace (contrast the long arising in vv. 3–5 to the quick fleeing in v. 6); to irony (v. 7, where the guards, not the woman's lover, strip her); and to the highly unusual poetic structure of the center of verse 2, a string of three-syllable words all ending in -*i* (*pithi-li* [open] '*ahoti ra'yati yonati tammati sheroshi* 'for my head'). Finally, I discuss the problem of deciding where the unit beginning in 5.2 ends (v. 8? v. 16? 6.3? v. 9?). I conclude with a brief analysis of how the ambiguities of the Song might function within different secular interpretive frameworks. For example, are the "daughters of Jerusalem" (v. 8) a chorus at a wedding, participants in a drama, or all women who are being "addressed" by a woman engaged in a complex sexual fantasy? Other units in the Song may be used to explore the issue of ambiguity and interpretation, and many works exist to guide the novice through it (esp. Pope; Falk; Landy). Few units, however, are as elusive and absorbing as 5.2 and following.

I try hard not to resolve the difficulties of interpreting the Song; no one "key" should be supplied to Saadya's simile, but the diamondlike brilliance of this poem should nevertheless shine through. The students should be made to feel comfortable with the notion that the harder one tries to pin down one reading of the Song, whether sacred or sublime, allegorical, cultic, or ritualistic, the more elusive interpretation becomes. Indeed, the definitive interpretation of this work is best compared to the male lover at its conclusion, bolting away like a buck or stag.

CONTRIBUTORS TO THE VOLUME AND SURVEY PARTICIPANTS

The following scholars and teachers participated in the survey of approaches to teaching the Hebrew Bible that preceded the preparation of this volume. It is a pleasure to acknowledge their very generous assistance, without which the volume would not have been written, and also their enthusiastic support, confirming the need for such a book.

James S. Ackerman, Indiana University, Bloomington; Ruth Adler, Baruch College, City University of New York; Robert Alter, University of California, Berkeley; Ruth apRoberts, University of California, Riverside; David Bakan, York University; Mieke Bal, University of Rochester; Adele Berlin, University of Maryland, College Park; John Bligh, University of Guelph; Marc Brettler, Brandeis University; Margaret Conrow, Kansas State University; Alan Cooper, McMaster University; Robert C. Culley, McGill University; Pinchas Doron, Queens College, City University of New York; Harold H. P. Dressler, Northwest Baptist Theological College and Seminary; Diane T. Edwards, University of Victoria; Ann W. Engar, University of Utah; Lyle Eslinger, University of Calgary; Yael Feldman, Columbia University; Ernest S. Frerichs, Brown University; Kenneth Frieden, Yale University; Richard E. Friedman, University of California, San Diego; Raymond-Jean Frontain, University of Tennessee; Northrop Frye, University of Toronto; Roland Mushat Frye, University of Pennsylvania; Phillip J. Gallagher, University of Texas, El Paso; John Gammie, University of Tulsa; Stephen A. Geller, Dropsie College; Yehoshua Gitay, Wesleyan University; Alexander Globe, University of British Columbia; Edwin M. Good, Stanford University; Norman K. Gottwald, New York Theological Seminary; Edward L. Greenstein, Jewish Theological Seminary of America; Baruch Halpern, York University; Alan J. Hauser, Appalachian State University; Leslie J. Hoppe, Catholic Theological Union; Robert E. Hosmer, Jr., University of Massachusetts, Amherst; David L. Jeffrey, University of Ottawa; Bruce W. Jones, California State College, Bakersfield; Isaac Kikawada, University of California, Berkeley; William Kinsley, University of Montreal; Francis Landy, University of Alberta; Herbert J. Levine, Franklin and Marshall College; M. H. Levine, Eastern Connecticut State College; Aaron Lichtenstein, Baruch College, City University of New York; John Maier, State University of New York, Brockport; Edmund Miller, Long Island University; Donn F. Morgan, Church Divinity School of the Pacific; Barry N. Olshen, Glendon College, York University; C. Haldor Parker, Queen's University, Kingston; Elizabeth Popham, Memorial University of Newfoundland; Arthur Quinn, University of California, Berkeley; Gila Ramras-Rauch, Hebrew College; Gary A. Rendsburg, Canisius College; Vernon K. Robbins, Emory University; Stanley N. Rosenbaum, Dickinson College; Donna Runnalls, McGill University; Leland Ryken, Wheaton College; John Sandys-Wunsch, Thorneloe College; Donald G. Schley, Jr., Emory University; Herbert N. Schneidau, University of Arizona; Ray Shankman, Vanier College, Montreal; Robert E. Simmons, Glendon College, York University; Theodore L. Steinberg, State University of New York, Fredonia; Johanna H. Stuckey, York University, Toronto; Sol Tanenzapf, York University; Leonard Thompson, Lawrence University; Mordechai Wasserman, York University; William Whallon, Michigan State University; Jan Wojcik, Clarkson University; Tadanori Yamashita, Mount Holyoke College.

WORKS CITED

English Versions and Translations

The Jerusalem Bible (JB). 1966.
The King James Version (KJV), or "Authorized" Version (AV). 1611.
The Living Bible (LB). 1967, 1971.
The New American Bible (NAB). 1970.
The New American Standard Bible (NASB). 1963, 1971.
The New English Bible (NEB). 1961, 1970.
The New International Version (NIV). 1973, 1978.
The New Jewish Version (NJV), or the New Jewish Publication Society Version (New JPS Version). 1962, 1978, 1982.
The New King James Version (NKJV). 1979, 1980, 1982.
The Revised Standard Version (RSV). 1946, 1952, 1957, 1965, 1966, 1977.
Today's English Version (TEV), or "The Good News Bible." 1966, 1976.

Special English Editions

Fox, Everett, ed. and trans. *In the Beginning: A New English Rendition of the Book of Genesis*. New York: Schocken, 1983.
———, ed. and trans. *Now These Are the Names: A New English Rendition of the Book of Exodus*. New York: Schocken, 1986.
Green, Jay P., Sr., ed. and trans. *The Interlinear Bible: Hebrew/English*. 3 vols. Grand Rapids: Baker, 1980.
Kaplan, Aryeh, ed. and trans. *The Living Torah: The Five Books of Moses*. New York: Maznaim, 1981.
Mack, Maynard, gen. ed. *The Norton Anthology of World Masterpieces*. Vol. 1. 5th ed. New York: Norton, 1985.
The New Chain-Reference Bible. 4th ed. Indianapolis: Kirkbride Bible, 1964.
The New English Bible with the Apocrypha: Oxford Study Edition. New York: Oxford UP, 1976.
The New Oxford Annotated Bible with the Aprocrypha: Revised Standard Version. New York: Oxford UP, 1977.
The New Scofield Reference Bible: King James Version Text. New York: Oxford UP, 1967.
The Ryrie Study Bible: New American Standard Translation. Chicago: Moody, 1978.

Scholarly, Critical, and Miscellaneous Works

Abrams, M. H. "Apocalypse: Theme and Variations." *The Apocalypse in English Renaissance Thought and Literature: Patterns, Antecedents, and Repercussions*. Ed. Joseph Anthony Wittreich and C. A. Patrides. Manchester: Manchester UP, 1984. 342–68.

Ackerman, James S. "The Literary Context of the Moses Birth Story." *Literary Interpretations of Biblical Narratives.* Vol. 1. Ed. Kenneth R. R. Gros Louis, James S. Ackerman, and Thayer S. Warshaw. Nashville: Abingdon, 1974. 74–119.

Ackerman, James S., Alan Wilkin Jenks, Edward B. Jenkinson, and Jan Blough. *Teaching the Old Testament in English Classes.* Bloomington: Indiana UP, 1973.

Ackroyd, Peter R., ed. *Bible Bibliography 1967–1973, Old Testament.* Oxford: Blackwell, 1974.

Adar, Zvi. *The Biblical Narrative.* Trans. Misha Louvish. Jerusalem: Dept. of Education and Culture, World Zionist Org., 1959.

———. *Humanistic Values in the Bible.* Trans. Mrs. Victor Tcherikover. New York: Reconstructionist, 1967.

Aharoni, Yohanan, and Michael Avi-Yonah, eds. *The Macmillan Bible Atlas.* New York: Macmillan, 1968.

Albright, William F. *Archaeology and the Religion of Israel.* 2nd ed. Baltimore: Johns Hopkins UP, 1946. New York: Doubleday, 1969.

———. *The Biblical Period from Abraham to Ezra.* 1950. New York: Harper, 1963.

———. *From the Stone Age to Christianity: Monotheism and the Historical Process.* Baltimore: Johns Hopkins UP, 1940. Rev. ed. New York: Anchor-Doubleday, 1957.

Alonso Schökel, Luis. *The Inspired Word: Scripture in the Light of Language and Literature.* Trans. Francis Martin. New York: Herder, 1965.

Alter, Robert. *The Art of Biblical Narrative.* New York: Basic, 1981.

———. *The Art of Biblical Poetry.* New York: Basic, 1985.

Alter, Robert, and Frank Kermode. *The Literary Guide to the Bible.* Cambridge: Harvard UP, 1987.

Andersen, Francis I., and David Noel Freedman. *Hosea: A New Translation with Introduction and Commentary.* Anchor Bible. Garden City: Doubleday, 1980.

Anderson, Bernhard W. *Understanding the Old Testament.* 4th ed. Englewood Cliffs: Prentice, 1986.

Anderson, G. W., ed. *A Decade of Bible Bibliography.* Oxford: Blackwell, 1967.

———, ed. *Tradition and Interpretation: Essays by Members of the Society for Old Testament Study.* Oxford: Clarendon, 1979.

Andriolo, Karin R. "A Structural Analysis of Genealogy and Worldview in the Old Testament." *American Anthropologist* 75 (1973): 1657–69.

apRoberts, Ruth. "Old Testament Poetry: The Translatable Structure." *PMLA* 92 (1977): 987–1003.

Asimov, Isaac. *The Old Testament.* New York: Equinox-Avon, 1968. Vol. 1 of *Asimov's Guide to the Bible.* 2 vols. 1968–69.

Auerbach, Erich. "Figura." *Scenes from the Drama of European Literature.* Trans. Ralph Manheim. New York: Meridian, 1959. 11–76.

———. *Mimesis: The Representation of Reality in Western Literature.* Trans. Willard Trask. Princeton: Princeton UP; Garden City: Anchor-Doubleday, 1953.

Bailey, Lloyd R., ed. *The Word of God: A Guide to English Versions of the Bible.* Atlanta: Knox, 1982.

Baird, J. Arthur, and David Noel Freedman, eds. *The Computer Bible.* Multivol. work. In progress.

Bakan, David. *The Duality of Human Existence: An Essay on Psychology and Religion.* Chicago: Rand, 1966.

Baker, Dom Aelred. "Visual Imagination and the Bible." *Downside Review* 84 (1966): 349–60.

Bal, Mieke. *Death and Dissymmetry: The Politics of Coherence in the Book of Judges.* Chicago: U of Chicago P, 1988.

———. *Lethal Love: Feminist Literary Readings of Biblical Love Stories.* Bloomington: Indiana UP, 1987.

———. *Narratology: Introduction to the Theory of Narrative.* Toronto: U of Toronto P, 1985.

Barthes, Roland. *The Pleasure of the Text.* Trans. Richard Miller. New York: Hill, 1975.

Barthes, Roland, and F. Bovon, F.-J. Leenhardt, R. Martin-Achard, and J. Starobinski. *Structural Analysis and Biblical Exegesis: Interpretational Essays.* Trans. Alfred M. Johnson, Jr. Pittsburgh: Pickwick, 1974.

Becker, John E. "The Law, the Prophets, and Wisdom: On the Functions of Literature." *College English* 37 (1975): 254–64.

Berlin, Adele. *The Dynamics of Biblical Parallelism.* Bloomington: Indiana UP, 1985.

———. *Poetics and Interpretation of Biblical Narrative.* Sheffield: Almond, 1983.

Beyerlin, Walter, et al., eds. *Near Eastern Religious Texts Relating to the Old Testament.* Trans. John Bowden. London: SCM; Philadelphia: Westminster, 1978.

Bickerman, Elias J. *Four Strange Books of the Bible: Jonah, Daniel, Koheleth, Esther.* New York: Schocken, 1967.

Biggs, Robert. *Sa. Zi. Ga.: Ancient Mesopotamian Potency Incantations.* Texts from Cuneiform Sources. Vol. 2. Locust Valley: Augustin, 1967.

Black, Matthew, and H. H. Rowley, eds. *Peake's Commentary on the Bible.* 1919. Rev. ed. London: Nelson, 1962.

Blackman, Philip, trans. and ed. *The Mishnah.* 7 vols. New York: Judaica, 1964.

Blenkinsopp, Joseph. *A History of Prophecy in Israel: From the Settlement in the Land to the Hellenistic Period.* Philadelphia: Westminster, 1983.

Borges, Jorge Luis. "Pierre Menard, Author of *Don Quixote." Ficciones.* New York: Grove, 1962. 45–55.

Botterweck, G. J., and Helmer Ringgren, eds. *The Theological Dictionary of the Old Testament.* Trans. J. T. Willis et al. 5 vols. Grand Rapids: Eerdmans; London: SCM, 1977–81.

Brams, Steven J. *Biblical Games: A Strategic Analysis of Stories in the Old Testament.* Cambridge: MIT, 1980.

Bromiley, Geoffrey W., et al., eds. *The International Standard Bible Encyclopedia.* Rev. ed. 4 vols. Grand Rapids: Eerdmans, 1979–88.

Brown, Francis, S. R. Driver, and Charles Briggs. *A Hebrew and English Lexicon of the Old Testament, with an Appendix Containing the Biblical Aramaic. Based on the Lexicon of William Gesenius, as Translated by Edward Robinson.* 1906. Oxford: Clarendon, 1957.

Brown, Raymond E., Joseph A. Fitzmyer, and Roland E. Murphy, eds. *Jerome Biblical Commentary.* Englewood Cliffs: Prentice, 1968.

Bright, John. *A History of Israel.* 3rd ed. Philadelphia: Westminster, 1981.

Burke, Kenneth. "The First Three Chapters of Genesis." *The Rhetoric of Religion: Studies in Logology.* Boston: Beacon, 1961. 172–272.

Buss, Martin J., ed. *Encounter with the Text: Form and History in the Hebrew Bible.* Semeia supps. 8. Philadelphia: Fortress; Missoula: Scholars, 1979.

Buttrick, George Arthur, ed. *The Interpreter's Bible.* 12 vols. New York: Abingdon, 1951–57.

———. *The Interpreter's Dictionary of the Bible: An Illustrated Encyclopedia.* 4 vols. New York: Abingdon, 1962.

Cahill, P. Joseph. "Literary Criticism, Religious Literature, and Theology." *Studies in Religion* 12 (1983): 51–62.

The Cambridge History of the Bible. Vol. 1. *From the Beginnings to Jerome.* Ed. P. R. Ackroyd and C. F. Evans. Vol. 2. *The West from the Fathers to the Reformation.* Ed. G. W. H. Lampe. Vol. 3. *The West from the Reformation to the Present Day.* Ed. S. L. Greenslade. Cambridge: Cambridge UP, 1963–70.

Camp, Claudia V. "The Wise Women of 2 Samuel: A Role Model for Women in Early Israel?" *Catholic Biblical Quarterly* 43 (1981): 14–29.

Campbell, Edward F., Jr. *Ruth: A New Translation with Introduction, Notes, and Commentary.* Anchor Bible. Garden City: Doubleday, 1975.

Campbell, Joseph. *The Hero with a Thousand Faces.* 2nd ed. Princeton: Princeton UP, 1968.

———. *The Masks of God.* 4 vols. New York: Viking, 1959–68.

Campbell, Richard H., and Michael R. Pitts. *The Bible on Film: A Checklist, 1897–1980.* Metuchen: Scarecrow, 1981.

Carroll, Michael P. "Leach, Genesis, and Structural Analysis: A Critical Evaluation." *American Ethnologist* 4 (1977): 663–77.

Cassuto, Umberto. *A Commentary on the Book of Genesis.* Vol. 1. *From Adam to Noah.* Vol. 2. *From Noah to Abraham.* Trans. Israel Abrahams. Jerusalem: Magnes, 1961, 1964.

———. *The Documentary Hypothesis and the Composition of the Pentateuch: Eight Lectures.* Jerusalem: Magnes, 1961.

Chase, Mary Ellen. *The Bible and the Common Reader.* Rev. ed. New York: Macmillan, 1952.

———. *Life and Language in the Old Testament.* New York: Norton, 1955.

Chasseguet-Smirgel, J. "Perversion and the Universal Law." *International Review of Psycho-Analysis* 10 (1983): 293–301.

Childs, Brevard S. *Exodus: A Commentary.* London: SCM, 1974.

———. *Introduction to the Old Testament as Scripture.* Philadelphia: Fortress, 1979.

———. *Myth and Reality in the Old Testament.* London: SCM, 1960.

———. *Old Testament Books for Pastor and Teacher.* Philadelphia: Westminster, 1977.

Clements, Ronald E. *A Century of Old Testament Study.* Guildford: Lutterworth, 1976.

Clifford, Richard J. *The Cosmic Mountain in Canaan and the Old Testament.* Cambridge: Harvard UP, 1972.

Clines, David J. A., David M. Gunn, and Alan J. Hauser, eds. *Art and Meaning: Rhetoric in Biblical Literature. Journal for the Study of the Old Testament* supp. ser. 19. Sheffield: JSOT, 1982.

Cohen, A., ed. *Joshua. Judges. Hebrew Text and English Translation, with Introduction and Commentary.* 1950. London: Soncino, 1980.

———, ed. *Soncino Books of the Bible.* 14 vols. New York: Soncino, 1946–52.

Cohn, Robert L. "Narrative Structure and Canonical Perspective in Genesis." *Journal for the Study of the Old Testament* 25 (1983): 3–16.

———. *The Shape of Sacred Space: Four Biblical Studies.* Chico: Scholars, 1981.

Conroy, Charles. *Absalom Absalom! Narrative and Language in 2 Sam. 13–20.* Rome: Biblical Inst., 1978.

Cosby, Bill. "Noah." *Bill Cosby Is a Very Funny Fellow, Right?* Warner Bros., WS-1518, n.d.

Crenshaw, James L. *A Whirlpool of Torment: Israelite Traditions of God as an Oppressive Presence.* Philadelphia: Fortress, 1984.

Crim, Keith, ed. Supp. vol. Buttrick, *The Interpreter's Dictionary of the Bible.*

Cross, Frank Moore. *Canaanite Myth and Hebrew Epic: Essays in the History of the Religion of Israel*. Cambridge: Harvard UP, 1973.

Crossan, John Dominic, ed. *Paul Ricoeur on Biblical Hermeneutics*. Spec. issue of *Semeia* 4 (1975).

Cruden, Alexander. *Cruden's Complete Concordance to the Bible*. 1737. Ed. C. H. Irwin, A. D. Adams, and S. A. Waters. Rev. ed. London: Lutterworth, 1954.

Culley, Robert C., ed. *Classical Hebrew Narrative*. Spec. issue of *Semeia* 3 (1975).

———, ed. *Oral Tradition and Old Testament Studies*. Spec. issue of *Semeia* 5 (1976).

———. "Structural Analysis: Is It Done with Mirrors?" *Interpretation* 28 (1974): 165–81.

———. *Studies in the Structure of Hebrew Narrative*. Semeia supps. 3. Philadelphia: Fortress; Missoula: Scholars, 1976.

Dahood, Mitchell J. "Poetry, Hebrew." Crim.

Daly, Mary. *Beyond God the Father: Toward a Philosophy of Women's Liberation*. Boston: Beacon, 1973.

Damrosch, David. *The Narrative Covenant*. New York: Harper, 1987.

Danby, Herbert, trans. and ed. *The Mishnah*. London: Oxford UP, 1933.

Davidson, Robert. *The Courage to Doubt*. London: SCM, 1983.

Davis, Elizabeth Gould. *The First Sex*. New York: Putnam's, 1971.

de Vaux, Roland. *Ancient Israel*. Trans. John McHugh. 1961. Vol. 1. *Social Institutions*. Vol. 2. *Religious Institutions*. New York: McGraw, 1965.

Denton, Robert C., ed. *The Idea of History in the Ancient Near East*. New Haven: Yale UP, 1955.

Driver, G. R. *Canaanite Myths and Legends*. Edinburgh: Clark, 1956.

Driver, G. R., and John C. Miles, eds. and trans. *The Assyrian Laws*. Oxford: Clarendon, 1935.

———, eds. and trans. *The Babylonian Laws*. 2 vols. Oxford: Clarendon, 1952–55.

Dundes, Alan. *Analytic Essays in Folklore*. The Hague: Mouton, 1975.

Eban, Abba, narrator and host. *Heritage: Civilization and the Jews*. 9-pt. documentary. WNET, New York, 1984.

Eichrodt, Walther. *Theology of the Old Testament*. Trans. J. A. Baker. 2 vols. Philadelphia: Westminster, 1961, 1967.

Eissfeldt, Otto. *The Old Testament: An Introduction . . . .: The History of the Formation of the Old Testament*. Trans. Peter R. Ackroyd. Oxford: Blackwell; New York: Harper, 1965.

Eliade, Mircea. *The Myth of the Eternal Return: Or, Cosmos and History*. 1949. Trans. Willard R. Trask. Princeton: Princeton UP, 1954. Rpt. as *Cosmos and History: The Myth of the Eternal Return*. New York: Harper, 1969.

———. *Patterns in Comparative Religion*. Trans. Rosemary Sheed. 1958. New York: Meridian-World, 1963.

———. *The Sacred and the Profane: The Nature of Religion*. 1957. Trans. Willard R. Trask. New York: Harcourt, 1959.

Elley, Derek. *The Epic Film: Myth and History*. London: Routledge, 1984.

Elliger, K., and W. Rudolph, eds. *Biblia Hebraica Stuttgartensia*. Stuttgart: Deutsche Bibelstiftung, 1977.

Ellison, John W. *Nelson's Complete Concordance of the Revised Standard Version Bible*. New York: Nelson, 1957.

The Encyclopaedia Judaica. 16 vols. New York: Macmillan; Jerusalem: Keter, 1971–72.

Epstein, I., ed. *The Babylonian Talmud*. 18 vols. London: Soncino, 1961.

Evans, Carl D., William W. Hallo, and John B. White, eds. *Scripture in Context: Essays on the Comparative Method*. Pittsburgh: Pickwick, 1980.

Falk, Marcia. *Love Lyrics from the Bible: A Translation and Literary Study of the Song of Songs*. Sheffield: Almond, 1982.

Fisch, H. "The Analogy of Nature: A Note on the Structure of Old Testament Imagery." *Journal of Theological Studies* 6 (1955): 161–73.

Fishbane, Michael A. "The Sacred Center: The Symbolic Structure of the Bible." *Texts and Responses: Studies Presented to Nahum N. Glatzer on the Occasion of His Seventieth Birthday by His Students*. Ed. Michael A. Fishbane and Paul R. Flohr. Leiden: Brill, 1975. 6–27.

———. "Sin and Judgement in the Prophecies of Ezekiel." *Interpretation* 38 (1984): 131–50.

———. *Text and Texture: Close Readings of Selected Biblical Texts*. New York: Schocken, 1979.

Fokkelman, J. P. *Narrative Art and Poetry in the Books of Samuel*. Vol. 1. *King David*. Assen: Van Gorcum, 1981– .

———. *Narrative Art in Genesis: Specimens of Stylistic and Structural Analysis*. Assen: Van Gorcum, 1975.

Frankfort, Henri. *Kingship and the Gods: A Study of Ancient Near Eastern Religion as the Integration of Society and Nature*. Chicago: U of Chicago P, 1948.

Frankfort, Henri, H. A. Frankfort, Thorkild Jacobsen, and John A. Wilson. *The Intellectual Adventure of Ancient Man: An Essay on Speculative Thought in the Ancient Near East*. Chicago: U of Chicago P, 1946. Rpt. as *Before Philosophy*. New York: Penguin, 1949.

Frazer, James G. *Folklore in the Old Testament*. 3 vols. London: Macmillan, 1918.

Freedman, David Noel. *Pottery, Poetry, and Prophecy: Studies in Early Hebrew Poetry*. Winona Lake: Eisenbrauns, 1980.

Freedman, H., and Maurice Simon, eds. *The Midrash Rabbah*. 10 vols. New York: Soncino, 1939.

Freud, Sigmund. "Beyond the Pleasure Principle." 1920. *Standard Edition* 18: 3–64.

———. *The Future of an Illusion*. 1927. *Standard Edition* 21: 3–56.

———. *Moses and Monotheism*. 1930. Vol. 23 of *Standard Edition*.

———. "Remembering, Repeating and Working-Through." 1914. *Standard Edition* 12: 145–56.

———. *The Standard Edition of the Complete Psychological Works of Sigmund Freud*. Ed. James Strachey. 24 vols. London: Hogarth, 1953–74.

———. "The Taboo of Virginity." *Standard Edition* 11:191–208.

Frye, Northrop. *Anatomy of Criticism: Four Essays*. Princeton: Princeton UP, 1957.

———. *The Bible and Literature*. 30-pt. videocassette ser. 30 min. ea. Media Center, U of Toronto, 1981.

———. *The Great Code: The Bible and Literature*. New York: Harcourt, 1982.

———. "History and Myth in the Bible." *The Literature of Fact: Selected Papers from the English Institute*. Ed. Angus Fletcher. New York: Columbia UP, 1976. 1–19.

Frymer-Kensky, Tikva. "The Atrahasis Epic and Its Significance for Our Understanding of Genesis 1–9." *Biblical Archaeologist* 40 (1977): 147–55.

Fuchs, Esther. *Sexual Politics in the Biblical Narrative*. Bloomington: Indiana UP, forthcoming.

Fuentes, Carlos. "The Novel Always Says: The World Is Unfinished." *New York Times Book Review* 16 Feb. 1986: 25.

Gardner, John, and John Maier, trans. Gilgamesh, *Translated from the Sinlegi-unninni Version.* New York: Knopf, 1984.

Gaster, Theodor H. *Myth, Legend, and Custom in the Old Testament: A Comparative Study with Chapters from Sir James G. Frazer's* Folklore in the Old Testament. 2 vols. New York: Harper, 1969. Gloucester: Smith, 1981.

——, ed. *The New* Golden Bough: *A New Abridgment of the Classic Work by Sir James George Frazer.* 1959. New York: Mentor-NAL, 1964.

Geller, Stephen. *Parallelism in Early Biblical Poetry.* Missoula: Scholars, 1979.

——. "The Struggle at the Jabbok: The Uses of Enigma in a Biblical Narrative." *Journal of the Ancient Near Eastern Society* 14 (1982): 37–60.

Gill, Merton M. "The Analysis of the Transference." *Journal of the American Psychoanalytic Association* 27, supp. (1979): 263–87.

Ginsberg, H. L., et al. *The Five Megilloth and Jonah: A New Translation.* 2nd ed. Philadelphia: JPS, 1974.

Ginzberg, Louis. *Legends of the Jews.* 7 vols. Philadelphia: JPS, 1909–38.

Gitay, Yehoshua. *Prophecy and Persuasion: A Study of Isaiah 40–48.* Bonn: Linguistica Biblica, 1981.

Gizelis, Gregory. "Historical Event into Song." *Folklore* 83 (1972): 302–20.

Good, Edwin M. *Irony in the Old Testament.* Philadelphia: Westminster, 1965. 2nd ed. Sheffield: Almond, 1981.

Gordon, Cyrus H. "Abraham and the Merchants of Ura." *Journal of Near Eastern Studies* 17 (1958): 28–31.

Gottcent, John H. *The Bible as Literature: A Selective Bibliography.* Boston: Hall, 1979.

Gottwald, Norman K., ed. *The Bible and Liberation: Political and Social Hermeneutics.* Rev. ed. Maryknoll: Orbis, 1983.

——. *The Hebrew Bible: A Socio-Literary Introduction.* Philadelphia: Fortress, 1985.

——. "Poetry, Hebrew." Buttrick, *Interpreter's Dictionary.*

——. *The Tribes of Yahweh: A Sociology of the Religion of Liberated Israel, 1250–1050 B.C.E.* Maryknoll: Orbis, 1979. Corrected 2nd printing, 1981.

Grant, Robert M., with David Tracy. *A Short History of the Interpretation of the Bible.* 2nd ed. Rev. and enlarged. Philadelphia: Fortress, 1984.

Gray, George B. *The Forms of Hebrew Poetry: Considered with Special Reference to the Criticism and Interpretation of the Old Testament.* 1915. Rpt. with prolegomenon by David Noel Freedman. New York: Ktav, 1972.

Greenberg, Moshe. "The Design and Themes of Ezekiel's Program of Restoration." *Interpretation* 38 (1984): 181–208.

——. *Ezekiel 1–20: A New Translation with Introduction and Commentary.* Anchor Bible. Garden City: Doubleday, 1983.

——. "Some Postulates of Biblical Criminal Law." *Yehezkel Kaufmann Jubilee Volume.* Ed. M. Haran. Jerusalem: Magnes, 1960. Rpt. as *The Jewish Expression.* Ed. Judah Goldin. New Haven: Yale UP, 1976. 18–37.

——. *Understanding Exodus.* New York: Behrman, 1969.

Greenstein, Edward L. "How Does Parallelism Mean?" *A Sense of Text. Jewish Quarterly Review* supp. Winona Lake: Eisenbrauns, 1982. 41–70.

——. "The Riddle of Samson." *Prooftexts* 1 (1981): 237–60.

——. "Theories of Modern Bible Translation." *Prooftexts* 3 (1983): 9–39.

Greenstein, Edward L., and Alex Preminger, eds. *The Hebrew Bible in Literary Criticism.* New York: Ungar, 1986.

Gros Louis, Kenneth R. R., James S. Ackerman, and Thayer S. Warshaw, eds. *Literary nterpretations of Biblical Narratives.* 2 vols. Nashville: Abingdon, 1974, 1982.

Grünbaum, Adolf. *The Foundations of Psychoanalysis: A Philosophical Critique.* Berkeley: U of California P, 1984.

Gunkel, Hermann. *The Legends of Genesis: The Biblical Saga and History.* Trans. W. H. Carruth. New York: Schocken, 1984.

Gunn, D. M. *The Fate of King Saul: An Interpretation of a Biblical Story. Journal for the Study of the Old Testament* supp. ser. 14. Sheffield: JSOT, 1980.

——. *The Story of King David: Genre and Interpretation. Journal for the Study of the Old Testament* supp. ser. 6. Sheffield: JSOT, 1978.

Habel, Norman C. *Literary Criticism of the Old Testament.* Philadelphia: Fortress, 1971.

Hahn, Herbert F. *The Old Testament in Modern Research.* 3rd ed. Rev. bibliographical essay by Horace D. Hummel. Philadelphia: Fortress, 1970.

Hallo, William W., J. C. Meyer, and L. G. Perdue, eds. *Scripture in Context II: More Essays on the Comparative Method.* Winona Lake: Eisenbrauns, 1983.

Handelman, Susan A. *The Slayers of Moses: The Emergence of Rabbinic Interpretation in Modern Literary Theory.* Albany: State U of New York P, 1982.

Harrelson, Walter. *Interpreting the Old Testament.* New York: Holt, 1964.

Harrington, Daniel J. *Interpreting the Old Testament: A Practical Guide.* Wilmington: Glazier, 1981.

Hartman, Louis F., and Alexander A. Di Lella. *The Book of Daniel: A New Translation with Notes and Commentary.* Anchor Bible. Garden City: Doubleday, 1978.

Havlice, Patricia Pate. *World Painting Index.* Vol. 1. *Bibliography, Paintings by Unknown Artists, Painters and Their Works.* Vol. 2. *Titles of Works and Their Painters.* Metuchen: Scarecrow, 1977.

——. *World Painting Index: First Supplement, 1973–1980.* 2 vols. Metuchen: Scarecrow, 1982.

Hayes, John H. *An Introduction to Old Testament Study.* Nashville: Abingdon, 1979.

——, ed. *Old Testament Form Criticism.* San Antonio: Trinity UP, 1974.

Hayes, John H., and Carl R. Holladay. *Biblical Exegesis: A Beginner's Handbook.* Atlanta: Knox, 1982.

Hayes, John H., and J. Maxwell Miller, eds. *Israelite and Judaean History.* Philadelphia: Westminster, 1977.

Heidel, Alexander. *The Babylonian Genesis: The Story of Creation.* 2nd ed. Chicago: U of Chicago P, 1951.

——. *The Gilgamesh Epic and Old Testament Parallels.* 2nd ed. Chicago: U of Chicago P, 1949.

Henn, T. R. *The Bible as Literature.* New York: Oxford UP, 1970.

Herrmann, Siegfried. *A History of Israel in Old Testament Times.* Trans. John Bowden. London: SCM; Philadelphia: Fortress, 1975. 2nd ed. Philadelphia: Fortress, 1981.

Hertz, Joseph, ed. *The Pentateuch and Haftorahs.* 2nd ed. New York: Soncino, 1960.

Heschel, Abraham Joshua. *The Prophets.* 1962. 2 vols. New York: Harper, 1969.

Hoberman, Barry. "Translating the Bible." *Atlantic Monthly* Feb. 1985: 43–58.

Hoffman, Daniel G. "Historic Truth and Ballad Truth: Two Versions of the Capture of New Orleans." *Journal of American Folklore* 65 (1952): 295–303.

Holtz, Barry W., ed. *Back to the Sources: Reading the Classic Jewish Texts.* New York: Summit, 1984.

Hooke, Sidney H. *Middle Eastern Mythology.* Baltimore: Penguin, 1963.

——, ed. *Myth and Ritual: Essays on the Myth and Ritual of the Hebrews in Relation to the Culture Pattern of the Ancient East*. London: Oxford, 1933.

——, ed. *Myth, Ritual, and Kingship: Essays on the Theory and Practice of Kingship in the Ancient Near East and in Israel*. Oxford: Clarendon, 1958.

Hornsby, Samuel. "Style in the Bible: A Bibliography." *Style* 7 (1973): 349–74.

Hrushovski, Benjamin. "Prosody, Hebrew." *Encyclopaedia Judaica*.

Hughes, John J. *Bits, Bytes, and Biblical Studies: A Resource Guide for the Use of Computers in Biblical and Classical Studies*. Grand Rapids: Zondervan, 1987.

Jacobson, Richard. "The Structuralists and the Bible." *Interpretation* 28 (1974): 146–64.

Jeffrey, David L., gen. ed. *A Dictionary of the Bible and Biblical Tradition in English Literature*. In progress.

Jobling, David. *The Sense of Biblical Narrative: Three Structural Analyses in the Old Testament*. Sheffield: JSOT, 1978.

Johnson, Alfred M., Jr., ed. and trans. *Structuralism and Biblical Hermeneutics: A Collection of Essays*. Pittsburgh: Pickwick, 1979.

Kasher, Menachem M. *Encyclopedia of Biblical Interpretation: Torah Shelemah, a Millennial Anthology*. Trans. and ed. Harry Freedman. 9 vols. New York: American Biblical Encyclopedia Soc., 1953– .

Kaufmann, Yehezkel. *The Religion of Israel: From Its Beginnings to the Babylonian Exile*. Trans. and abr. Moshe Greenberg. Chicago: U of Chicago P, 1960. New York: Schocken, 1972.

Keel, Othmar. *The Symbolism of the Biblical World: Ancient Near Eastern Iconography and the Book of Psalms*. 1972. Trans. Timothy J. Hallett. New York: Seabury, 1978.

Kermode, Frank. "Freud and Interpretation." *International Review of Psycho-Analysis* 12 (1985): 3–12.

Kikawada, Isaac M., and Arthur Quinn. *Before Abraham Was: The Unity of Genesis 1–11*. Nashville: Abingdon, 1985.

Kilmer, Anne Daffkorn. "The Mesopotamian Concept of Overpopulation and Its Solution as Reflected in the Mythology." *Orientalia* 41 (1972): 160–77.

King, Martin Luther, Jr. "I Have a Dream." *In Search of Freedom*. Mercury, SR 61170, n.d.

Klein, Ralph W. *Textual Criticism of the Old Testament*. Philadelphia: Fortress, 1974.

Knight, Douglas A., and Gene M. Tucker, eds. *The Hebrew Bible and Its Modern Interpreters*. Philadelphia: Fortress; Chico: Scholars, 1985.

Koch, Klaus. *The Growth of the Biblical Tradition: The Form-Critical Method*. Trans. S. M. Cupitt. New York: Scribner's, 1969.

——. *The Prophets*. 2 vols. Philadelphia: Fortress, 1983.

Kramer, Samuel Noah. *History Begins at Sumer: Thirty-Nine Firsts in Man's Recorded History*. 1959. Rev. ed. Philadelphia: U of Pennsylvania P, 1981.

——, ed. *Mythologies of the Ancient World*. Chicago: Quadrangle; Garden City: Anchor-Doubleday, 1961.

——. *The Sumerians: Their History, Culture, and Character*. Chicago: U of Chicago P, 1963.

Krentz, Edgar. *The Historical-Critical Method*. Philadelphia: Fortress, 1975.

Kristeva, Julia. "Semiotics of Biblical Abomination." *Powers of Horror: An Essay on Abjection*. Trans. Leon S. Roudiez. New York: Columbia UP, 1982. 90–112.

Kugel, James L. *The Idea of Biblical Poetry: Parallelism and Its History*. New Haven: Yale UP, 1981.

Kuntz, J. Kenneth. *The People of Ancient Israel: An Introduction to Old Testament Literature, History, and Thought.* New York: Harper, 1974.

Kupper, Jean-Robert. *Les nomades en Mésopotamie au temps des rois de Mari.* Paris: Société d'Edition, 1957.

Lacan, Jacques. *The Four Fundamental Concepts of Psycho-Analysis.* Trans. Alan Sheridan. Ed. Jacques-Alain Miller. New York: Norton, 1981.

Lakoff, George, and Mark Johnson. *Metaphors We Live By.* Chicago: U of Chicago P, 1980.

Lambert, Wilfred G. *Babylonian Wisdom Literature.* Oxford: Oxford UP, 1960.

——. "A New Look at the Babylonian Background of Genesis." *Journal of Theological Studies* 16 (1965): 287–300.

Lambert, Wilfred G., and A. R. Millard. *Atra-hasis: The Babylonian Story of the Flood.* Oxford: Clarendon, 1969.

Lance, H. Darrell. *The Old Testament and the Archaeologist.* Philadelphia: Fortress, 1981.

Landy, Francis. *Paradoxes of Paradise: Identity and Difference in the Song of Songs.* Sheffield: Almond, 1983.

Langevin, Paul-Emile. *Bibliographie Biblique/Biblical Bibliography 1930–1983.* 3 vols. Québec: PU Laval, 1972–85.

Lauterbach, Jacob, trans. *Mekilta de-Rabbi Ishmael.* 3 vols. Philadelphia: JPS, 1976.

Layman, Charles M., ed. *The Interpreter's One-Volume Commentary on the Bible.* Nashville: Abingdon, 1971.

Leach, Edmund. *Genesis as Myth and Other Essays.* London: Cape, 1969.

Leach, Edmund, and D. Alan Aycock. *Structuralist Interpretations of Biblical Myth.* Cambridge: Cambridge UP, 1983.

Lemke, Werner E. "Life in the Present and Hope for the Future." *Interpretation* 38 (1984): 165–80.

Levenson, Jon D. *Sinai and Zion: An Entry into the Jewish Bible.* Minneapolis: Winston, 1985.

Lévi-Strauss, Claude. *The Elementary Structures of Kinship.* Rev. ed. Trans. J. H. Bell and J. R. von Sturmer. Ed. R. Needham. Boston: Beacon, 1969.

——. *The Raw and the Cooked: Introduction to a Science of Mythology.* Vol. 1. Trans. John Weightman and Doreen Weightman. Chicago: U of Chicago P, 1969.

——. *Structural Anthropology.* Vol. 1. Trans. Claire Jacobson and Brooke G. Schoepf. Vol. 2. Trans. Monique Layton. New York: Basic, 1963, 1976.

——. "The Structural Study of Myth." *Journal of American Folklore* 68 (1955): 428–44.

Lewis, Jack P. *The English Bible from KJV to NIV: A History and Evaluation.* Grand Rapids: Baker, 1982.

Licht, Jacob. *Storytelling in the Bible.* Jerusalem: Magnes, 1978.

Lichtheim, Miriam. *Ancient Egyptian Literature: A Book of Readings.* Vol. 2. Berkeley: U of California P, 1976.

Lindberg, Bo. *William Blake's Illustrations to the Book of Job.* Abo, Finland: Abo Akademi, 1973.

Lindblom, Johannes. *Prophecy in Ancient Israel.* Oxford: Blackwell, 1962.

Littledale, Richard Frederick. *A Commentary on the Song of Songs from Ancient and Mediaeval Sources.* London: Masters, 1869.

Long, Burke O., ed. *Images of Man and God: Old Testament Short Stories in Literary Focus.* Sheffield: Almond, 1981.

Lowth, Robert. *De sacra poesi Hebraeorum.* 1754. New York: Garland, 1971.

Lyotard, Jean François. "Jewish Oedipus." *Genre* 10 (1977): 395–411.

Maccoby, Hyam. *The Sacred Executioner: Human Sacrifice and the Legacy of Guilt.* New York: Thames, 1982.

Maier, John R. "The 'Truth' of a Most Ancient Work: Interpreting a Poem Addressed to a Holy Place." *Centrum* 2 (1982): 27–44.

Maier, John R., and Vincent L. Tollers, eds. *The Bible in Its Literary Milieu: Contemporary Essays.* Grand Rapids: Eerdmans, 1979.

Maimonides, Moses. *The Guide of the Perplexed.* Vol. 1. Trans. Shlomo Pines. Chicago: U of Chicago P, 1963.

Magonet, Jonathan. *Form and Meaning: Studies in Literary Techniques in the Book of Jonah.* Sheffield: Almond, 1983.

Mandelkern, Salomon. *Konkordantsyah la-Tanakh* (*Veteris Testamenti Concordantiae Hebraicae atque Chaldaicae*). 1896. Supps. by Moshe H. Goshen-Gottstein. 9th ed. Jerusalem: Schocken, 1971.

Marrow, Stanley B. *Basic Tools of Biblical Exegesis: A Student's Manual.* 2nd ed. Rome: Biblical Inst., 1978.

Marshall, Robert C. "Heroes and Hebrews: The Priest in the Promised Land." *American Ethnologist* 6 (1979): 772–90.

Mason, Herbert, trans. Gilgamesh: *A Verse Narrative.* 1970. New York: Mentor-NAL, 1972.

Mauser, Ulrich. *Christ in the Wilderness: The Wilderness Theme in the Second Gospel and Its Basis in the Biblical Tradition.* Naperville: Allenson, 1963.

May, Herbert G., ed. *Oxford Bible Atlas.* Rev. John Day. 3rd ed. London: Oxford UP, 1985.

Mays, James L., et al., eds. *Harper's Bible Commentary.* San Francisco: Harper, 1988.

McClintock, Marsha Hamilton. *The Middle East and North Africa on Film: An Annotated Filmography.* New York: Garland, 1982.

McFague, Sallie. *Metaphorical Theology: Models of God in Religious Language.* Philadelphia: Fortress, 1982.

McKenzie, John L. *Dictionary of the Bible.* Milwaukee: Bruce, 1965.

McKnight, Edgar V. *The Bible and the Reader: An Introduction to Literary Criticism.* Philadelphia: Fortress, 1985.

———. *What Is Form Criticism?* Philadelphia: Fortress, 1969.

Meletinsky, Eleasar M. "Structural-Typological Study of the Folktale." *Genre* 4 (1971): 249–79.

Mendenhall, George E. *The Tenth Generation: The Origins of the Biblical Tradition.* Baltimore: Johns Hopkins UP, 1973.

Miller, J. Maxwell. *The Old Testament and the Historian.* Philadelphia: Fortress, 1976.

Miller, J. Maxwell, and John H. Hayes. *A History of Ancient Israel and Judah.* Philadelphia: Westminster, 1986.

Millett, Kate. *Sexual Politics.* New York: Avon, 1971.

Miscall, Peter D. *1 Samuel: A Literary Reading.* Bloomington: Indiana UP, 1986.

———. *The Workings of Old Testament Narrative.* Philadelphia: Fortress; Chico: Scholars, 1983.

Modern Language Bible. Grand Rapids: Zondervan, 1969.

Monro, Isabel Stevenson, and Kate M. Monro. *Index to Reproductions of American Paintings: A Guide to Pictures Occurring in More Than Eight Hundred Books.* New York: Wilson, 1948.

———. *Index to Reproductions of American Paintings, First Supplement: A Guide to Pictures Occurring in More Than Four Hundred Works.* New York: Wilson, 1964.

——— . *Index to Reproductions of European Paintings: A Guide to Pictures in More Than Three Hundred Books*. New York: Wilson, 1956.

Moore, George Foot. *A Critical and Exegetical Commentary on Judges*. Edinburgh: Clark; New York: Scribner's, 1895.

Morgenstern, Julian. "Additional Notes on 'Beena Marriage (Matriarchat) in Ancient Israel and Its Historical Implications.'" *Zeitschrift für die Alttestamentliche Wissenschaft* 49 (1931): 46–58.

——— . "*Beena* Marriage (Matriarchat) in Ancient Israel and Its Historical Implications." *Zeitschrift für die Alttestamentliche Wissenschaft* 47 (1929): 91–110.

Muilenburg, James. "Biblical Poetry." (s.v. "Poetry"). *Encyclopaedia Judaica*.

——— . "Form Criticism and Beyond." *Journal of Biblical Literature* 88 (1969): 1–18.

——— . "Preface to Hermeneutics." *Journal of Biblical Literature* 77 (1958): 18–26.

——— . "A Study in Hebrew Rhetoric: Repetition and Style." *Supplements to Vetus Testamentum*. Vol. 1. Leiden: Brill, 1953. 97–111.

Neusner, Jacob. *Invitation to the Talmud*. 1973. Rev. ed. New York: Harper, 1984.

——— , gen. ed. *The Talmud of the Land of Israel*. Chicago: U of Chicago P. In progress.

Newsome, Carol A. "A Maker of Metaphors: Ezekiel's Oracles against Tyre." *Interpretation* 38 (1984): 151–64.

Noth, Martin. *The History of Israel*. 2nd ed. Trans. Stanley Godman. Rev. P. R. Ackroyd. London: Black; New York: Harper, 1960.

Ohlsen, Woodrow. *Perspectives on Old Testament Literature*. New York: Harcourt, 1978.

Orlinsky, Harry M. *Ancient Israel*. 1954. 2nd ed. Westport: Greenwood, 1982.

Otto, Rudolph. *The Idea of the Holy*. 2nd ed. Trans. John W. Harvey. London: Oxford UP, 1950.

Patai, Raphael. *Sex and Family in the Bible and the Middle East*. New York: Doubleday, 1959.

Patte, Daniel. *What Is Structural Exegesis?* Philadelphia: Fortress, 1976.

Patte, Daniel, and Aline Patte. *Structural Exegesis: From Theory to Practice*. Philadelphia: Fortress, 1978.

Payne, D. F. "A Perspective on the Use of Simile in the Old Testament." *Semitics* 1 (1970): 111–25.

Pedersen, Johannes. *Israel: Its Life and Culture*. Vols. 1 and 2. Trans. Aslang Møller. London: Oxford UP, 1926. Vols. 3 and 4. Trans. Annie I. Fausbøll. London: Oxford UP, 1940.

Perrin, Norman. *What Is Redaction Criticism?* Philadelphia: Fortress, 1969.

Plaut, W. Gunther, ed. *The Torah: A Modern Commentary*. New York: Union of American Hebrew Congregations, 1981.

Poland, Lynn M. *Literary Criticism and Biblical Hermeneutics: A Critique of Formalist Approaches*. Chico: Scholars, 1985.

Polzin, Robert M. *Biblical Structuralism: Method and Subjectivity in the Study of Ancient Texts*. Semeia supps. Philadelphia: Fortress; Missoula: Scholars, 1977.

——— . "The Framework of the Book of Job." *Interpretation* 28 (1974): 182–200.

——— . *Moses and the Deuteronomist: A Literary Study of the Deuteronomic History*. New York: Seabury, 1980.

Polzin, Robert M., and Eugene Rothman, eds. *The Biblical Mosaic: Changing Perspectives*. Philadelphia: Fortress; Chico: Scholars, 1982.

Pope, Marvin, ed. and trans. *The Song of Songs*. Anchor Bible. Garden City: Doubleday, 1977.

Pritchard, James B., ed. *The Ancient Near East: An Anthology of Texts and Pictures.* Vol. 2. *The Ancient Near East: A New Anthology of Texts and Pictures.* Princeton: Princeton UP, 1958, 1975.

———, ed. *The Ancient Near East in Pictures Relating to the Old Testament.* 2nd ed. Princeton: Princeton UP, 1969.

———, ed. *Ancient Near Eastern Texts Relating to the Old Testament.* 3rd ed. Princeton: Princeton UP, 1969.

Propp, Vladimir. *Morphology of the Folktale.* 1928. Trans. Laurence Scott. Ed. Louis A. Wagner. Austin: U of Texas P, 1968.

Radday, Yehuda T. "Chiasm in Kings." *Linguistica Biblica* 31 (1974): 52–67.

———. "Chiasmus in Hebrew Biblical Narrative." Welch 50–117.

[Rashi]. *Pentateuch with Targum Onkelos, Haphtaroth and Rashi's Commentary.* Trans. and ed. M. Rosenbaum and A. M. Silbermann. 5 vols. 1929–34. Jerusalem: Silbermann Family with Routledge; New York: Feldheim, 1973.

Rast, Walter E. *Tradition History and the Old Testament.* Philadelphia: Fortress, 1972.

Reik, Theodor. *The Creation of Woman.* New York: Braziller, 1960.

———. "A Discovery in Archeological Psychoanalysis." *Mystery on the Mountain: The Drama of the Sinai Revelation.* New York: Harper, 1959.

Ricoeur, Paul. *The Conflict of Interpretations: Essays in Hermeneutics.* Ed. Don Ihde. Evanston: Northwestern UP, 1974.

———. *Essays on Biblical Interpretation.* Ed. Lewis S. Mudge. Philadelphia: Fortress, 1980.

———. *Freud and Philosophy.* New Haven: Yale UP, 1970.

———. "The Question of Proof in Freud's Psychoanalytic Writings." *Journal of the American Psychoanalytic Association* 25 (1977): 835–71.

———. *The Rule of Metaphor.* Trans. Robert Czerny et al. Toronto: U of Toronto P, 1977.

———. *The Symbolism of Evil.* Trans. Emerson Buchanan. New York: Harper, 1967.

Ringgren, Helmer. *Israelite Religion.* Trans. David E. Green. Philadelphia: Fortress, 1966.

Roberts, Helene E. *Iconographic Index to Old Testament Subjects Represented in Photographs and Slides of Paintings in the Visual Collections, Fine Arts Library, Harvard University.* New York: Garland, 1987.

Robertson, David. *The Old Testament and the Literary Critic.* Philadelphia: Fortress, 1977.

Robinson, Theodore H. *The Poetry of the Old Testament.* London: Duckworth, 1947.

Rogerson, John. *Old Testament Criticism in the Nineteenth Century: England and Germany.* London: SPCK, 1984.

Roheim, Geza. "The Garden of Eden." *Psychoanalytic Review* 27 (1940): 1–26, 177–99.

Roitman, Betty. "Sacred Language and Open Text." *Midrash and Literature.* Ed. Geoffrey Hartman and Sanford Budick. New Haven: Yale UP, 1986. 159–75.

Rollins, Hyder E., and Herschel Baker, eds. *The Renaissance in England: Non-Dramatic Prose and Verse of the Sixteenth Century.* Lexington: Heath, 1954.

Rosner, Dov. "The Simile and Its Use in the Old Testament." *Semitics* 4 (1974): 37–46.

Rowley, H. H., ed. *Eleven Years of Bible Bibliography.* Indian Hills: Falcon's Wing, 1957.

Ruether, Rosemary Radford. *Faith and Fratricide.* New York: Seabury, 1974.

———, ed. *Religion and Sexism: Images of Woman in the Jewish and Christian Traditions.* New York: Simon, 1974.

Russell, Letty M., ed. *Feminist Interpretation of the Bible.* Philadelphia: Westminster, 1985.

——, ed. *The Liberating Word: A Guide to Nonsexist Interpretation of the Bible*. Philadelphia: Westminster, 1978.

Ryken, Leland. *How to Read the Bible as Literature*. Grand Rapids: Zondervan, 1984.

——. *The Literature of the Bible*. Grand Rapids: Zondervan, 1974.

Sacks, Sheldon. *Fiction and the Shape of Belief*. Berkeley: U of California P, 1964.

Sandars, N. K., trans. *Epic of Gilgamesh*. 1960. 2nd ed. Harmondsworth: Penguin, 1972.

Sanders, James A. *Canon and Community: A Guide to Canonical Criticism*. Philadelphia: Fortress, 1984.

Sandmel, Samuel. *The Enjoyment of Scripture*. London: Oxford UP, 1972.

——. *The Hebrew Scriptures: An Introduction to Their Literature and Religious Ideas*. New York: Knopf, 1963.

——. "Parallelomania." *Journal of Biblical Literature* 81 (1962): 1–13.

Santillana, Giorgio de, and Hertha von Dechend. *Hamlet's Mill: An Essay on Myth and the Frame of Time*. Boston: Godine, 1977.

Sarna, Nahum M. *Exploring Exodus*. New York: Schocken, 1986.

——. *Understanding Genesis*. New York: Schocken, 1966.

Sasson, Jack M. *Ruth: A New Translation with a Philological Commentary and a Formalist-Folklorist Interpretation*. Baltimore: Johns Hopkins UP, 1979.

Schafer, Roy. "The Appreciative Analytic Attitude and the Construction of Multiple Histories." *Psychoanalytic and Contemporary Thought* 2 (1979): 3–24.

——. "Narration in the Psychoanalytic Dialogue." *The Analytic Attitude*. New York: Basic, 1983. 212–39.

Schlossman, Howard. "God the Father and His Sons." *American Imago* 29 (1972): 35–52.

Schneidau, Herbert N. *Sacred Discontent: The Bible and Western Tradition*. Baton Rouge: Louisiana State UP, 1976.

Scholem, Gershom G. *Jewish Gnosticism, Merkabah Mysticism, and Talmudic Tradition*. 2nd ed. New York: Jewish Theological Seminary, 1965.

——. *Major Trends in Jewish Mysticism*. Jerusalem: Schocken, 1941.

——. *On the Kabbalah and Its Symbolism*. Trans. Ralph Manheim. New York: Schocken, 1965.

Scholes, Robert. *Structuralism in Literature: An Introduction*. New Haven: Yale UP, 1974.

Scolnic, Benjamin E. "Theme and Context in Biblical Lists." Diss. Jewish Theological Seminary of America, 1987.

Shoham, Giora S. "The Isaac Syndrome." *American Imago* 33 (1976): 329–49.

Short, Robert. *A Time to Be Born—a Time to Die*. New York: Harper, 1973.

Simon, Maurice, and Harry Sperling, trans. *The Zohar*. 5 vols. London: Soncino, 1934.

Simon, Ulrich. *Story and Faith in the Biblical Narrative*. London: SPCK, 1975.

Skura, Meredith Anne. *The Literary Uses of the Psychoanalytic Process*. New Haven: Yale UP, 1981.

Slater, Philip. *The Glory of Hera: Greek Mythology and the Greek Family*. Boston: Beacon, 1968.

Smith, Lyn Wall, and Nancy Dustin Wall Moure. *Index to Reproductions of American Paintings Appearing in More Than Four Hundred Books, Mostly Published since 1960*. Metuchen: Scarecrow, 1977.

Soggin, J. A. *Introduction to the Old Testament, from Its Origins to the Closing of the Alexandrian Canon*. Trans. John Bowden. Rev. ed. Philadelphia: Westminster, 1982.

Solomon, Jon. *The Ancient World in the Cinema*. New York: Barnes; London: Yoseloff, 1978.

Soloveitchik, Joseph B. "Confrontation." *Tradition* 6.2 (1964): 5–29.

Soulen, Richard N. *Handbook of Biblical Criticism.* 2nd ed. Atlanta: Knox, 1981.

Speiser, Ephraim A. *Genesis.* Anchor Bible. Garden City: Doubleday, 1964.

Spence, Donald P. "Narrative Recursion." *Discourse in Psychoanalysis and Literature.* Ed. Shlomit Rimon-Kenan. New York: Methuen, 1987. 188–211.

———. *Narrative Truth and Historical Truth: Meaning and Interpretation in Psychoanalysis.* New York: Norton, 1982.

Spiegel, Shalom. *The Last Trial: On the Legends and Lore of the Command to Abraham to Offer Isaac as a Sacrifice, the Akedah.* 1950. Trans. and introd. Judah Goldin. New York: Behrman, 1979.

Spitz, Ellen Handler. *Art and Psyche: A Study in Psychoanalysis and Aesthetics.* New Haven: Yale UP, 1985.

Spivey, Robert A. "Structuralism and Biblical Studies: The Uninvited Guest." *Interpretation* 28 (1974): 133–45.

Steinbeck, John. *East of Eden.* New York: Penguin, 1979.

Sternberg, Meir. *The Poetics of Biblical Narrative: Ideological Literature and the Drama of Reading.* Bloomington: Indiana UP, 1985.

Strong, James. *The Exhaustive Concordance of the Bible.* 1890. New York: Abingdon, 1955.

Thomas, D. Winton, ed. *Documents from Old Testament Times.* London: Nelson, 1958. New York: Torchbooks-Harper, 1961.

Thompson, J. A. *The Book of Jeremiah.* Grand Rapids: Eerdmans, 1980.

Thompson, Leonard L. *Introducing Biblical Literature: A More Fantastic Country.* Englewood Cliffs: Prentice, 1978.

Tigay, Jeffrey H., ed. *Empirical Models for Biblical Criticism.* Philadelphia: U of Pennsylvania P, 1985.

———. *The Evolution of the* Gilgamesh Epic. Philadelphia: U of Pennsylvania P, 1982.

Tolbert, Mary Ann, ed. *The Bible and Feminist Hermeneutics. Semeia* supps. 28. Missoula: Scholars, 1983.

Tollers, Vincent, and John Maier, eds. *The Bible in Its Literary Milieu: Contemporary Essays.* Grand Rapids: Eerdmans, 1979.

Trible, Phyllis. *God and the Rhetoric of Sexuality.* Philadelphia: Fortress, 1978.

———. *Texts of Terror: Literary-Feminist Readings of Biblical Narratives.* Philadelphia: Fortress, 1984.

Tsevat, Matitiahu. "Israelite History and the Historical Books of the Old Testament." *The Meaning of the Book of Job and Other Biblical Studies.* New York: Ktav, 1980. 177–87.

Tucker, Gene M. *Form Criticism of the Old Testament.* Philadelphia: Fortress, 1971.

Via, Dan O., Jr. "A Structuralist Approach to Paul's Old Testament Hermeneutic." *Interpretation* 28 (1974): 201–20.

von Rad, Gerhard. *Old Testament Theology.* Trans. D. M. G. Stalker. Vol. 1. *The Theology of Israel's Historical Traditions.* Vol. 2. *The Theology of Israel's Prophetic Traditions.* New York: Harper, 1962, 1965.

———. *Wisdom in Israel.* Trans. James D. Martin. London: SCM, 1972.

Warshaw, Thayer S. *Handbook for Teaching the Bible in Literature Classes.* Nashville: Abingdon, 1978.

Warshaw, Thayer S., Betty Lou Miller, and James S. Ackerman, eds. *Bible-Related Curriculum Materials: A Bibliography.* New York: Abingdon, 1976.

Watson, Wilfred G. "Chiastic Patterns in Biblical Hebrew Poetry." Welch 119–68.

———. *Classical Hebrew Poetry: A Guide to Its Techniques. Journal for the Study of the Old Testament* supp. ser. 26. Sheffield: JSOT, 1984.

Welch, John W., ed. *Chiasmus in Antiquity: Structures, Analyses, Exegesis.* Hildesheim: Gerstenberg, 1981.

Wellhausen, Julius. *Prolegomena to the History of Israel.* 1878. Trans. J. Sutherland Black and Allan Menzies. 1885. Rpt. as *Prolegomena to the History of Ancient Israel.* New York: Harper, 1957.

Wellisch, Erich. *Issac and Oedipus: A Study in Biblical Psychology of the Sacrifice of Isaac.* London: Routledge, 1954.

Wenham, Gordon J. "The Coherence of the Flood Narrative." *Vetus Testamentum* 28 (1978): 336–48.

Whallon, William. *Formula, Character, and Context: Studies in Homeric, Old English, and Old Testament Poetry.* Washington: Center for Hellenic Studies, 1969.

———. "Old Testament Poetry and Homeric Epic." *Comparative Literature* 18 (1966): 113–31.

Widengren, George. "Myth and History in Israelite-Jewish Thought." *Culture in History: Essays in Honor of Paul Radin.* Ed. Stanley Diamond. New York: Columbia UP, 1960. 467–95.

Williams, James G. *Women Recounted: Narrative Thinking and the God of Israel.* Sheffield: Almond, 1982.

Wilson, Robert R. *Genealogy and History in the Biblical World.* Yale Near Eastern Researches 7. New Haven: Yale UP, 1977.

———. "Prophecy in Crisis: The Call of Ezekiel." *Interpretation* 38 (1984): 117–30.

———. *Sociological Approaches to the Old Testament.* Philadelphia: Fortress, 1984.

Wright, Elizabeth E. *Psychoanalytic Criticism: Theory in Practice.* London: Methuen, 1984.

Wright, G. Ernest, and Floyd V. Filson, eds. *The Westminster Historical Atlas to the Bible.* Rev. ed. Philadelphia: Westminster, 1956.

Young, Robert. *Young's Analytical Concordance to the Bible.* 1879. 8th ed. 1939. Rev. ed. New York: Nelson, 1982.

Zeligs, Dorothy F. *Moses: A Psychodynamic Study.* New York: Human Sciences, 1986.

———. *Psychoanalysis and the Bible: A Study in Depth of Seven Leaders.* New York: Bloch, 1974.

Zimmerli, Walther. *Old Testament Theology in Outline.* Trans. David E. Green. Atlanta: Knox, 1978.

INDEX